THE NEW **URBAN** **RENEWAL**

THE NEW **URBAN RENEWAL**

The Economic Transformation of Harlem and Bronzeville

Derek S. Hyra

THE UNIVERSITY OF CHICAGO PRESS   Chicago and London

Derek S. Hyra is a community development expert in the Office of the Comptroller of the Currency in the U.S. Treasury Department. He teaches urban sociology at The George Washington University and is a research affiliate of the National Poverty Center.

The University of Chicago Press, Chicago 60637
The University of Chicago Press, Ltd., London
© 2008 by The University of Chicago
All rights reserved. Published 2008
Printed in the United States of America

17 16 15 14 13 12 11 10 09 08   1 2 3 4 5

ISBN-13: 978-0-226-36604-3 (cloth)

ISBN-10: 0-226-36604-9 (cloth)

Library of Congress Cataloging-in-Publication Data

Hyra, Derek.
  The new urban renewal : the economic transformation of Harlem and Bronzeville / Derek Hyra.
    p. cm.
  Includes bibliographical references.
  ISBN-13: 978-0-226-36604-3 (cloth : alk. paper)
  ISBN-10: 0-226-36604-9 (cloth : alk. paper)   1. Urban renewal—New York (State)—New York.   2. Harlem (New York, N.Y.)—Economic conditions.
3. Urban renewal—Illinois—Chicago.   4. Bronzeville (Chicago, Ill.)—Economic conditions.   I. Title.
  HT177.N5H97   2008
  307.3′41609747—dc22

                                                      2007034707

All photos by Derek Hyra.

♾ The paper used in this publication meets the minimum requirements of the American National Standard for Information Sciences—Permanence of Paper for Printed Library Materials, ANSI Z39.48-1992.

To Mom, Dad, and Allison

Contents

Illustrations

Tables

Preface

In the 1990s, urban sociology's central debate concerned the factors contributing to the creation of impoverished black "hyper-ghettos." The two most influential figures in this dispute were William Julius Wilson and Douglas Massey, both professors in the Sociology Department at the University of Chicago who used Bronzeville, on Chicago's South Side, as their laboratory to understand the factors associated with neighborhood poverty. Following in the footsteps of these renowned scholars, I began to examine the disadvantaged conditions in Bronzeville when I arrived as a graduate student at the University of Chicago in 1999.

In Bronzeville, I discovered not a laboratory of inner city decline, but a prime locality for investigating the process of inner city revitalization. To my surprise, the City of Chicago had begun to invest in the area. The city moved the police headquarters from its downtown location to the center of Bronzeville. The Illinois Institute of Technology, a large university in the neighborhood, declared it would proceed with a multimillion dollar campus renovation and expansion. And finally the city announced a plan to destroy all of the community's high-rise public housing and replace it with mixed-income housing developments. The development snowballed and almost overnight, vacant lots untouched for years had signs promoting soon-to-come half-million dollar luxury townhomes. At the same time, an upscale bed and breakfast and several coffeehouses opened. Many private, market rental buildings converted to condominium units, and banking institutions not only began to make loans in the area but were also opening new commercial branches. The black middle class that a generation ago abandoned this community was returning.

I studied Bronzeville for three years, from 1999 to 2001, and wanted to compare its redevelopment to another black gentrifying community. There have been numerous case studies of neighborhood development, but far fewer comparative studies. I knew that the comparative angle would provide an opportunity to produce a more robust and insightful study, and Harlem seemed the ideal comparison community because of its similarity to Bronzeville. In 2002, I moved to Harlem and began my comparative exploration.

Harlem and Bronzeville have undergone two similar transitions: changing from affluent white areas to significant black communities in the early 1900s, then from mixed-income black areas to highly concentrated poor neighborhoods. Each alteration has prompted several noteworthy studies highlighting how industrialization, patterns of black urban migration, antagonistic race relations, and government action affect these neighborhoods and other black communities across urban America. Today Harlem and Bronzeville are undergoing a third major transformation: their "second renaissance." This book follows in the tradition of previous research and highlights the comprehensive set of dynamics related to the monumental economic changes taking place in these historic African-American communities.

Acknowledgments

This book could not have been written without the support of numerous people and institutions. At the University of Chicago, Richard Taub, Michael Dawson, Saskia Sassen, and Omar McRoberts provided invaluable feedback and encouragement throughout the formulation, research, and writing. Richard has been an incredible advisor, mentor, and friend. He not only persuaded me to take on the comparative nature of this project, but helped me, on several occasions, secure funding that made this research endeavor feasible. Additionally, Richard's insightful comments and suggestions have challenged me and greatly improved this manuscript. I hope I can someday help a budding scholar as much as he has assisted me. Michael has served as an inspirational guide during every stage of this project. Michael hired me as a graduate research assistant when I first stepped foot on the University of Chicago campus and instantly changed the way I thought about urban politics. His continual support has enabled me to accomplish this work. Saskia and Omar have provided invaluable feedback on several drafts of this manuscript and I thank them for their constant encouragement.

Several other individuals contributed immensely to this book. Vincent Carretta, whom I met while we were Fellows at the W. E. B. Du Bois Institute at Harvard University, made numerous suggestions that have enhanced this body of work. I cannot thank Vin enough for his guidance, encouragement, and friendship. Herbert Gans, one of the greatest ethnographers, trained me in participant observation. While conducting my research in Harlem, we met on several occasions and he was an excellent mentor whose door was always open. Manning Marable has been a tremendous guide throughout the research process. He also provided me with ample assistance and support while I conducted my fieldwork in Harlem.

Others provided me with comments on the entire or specific sections of the manuscript, and I thank them for their help. They include Janet Abu-Lughod, Scott Allard, Terry Clark, Cathy Cohen, Barbara Ferman, Lance Freeman, Bill Grimshaw, Nicole Marwell, John Mollenkopf, Mary Pattillo, Michael Schill, Carmi Schooler, Bill Sites, Phil Thompson, and Bill Wilson. In addition to these scholars, two close friends and colleagues, Dave Kirk and Percival Matthews, have contributed immensely by providing substantial feedback on numerous drafts. Their feedback has greatly improved this work. I thank my former U.S. Department of Housing and Urban Development colleagues, John Carruthers, Marge Martin, and Mark Shroder, who commented on various chapters and provided meaningful encouragement during the final stages of this project. I also thank Robert Renner for his assistance in constructing the maps that appear in the manuscript.

I am grateful for having such a wonderful staff at the University of Chicago Press: Doug Mitchell supported this project from its origin and was always willing to listen to and shape my fledgling manuscript ideas over beers and jazz at Jimmy's, Mara Naselli's superb manuscript editing helped to transform a dissertation into a polished book, and Tim McGovern magnificently coordinated all of the necessary pieces that resulted in the final product.

Certain parts of this manuscript appear in other journals and books. Sections of chapter six are found in a 2006 publication, "City Politics and Black Protest: The Economic Transformation of Harlem and Bronzeville," in *Souls*, 8(3), 176–196. I thank Taylor and Francis and the Trustees of Columbia University for granting permission to reprint this material. Portions of chapter six are also in "City Politics and Black Civil Society: The Transformation of Harlem and Bronzeville," forthcoming in *Race and Civil Society*, edited by Michael Dawson. I am grateful to the Russell Sage Foundation for reprint permission. A version of chapter seven appears as a 2006 article entitled, "Racial Uplift? Intra-racial Class Conflict and the Economic Revitalization of Harlem and Bronzeville," in *City and Community*, 5(1), 71–92. I thank the journal, Blackwell, and the American Sociological Association for granting permission to reprint this material.

Financial resources from a number of institutions supported various aspects of this research. I thank the Rockefeller Foundation's Working Communities Program and the U.S. Department of Housing and Urban Development for providing resources that aided in the analysis and writing. My fieldwork was supported with grants from the Social Science Research Council's Program in Applied Economics and the Center for the Study of Race, Politics and Culture, and a graduate internship from the New York State Assembly. I also thank the Joint Center for Poverty Research, the Institute for Research in African-American Studies, and the Division of the Social Sciences at the University of Chicago for the financial support that helped initiate this project. Much of this work was written while I was a fellow at the W. E. B. Du Bois Institute at Harvard University. This fellowship program provided me with an ideal intellectual environment in which to write a large portion of this book.

Several community leaders assisted me during my fieldwork. In Harlem, Mayor David Dinkins and New York state assemblyman Keith Wright were instrumental. In Bronzeville, Sokoni Karanja and all of the members of the South Side Partnership helped me considerably. In addition, I want to thank Jamie Kalven, Danielle Walters, and Andre Williams for allowing me to work with them.

I owe a great deal to my family. Both my mom and dad have enthusiastically supported my academic pursuits. Their unconditional love has allowed me to stay focused on my research. I also want to thank John Wedges and Matthew Goodman, whose friendship throughout the years inspired me to take on this project. Lastly, I thank my wife, Allison. She is my partner, friend, and inspiration. Her commitment, love, and support, in so many ways, contributed to the completion of this work. Although I am indebted to many individuals and institutions that helped me finish this book, the views expressed, as well as any errors, are my own.

1

Introduction

From the intersection of 135th Street and 7th Avenue, Harlem's twenty-first century renaissance is ubiquitous. On the southwest corner, scaffolding covers a large abandoned building and construction workers repair the facade of a structure that once housed Smalls Paradise, a legendary 1920s jazz club. A few blocks away, a new luxury condominium complex rises from a once vacant lot. Around the corner, a new bank branch has opened as have a number of small boutique shops. Nearby rehabilitated brownstones command prices between $600,000 and $1,000,000.

While Harlem, and this intersection, is rapidly redeveloping, a Laundromat just north of 135th Street is still a remnant of the community's impoverished past. The shop is run down and the old washers and dryers often do not work. An outdated arcade video game stands in the back. In the front, two worn metal folding chairs and a small TV sit in a makeshift waiting area.

Lashanda, a petite woman in her late twenties, owns the business. Lashanda has lived in Harlem all her life. She grew up in one of Harlem's many public housing projects and now lives with her two-year old son in a market rate, $1,000-a-month one-bedroom apartment. While waiting for my laundry, Lashanda and I talk about the articles in the *Daily News*, the latest BET music videos, and Harlem's new posh nightclubs and bars.

Our conversations often center on the revitalization of the community. She says she does not mind the changes because her perception is that the neighborhood is improving. She expects her business will allow her to keep up with Harlem's rising costs. However, she declares that rents are becoming unaffordable for the majority of residents.

About a year after I first met Lashanda, I was walking up 7th Avenue past the Laundromat and noticed that it was closed, as were some of the other flanking businesses. Construction workers were tearing down the Laundromat's frontal signage. I immediately called Lashanda and asked her what had happened. She said the owner of the building did not renew her lease; he wanted to rehabilitate the building in order to rent to more upscale businesses. I asked if she was upset and she replied, "The one thing constant in life is change." She was not angry or highly distressed, as many of the other Harlem business owners faced with the prospects of displacement had been. Lashanda has a carefree way about her and per-haps compared to the tragedy of her boyfriend's death a few years ago, the loss of her business was minor. The commercial section that once housed Lashanda's Laundromat now contains high-end boutique clothing shops that serve the tastes of young black professionals, willing to pay $500 for a pair of stylish designer jeans.[1]

Economic development in Bronzeville on Chicago's South Side is just as pervasive as in Harlem. Until recently the community had one of the highest concentrations of public housing in the world, but now all of Bronzeville's high-rise housing projects are slated for demolition, and many will be replaced with $500,000 townhomes and luxury condomini-ums. With the public housing removed, major financial institutions that once neglected the community for decades are now eager to make loans, and are even establishing new branches in the area. Many of the beauti-ful graystones, which were built in the late nineteenth and early twentieth centuries, have been rehabilitated and are selling for upwards of $600,000. A number of coffeehouses, as well as a bed and breakfast, have opened. As the cover of a recent Chicago real estate publication emphatically states, "Bronzeville Is Booming," evidenced by Bronzeville's higher than city av-erage property value increase.[2]

My introduction to Bronzeville's public housing began while attend-ing a resident health fair at the Stateway Gardens housing project. My neighborhood connections suggested that this event might present a good opportunity to meet and talk with public housing residents. While at the all-day event, I decided, near the end of the day, to play basketball with a bunch of elementary-school aged boys. After I finished, Tre, who is in his late twenties, invited me to play basketball with some of the adults the next day. Through playing basketball most Saturdays and Sundays at Stateway for three years, Tre and I became good friends.

Tre, a man who stands almost six feet and is about 250 pounds, has lived at the Stateway Gardens housing project his entire life and comes from a family that is entrenched in its gang life. Nearly all of his brothers have been gang members, yet Tre, a high school dropout, has remarkably resisted gang involvement. Tre has experienced many hardships at Stateway. He has been robbed by a group of men carrying shotguns. He has seen his brothers go in and out of prison and has had to navigate the violence that occasionally erupts between rival gangs that control Stateway's drug trade. Regardless of the tragedies he has witnessed and experienced, Tre loves Stateway; it is his home.

Tre is a Stateway leader who is committed to improving people's lives. For the last six years, he has worked for several nonprofit groups. Tre connects Stateway residents to health care services, intervenes during instances of police brutality and harasses neglectful housing authority staff. Tre also coordinates an annual basketball tournament involving teams from various housing projects.

As each Stateway high-rise building is demolished, Tre moves to another one to remain at Stateway. He knows he can get a voucher for a private market apartment but Tre wants to stay at Stateway and in Bronzeville. With Bronzeville's real estate prices escalating and housing demand increasing, the community's landlords are reluctant to accept housing vouchers, especially from former public housing tenants. Tre eventually finds an apartment in a more distant South Side neighborhood; he is forced to watch Bronzeville's revitalization from afar.

The stories of Lashanda and Tre are not unique. Their situations are all too familiar to longtime residents and small business owners of revitalizing inner city areas. As redevelopment occurs, many of those with strong community roots are forced to relocate in response to mounting market pressures and government action. In the drama of the creative yet destructive forces impacting urban America, they are the victims.

To some, this scenario may seem reminiscent of the past urban renewal, however, the situation occurring in Harlem and Bronzeville is different. Urban renewal of the 1940s, '50s, and '60s was synonymous with "Negro Removal."[3] During this period in cities throughout the United States, large tracts of land were cleared for redevelopment and many African Americans were displaced to make room for highways, universities, large commercial developments, and new residential neighborhoods.

Most of the beneficiaries of this development were white. White residents, real estate developers, and construction companies benefited from the deployment of federal funds to revitalize central cities.

Today's urban renewal, evident in the redevelopment of Harlem and Bronzeville, is benefiting middle and upper-income African Americans, while lower-income members of this racial group are seeing their communities transformed into spaces they can no longer afford. As individuals like Lashanda and Tre are being left out, prominent black real estate developers are making millions building and selling luxury condominiums and townhomes. One black developer in Harlem estimates that he has already made nearly $10 million from one of the community's new upscale high-rise condominium buildings. He forecasts that his Harlem plans will eventually net his company approximately $40 million. In addition, numerous African-American homeowners in these communities are seeing their property values skyrocket. Unlike the past, the second round of urban renewal is benefiting certain segments of black America. The current urban renewal is not entirely race specific but involves an intersection of race and class.

While many developing inner city areas experience an influx of white residents, Harlem and Bronzeville are transforming without drastic racial changeover; they are experiencing "black gentrification." Instead of middle-class whites, middle-income blacks are replacing low-income African-American residents in these communities. Today, Harlem is nearly 80 percent African American and Bronzeville is 90 percent; the redevelopment of both areas is associated with the influx of the black middle class.

At the turn of the twenty-first century, America is experiencing a new round of urban renewal. Although concentrated poverty continues to plague many metropolitan neighborhoods across the United States, inner city, African-American communities in Boston, New York City, Philadelphia, Washington, D.C., Atlanta, Charlotte, Chicago, Minneapolis, and Los Angeles have transformed from concentrated pockets of poverty into trendy and expensive living spaces.[4] No two communities symbolize this revitalization trend more than Harlem and Bronzeville. These two neighborhoods were once among the most impoverished, declining, and destitute urban black ghettos in the country. In the 1970s and 1980s, violent crime, drug use, school dropout, teen pregnancy, and pervasive poverty were commonplace. In the last ten years, however, the economic conditions of these communities have dramatically changed: property values skyrocketed and median household income doubled. As massive amounts of residential and commercial investments have poured into these areas, the communities have gone from being red-lined to green-lined, from the crack house to the coffeehouse. It is imperative that scholars uncover the dynamics and consequences associated with these monumental transformations.

The primary purpose of this book is to highlight the dynamics that are leading to the changing conditions in redeveloping inner city neighborhoods. Harlem and Bronzeville have undergone two similar transitions in the twentieth century: changing from affluent white areas to significant black communities and then from mixed-income black areas to highly concentrated poor neighborhoods. Each alteration has highlighted major societal forces that have been instrumental in shaping America's urban landscape. The formation of these communities as culturally, politically, and economically self-contained black spaces—cities within cities in the 1920s—expressed the importance of industrialization, patterns of black urban migration, antagonistic black/white relations, and black solidarity on urban neighborhoods. Their second transition, from thriving, segregated communities, to what Kenneth Clark coined the "dark ghetto" in Harlem and Arnold Hirsch labeled the "second ghetto" in Bronzeville signaled how deindustrialization, concentrated public housing construction, persistent white racism, and black middle class movement to the suburbs merged to create extremely disadvantaged black neighborhoods that engendered America's urban "underclass."

As Harlem and Bronzeville experience their economic revival and "second renaissance," they once again reflect patterns and forces critical to the reconfiguration of urban America. Economic globalization, increasing interdependency among national economies around the world, is a major societal dynamic that is contributing to the inner city development in certain cities. The movement of industrial jobs to off-shore locations was one of the key factors related to the inner city decline, and now, downtown centralization, also influenced by international business, is associated with Harlem and Bronzeville's redevelopment.

Federal government action and resources are also critical factors. While national community development funds were severely cut during the 1980s, in the 1990s certain federal programs, most notably the Empowerment Zone (EZ) Initiative and the Housing Opportunities for People Everywhere (HOPE VI) program, steered billions of redevelopment dollars to some of the country's most blighted urban areas. The allocation of federal funding is one of the important backdrops that set the context for understanding contemporary inner city revitalization.

In the last three decades America's black middle class has tripled and the tastes and preferences, not to mention the increased purchasing power, of this group are reshaping the social, political and economic features of the urban landscape.[5] While the black middle class fled black ghettos to more prosperous and often less segregated communities in the late 1940s and 1950s after the abolishment of restrictive housing laws, a new crop of middle class African Americans returned in the 1990s. By moving into and participating in the redevelopment of historic African-American communities, this group is altering the notions of urban black America.

While these major redevelopment dynamics are influencing Harlem and Bronzeville, their consequences are different. For instance, Harlem has more commercial development. With the arrival of mainstream outlets such as Staples, Starbucks, Marshalls and Old Navy on 125th Street, greater displacement pressures are being faced by Harlem's longstanding small businesses. Furthermore, Bronzeville's high-rise public housing is being demolished while Harlem's public housing high-rises remain. Thus, in Bronzeville extensive displacement occurs among the poorest segments of the resident population. Greater public resistance to the revitalization exists in Harlem, even though one of the most visible signs of gentrification, the demolition of high-rise public housing, is not occurring there. I seek to explain both the parallels and inconsistencies related to the redevelopment processes in these historic African-American communities.

A critical dissimilarity between Harlem and Bronzeville is they are situated in cities with drastically different political landscapes. NYC has a fragmented government system and Chicago is a classic, centralized Democratic machine. This difference is essential for understanding the distinct consequences associated with the redevelopment of these communities. More than any other study on neighborhood redevelopment, this investigation uncovers how city politics mediate and alter the effects of community development forces.

Harlem and Bronzeville: Not Just Communities

In this book Harlem refers specifically to Central Harlem. It is located toward the northern tip of Manhattan, the main borough of New York City, and is bounded by Central Park at 110th Street to the south, 155th Street to the north, 5th Avenue on the east and Morningside and St. Nicholas Parks on the west. It houses many culturally significant black institutions including the Apollo Theatre, Abyssinian Baptist Church, once led by

Adam Clayton Powell, Jr., and the New York Urban League. Harlem is where Marcus Garvey and Malcolm X settled and established their political and social movements. Langston Hughes and Zora Neale Hurston wrote many of their famous literary works in Harlem, and renowned painter Jacob Lawrence lived there as well. Musicians Duke Ellington, Charlie Parker, and John Coltrane performed at venues such as Smalls Paradise, the Cotton Club and the Lenox Lounge. During the early and mid-twentieth century, these people and many other African-American artists, writers, performers, and political leaders developed Harlem's reputation as the "capital of black America."

Bronzeville is the Harlem of Chicago. It is located on the South Side of Chicago and is bounded by 26th Street to the north, 51st Street to the south, Cottage Grove Avenue to the east and the Dan Ryan Expressway to the west.[6] During its heyday, Bronzeville inspired the work of literary figures such as Richard Wright and Gwendolyn Brooks, as well as artists like Archibald J. Motley, Jr. It houses many important black institutions including the Chicago Urban League, Olivet Baptist Church, and the *Chicago Defender* newspaper, which still sponsors one of the largest annual African-American parades in the country. Moreover, this community is where the Johnson Publishing Company, with its signature African-American magazines *Ebony* and *Jet*, originally began. Many important political leaders such as Ida B. Wells, Oscar DePriest, and William Dawson resided in Bronzeville. During the 1920s, '30s, and '40s, numerous singers and musicians including Ella Fitzgerald, Louis Armstrong, and Earl Hines performed in neighborhood venues like the Regal Theater, the Palm Tavern, and the Parkway Ballroom.

Harlem and Bronzeville are not just geographic communities: they are symbols of the black experience in urban America. The fate of these communities is intimately tied to the prospects for African Americans living in cities throughout the United States. In *Black Metropolis*, St. Clair Drake and Horace Cayton state, "Understand Chicago's Black Belt and you will understand the Black Belts of a dozen large American cities."[7] Further, Roi Ottley in his masterpiece, *New World A-Coming*, claims that to comprehend black America. "One must put his finger on the pulse of Harlem."[8] More recent studies of Bronzeville and Harlem continue to stress the importance of these communities as critical black icons.[9] The study of these historic African-American communities illuminates the changing contours of black civil society and the complex set of forces affecting it.

Bronzeville and Harlem are similar on many levels. These communities have almost identical histories as well as other analogous qualities.[10]

Harlem and Bronzeville are located within global cities and are almost equally distant from the central business districts (CBD) of their respective cities.[11] Proximity to the CBD is important because of indications that distance from the central city relates to patterns of gentrification.[12] In addition, both communities are targets of similar federal initiatives, such as the Empowerment Zone Initiative, and are heavily concentrated with public housing. Bronzeville and Harlem have very similar social and economic demographics, including racial composition, income and educational levels, and homeownership rates (see appendix A). These similarities minimize the chances that distinct developmental trajectories result from differences in pre-existing community conditions, making the exploration of the unique citywide political environments a potentially worthwhile endeavor.

The Research

This book demonstrates the complex set of forces associated with the revitalization of inner city communities through a rigorous exploration of race, class, and politics within the framework of neighborhood change. It is not an investigation of black politics or black identity, although the patterns of community development will tell us something about the state of black civil society. Nor is it an evaluation of federal policy, although major urban federal community economic development and housing policies of the 1990s are assessed. Instead, this is a comprehensive study of community change. It considers the intersection of dynamics that originate beyond, and within these communities, and argues that a similar broad political and economic context influences urban redevelopment but that distinct citywide landscapes mediate forces that stem from outside, as well as inside these communities. This study does not pinpoint the most influential level of analysis, but rather demonstrates that interactions among multiple levels are critical to understanding neighborhood change.

How are economic globalization and national policies contributing to redevelopment of Harlem and Bronzeville? To what extent do distinct citywide political contexts mediate dynamics that facilitate community change? How do internal community structures affect the redevelopment process? Finally, what are the consequences associated with this development: who is benefiting from these changes, and who is being left out?

Harlem and Bronzeville continue to be the most researched communities in the country and numerous studies have explored the altering economic circumstances in Upper Manhattan and on the South Side of Chicago. Works by Michele Boyd, Lance Freeman, John Jackson, Mary Pattillo, and Monique Taylor, illustrate what the economic changes in these communities mean for notions of black identity.[13] By investigating the diverse set of behaviors and attitudes of residents with varying incomes, these studies debunk the notion of a homogenous black America. Other assessments focus on external community factors leading the changes taking place in these neighborhoods. Accounts of Harlem and Bronzeville's redevelopment by Mamadou Chinyelu, Lily Hoffman, David Ranney, and Neil Smith examine how aspects of economic globalization, federal policies, and city-generated programs affect the revitalization process.[14]

Notably, however, none of these examinations explore both of these communities simultaneously, nor do they rigorously investigate how internal community dynamics interact with forces that originate outside of these neighborhoods. Without a more comprehensive research approach, our understanding of the forces driving central city redevelopment, and associated outcomes, will remain fragmented and incomplete. This study, more than any other, highlights that multiple forces, both internal and external to these communities, come together to bring about inner city transformation. This book also provides great insights into how municipal governments mediate community development processes.

To understand the redevelopment of Harlem and Bronzeville, a distinct comparative ethnographic approach is applied. Ethnography and participant observation are excellent research techniques for understanding community redevelopment processes and consequences because they facilitate in-depth knowledge of revitalization forces as they are perceived and acted upon by individuals in their everyday lives. By using this approach in both communities, I am able to compare and contrast community change patterns, allowing for a more robust and nuanced picture of inner city development.

My research uses aspects of what Michael Burawoy and his colleagues coined the "extended case method."[15] This ethnographic approach encourages the researcher to be highly engaged in community activities, while remaining mindful of important factors that originate beyond the neighborhood. Some ethnographic studies are limited in scope because they focus excessively on community events and fail to discuss outlying redevelopment dynamics. This analysis of Harlem and Bronzeville is distinct from prior research, because it is grounded in these communities, yet extends vertically beyond the immediate neighborhoods.

Investigating multiple level forces in two different research sites is not easy, and I've had to sacrifice, to some extent, the thick descriptions that make the traditional community ethnography such a compelling research technique. But this is a worthwhile trade-off. The insight achieved by using a vertical, comparative perspective is something very few ethnographic studies possess. While choosing a particular community or a certain level of analysis might have led to a more detailed study, it would have been an incomplete story of the various processes related to neighborhood change. Several contemporary studies that focus on Harlem or Bronzeville center on one or two levels of analysis. This study takes a more comprehensive approach.

Three years (from 1999 to 2001) were spent exploring redevelopment in Bronzeville and two six-month periods (in 2002 and 2003) were spent in Harlem. While living in these communities, I frequented local restaurants, bars, coffee shops, barbershops and recreational centers, and, more importantly, embedded myself in associational life by attending hundreds of meetings hosted by homeownership block clubs, public housing tenant associations, coalitions of civic leaders, government agencies, and social service organizations. I interviewed thirty-five stakeholders in each community, speaking with heads of social service organizations, tenant rights organizations, community development corporations, elected officials, religious leaders, real estate developers, commercial bankers, city officials, and private foundation program officers.[16] Collecting and reading relevant community and citywide newspapers, city documents, community organization meeting minutes, and academic reports was another critical source of information. This archival material allowed me to stay connected to one community while actively studying the other.

The testimony of those interviewed and detailed descriptions of events provide evidence that certain processes are affecting these communities and do not infer causal linkages or concrete policy assessments. The presented data and analysis are primarily used to highlight the interactions among various redevelopment processes and should not be interpreted as precise empirical measurements or causal inferences.

When interpreting my analysis, readers should be aware of the potential insight and bias associated with the formal positions I held in these communities as well as my race. I performed various tasks in these neighborhoods and have been perceived as a researcher, member of an organizational coalition, employee of a social service agency, and aide to a political official. In addition, I am a white male who is participating in and studying the most well-known African-American communities. I reveal this information because my altering duties and race constructs the various lenses that guide my observations. Moreover, my roles and skin color influence the ways in which people initially respond to me.[17]

Accessing the Communities' Leadership

My research separates itself from other urban revitalization projects because of my unprecedented access to community leaders. I initially gained access in September of 1997 to Bronzeville as part of a research team from the University of Kansas documenting a comprehensive community initiative supported by the MacArthur Foundation. During the two years of this study, I established relationships with many of Bronzeville's institutional and organizational decision makers. In 1999, when the initial study ended, I formally began my own research and became a member of the South Side Partnership, a coalition of key organizations in Bronzeville. My induction into the group was facilitated by the relationships I developed with many of the members over the previous two years. Although some of the member organizations served public housing residents, formal public housing tenant leaders were absent. Therefore, to better document public housing resident engagement, I worked for a social service and advocacy organization located in Bronzeville's Stateway Gardens housing project.

Though I had a few personal contacts in Harlem, I did not have immediate access to the community's core leadership. During my first few months in Harlem, it was difficult to establish the same level of trusting relationships I had developed in Bronzeville. Then two critical events occurred: I met two influential political leaders, Mayor David Dinkins, New York City's first and only African-American mayor, and New York state assemblyman Keith Wright.

Mayor Dinkins was teaching at Columbia University while I conducted my Harlem research. Several Columbia University faculty members familiar with my study encouraged me to arrange an interview with Dinkins. After months of scheduling and rescheduling, I finally obtained the interview. As the interview came to an end, Dinkins asked if there were any individuals in Harlem that I had wanted to speak with but was not able to get on their schedules. I rattled off eight names and he graciously volunteered to notify them of my presence. Soon I received a call from Congressman Charles Rangel's office about setting up an interview. In contacting Harlem leaders, Dinkins not only opened up important institutions such as the Upper Manhattan Empowerment Zone, Abyssinian

Baptist Church, and the Schomburg Center for Research in Black Culture, but more importantly he brought legitimacy to my project.

While Dinkins's assistance was invaluable for acquiring interviews, my relationship with Assemblyman Wright granted me access to the inner workings of Harlem and provided me with intimate connections to its residents. I was walking west on 135th Street toward 7th Avenue when I heard someone in front of the Democratic Club call out, "Hey you, come over here." I looked over and immediately recognized Harlem's assemblyman, Keith Wright. He was dressed in sweat pants and a sweatshirt and smoking a cigarette. He had just finished playing basketball at the Harlem YMCA, where I had first met him after playing against him the previous week.

When I got over to the other side of the street he said, "You're the guy from Chicago living on 137th. What's your name again?" I thought it was pretty funny he remembered my address and not my name. He asked me to remind him what my research was about, and when I said Harlem's revitalization, he replied, "There is nothing wrong with development as long as it doesn't lead to displacement." He then said, "So, you're doing a study like Tally's Corner?" Later I would learn that he studied sociology at Tufts University. That day Keith invited me to attend his political club meetings and encouraged me to play ball at the Y the following Saturday. Through our athletic endeavors on the court, I got to know the assemblyman pretty well and eventually worked in his district office for six months. Working for Keith afforded me an extraordinary opportunity to interact with a wide range of individuals who had a stake in, or were being affected by, Harlem's redevelopment.

The Dynamics of Economic Transformation

The major contribution of this book is that it shows how global, federal, city, and community level forces simultaneously *interact* to produce inner city revitalization. The increased importance of the central business district, due to the global economy, relates to downtown centralization and subsequent inner city development in New York City and Chicago. However, city political action, such as the distribution of resources through tax incentives and locally developed housing, continues to attract investment to particular areas. Global and local forces interact to produce centralization and neighborhood gentrification, supporting the notion that a complex interplay between global dynamics and local political decisions shape the geography of the inner city. While global forces are becoming increasingly important, local political decisions remain central.

Political circumstances, particularly the structure of urban politics, continue to be essential for understanding how federal policies influence urban community development. In an era of devolution, local political circumstances are extremely crucial in determining how national politics are actually implemented. While external forces, like globalization and federal policies affect urban areas, they do not diminish the role that city politics have on mediating these forces by distributing public resources to certain communities. Scholars of urban growth and inner city development must seek to understand distinct citywide political climates to get a more nuanced grasp of policy implementation and corresponding outcomes that affect urban growth and neighborhood development in multiple settings.

Redevelopment in Harlem and Bronzeville forces us to rethink our understandings of black civil society. Within urban black communities, higher-income individuals see their interests as separate from more impoverished members of their racial group. This cleavage is apparent when affluent and middle-class dominated black organizations pursue political actions that contribute to the removal of low-income residents from their community. While the urban renewal of the 1960s did little to assist African Americans, today's urban renewal benefits a certain segment of affluent African Americans. The political power and preferences of the black middle class has increased and these individuals are aligning themselves more and more with the urban growth machine than with lower-income members of their race.

Where We Are Headed

The book begins by assessing more distal community redevelopment factors, such as the global economy, and works down to more proximal levels, like community action. While going from broad to specific, each chapter builds on the theme of variable interaction as the key to understanding community change. Chapter 2 constructs a multiple-level theoretical framework for analyzing community change. This chapter sets the theoretical orientation that guides the rest of the book. It is intended for those that have a keen interest in community development theory.

Chapter 3 focuses on the relationship between inner city development and the emergence of an expanded and more integrated worldwide economy. While many international forces influence the inner city, the global trend of central business district expansion and growth increases market demand for properties in nearby communities, such as Harlem and Bronzeville. However, the development process cannot be completely attributed to global dynamics given that city-initiated policies (e.g., Business Improvement Districts and Tax Increment Financing Districts) and city-generated housing plans also facilitate downtown growth and neighborhood gentrification. The rise in property values and the influx of capital into Harlem and Bronzeville result from an interaction between global and local economic and political forces.

Although federal dynamics play an important role spurring community revitalization, local political landscapes greatly shape the specific outcomes of national community economic development policy. Chapter 4 and 5, through an exploration of the implementation of the Empowerment Zones and recent public housing reforms, such as the HOPE VI program, demonstrate that Chicago's political machine and New York City's decentralized two-party system have important consequences for a variety of redevelopment outcomes. For instance, citywide political differences help explain why the New York City EZ is associated with a 17 percent job growth in Harlem, while the Chicago EZ creates little employment opportunities in Bronzeville. The municipal political systems also illuminate why nearly 17,000 public housing residents are being displaced from Bronzeville, while the public housing population remains in Harlem.

Chapters 6 and 7 explore the political actions of two groups internal to these communities: those facilitating the redevelopment and those resisting it. Chapter 6 shows how the local political environment shapes black protest stemming from those concerned with displacement. Chapter 7 focuses on the political action of middle-class residents who are promoting the revitalization. While displacement is associated with global, federal, and city factors beyond the control of these communities, the political action of community groups, composed of affluent and middle-class blacks, also plays a role.

Chapter 8 summarizes my results and critiques past paradigms of urban growth and theories of neighborhood development, particularly ones geared toward urban African-American communities. In this concluding chapter, I discuss the symbolic meaning of Harlem and Bronzeville's redevelopment for black/white relations and make policy recommendations to increase the likelihood that low-income residents benefit from the redevelopment of their communities. Now that investments have come to inner city areas, displacement of the poor is a serious concern. We must rethink policy prescriptions to ensure that equitable growth is achieved.

A Closing Comment: Staying Neutral

My research objective always compromised my passion to be an activist and advocate. Throughout my research one moral issue continually plagued me; I witnessed the forced relocation of many low-income people, particularly in Bronzeville, which I often considered unjust. During his research on the redevelopment and subsequent massive displacement in Boston's West End, Herbert Gans stated, "I was torn between my research role and my desire to correct what I felt to be a prime example of social injustice as well as poor planning."[18] I often felt the same way.

I considered advocating for displaced individuals but I knew activism would jeopardize the quality and objectivity of my research. If I participated in extensive community organizing efforts on behalf of low-income people, I would alienate factions critical to the redevelopment process, such as bankers, real estate developers, and some political officials. During my research I was constantly moving between competing groups and attempted to remain equally aligned with each. I knew that staying neutral was critical to understanding the overall process of neighborhood development, but by doing so I compromised my personal concern for the plight of the most vulnerable population. Ethnographic researchers always have to make tough choices about their participation. My goal was to immerse myself in Harlem and Bronzeville without choosing a particular faction. This was difficult to do because several people I spoke with felt their livelihoods were being taken away by forces beyond their control. My hope is that this research illuminates some of these forces and makes them more concrete, understandable, and actionable.

2

Building a Theoretical Framework
of Urban Transformation

Before assessing Harlem and Bronzeville's revitalization, it is important
to lay out my assumptions and perspectives to demonstrate why I chose
to focus on particular aspects of the redevelopment. This chapter includes
a review of previous theories of neighborhood change and a discussion
of why the conditions of gentrifying inner city communities can only be
fully understood by noting the interconnections among global, national,
municipal, and community dynamics.

Classic Paradigms of Urban Community Change

Social scientists are constantly grappling to fully theorize and concep-
tualize the dynamics shaping the urban landscape generally and inner
city neighborhoods particularly. In the past century, three successive
paradigms have emerged to explain urban growth and neighborhood development. In the early part of the twentieth century, Robert Park and
Ernest Burgess, the founders of the Chicago School of sociology, introduced the theory of human ecology to account for urban growth and
community change. This paradigm of urban growth and differentiation
was based primarily on patterns of movement occurring in plant life.
Park and Burgess argued that just as a pine forest takes over a prairie,
different populations compete over space within the city. They claimed

that two processes, invasion and succession, caused the segmentation of the metropolis into "a mosaic of little worlds" (Park and Burgess [1925] 1967, 40). According to their model, urban neighborhoods are inevitable by-products of natural differentiation processes by which residents select community areas based on their individual preferences. Neighborhood change arises when different ethnic or status groups attempt to expand their spatial niche into other segments of the city. Park and Burgess assume that as people acquire greater wealth they will prefer to move outward from the core of the city. The flow of populations from the central business district into outer sections of the city, according to Park and Burgess, is the critical dynamic that affects neighborhood growth.

Although this model for urban change was highly influential, it relies on some questionable assumptions, presuming, for instance, that individuals can freely choose neighborhoods consonant with their individual preferences. But we know this was not and is not the case. When Park and Burgess developed their theory in the early 1900s, many communities had restrictive covenants preventing the sale of property to African Americans. Second, their theory does not account for political actions that shape individual preferences for particular communities. People are often attracted to certain areas because of their proximity to transportation routes, park space, or cultural amenities, which are frequently the result of targeted, concrete government decisions. These public decisions, far from natural occurrences, were not seen by Park and Burgess as critical in altering the urban landscape or influencing individual preferences for certain neighborhoods.

The political economy paradigm was formulated to address the shortcomings of the human ecology perspective. Under this framework, urban neighborhood growth is seen as a created circumstance related to tangible economic structures and political decisions (Logan and Molotch 1987). It explains urban development patterns through the influence of the growth machine, which is composed of real estate speculators, insurance and title companies, owners of large department stores, political leaders, and universities. Actors within the growth machine are motivated to enhance property values in strategic places and increase the profitability, and influence, of their respective businesses and institutions. This theory presumes that key metropolitan political and economic actors have disproportionate amounts of power to implement public policies that benefit certain parts of the city at the expense of others.

Therefore, neighborhood growth and changing property values are associated with the actions of the ruling growth regime.[1]

While political economy paradigm scholars like John Logan and Harvey Molotch focus primarily on economic and political dynamics internal to cities, other scholars reposition this framework to center on national circumstances, contending that forces outside of the city are far more powerful than those originating within it (Halpern 1995; Peterson 1981; Wilson 1996). In his seminal 1981 study *City Limits,* Paul Peterson claims that competition for key industries between cities constrains local business elites and political actors, hampering their abilities to alter the circumstances in urban communities. Moreover, William Julius Wilson suggests that the structure of the national economy has the greatest impact on the urban terrain, particularly in declining inner city areas. Still others, like Robert Halpern, argue that national political decisions, such as the deployment of federal resources for public housing, have a significant influence. Although political economy researchers debate whether local or national circumstances are more important, those who subscribe to this paradigm acknowledge that city growth and decline is largely influenced by tangible economic and political actions.

A major critique of the political economy approach is that it fails to account for powerful forces beyond the city and nation-state. The global perspective deals with this shortcoming by emphasizing that economic and political pressures are increasingly international in scope (Castells 2000; Fainstein [1994] 2001; Feagin 1998; Sassen 1998; Ranney 2003). This paradigm insists that the relationship metropolitan regions have with the global economy determines urban community growth.

The global perspective presumes that international forces, more than federal or elite city actors, determine the metropolitan landscape and the fate of inner city areas. Global dynamics may influence cities in multiple ways. Some perceive that international financial transactions correspond to urban redevelopment by making development capital and credit more readily available (Ranney 2003). Others stress the emergence of multinational companies and international tourism as a development force (Chinyelu 1999; Hoffman 2000). Yet another group of scholars assumes that integrated worldwide financial markets and improved communication systems, set the conditions for the proliferation of global cities (Sassen 2000; Taylor 2004).[2]

Global city scholars claim that certain international municipalities form a strategic network of places that function as the "command and control" centers for the emerging international economy. Command and control cities, through multinational corporations, coordinate the production of products worldwide. Consequently, to handle this function, global cities must attract high-level managers. Cities positioned to attract multinational firms and high-wage service sector employees will boom, while nonglobal cities will decline or stagnate (Fainstein ([1994] 2001). In global cities, high-wage service sector expansion, particularly in the central business district, is associated with the gentrification of neighborhoods close to the downtown. Although the mechanism of change might vary for different globalists, they all presume that urban change stems from forces originating from the international economy.

Each of these broad perspectives has strengths and weaknesses. The ecological paradigm explains how population movement in one segment of the city affects other areas, but it says little about specific conditions that cause migration. The political economy approach highlights the importance of powerful city actors and national economic circumstances but tends to dismiss broader forces. The global perspective illuminates international dynamics, but does not address how more localized actions interact with processes stemming from the global economy. None of the paradigms stress the importance of interactions that occur among global, federal, and city-level dynamics. Furthermore, they leave little room for community action in the process of change. Relying relatively more heavily on the political economic and global perspectives in my investigation, I integrate aspects of these classic paradigms to explore the altering terrain of the inner city.

The Need for a Multilayered Analysis

Neighborhood change is a culmination of interactions among political and economic factors that originate from multiple levels. While some scholars view external neighborhood factors, such as economic globalization, federal policy, and citywide politics, as the driving forces related to inner city revitalization, others contend that internal variables, including neighborhood-based organizational efforts, are more important (Gittell 1992; Pattillo 2003; Taub, Taylor and Dunham 1984). To focus on either external or internal factors is shortsighted.

Two compelling studies on urban transformation highlight the interactions among these different levels of analysis. For example, William Julius Wilson maintains that external variables, such as the national economy, affect neighborhood conditions. In particular, he describes how deindustrialization has negatively impacted many African-American, inner city areas. However, he notes that internal organizational structures can buffer against neighborhood decay and thus affect community development. "The higher the density and stability of formal organizations," Wilson argues, "the less that illicit activities such as drug trafficking, crime, prostitution, and gang formation can take root in the neighborhood" (1996, 64). The actions of community-based organizations, according to Wilson, can mitigate negative neighborhood conditions brought on by the national economy.

Further, in her historic comparative study of New York, Chicago, and Los Angeles, Janet Abu-Lughod argues that "common forces originating at the level of the global economy" have differential effects on areas based on their local political structures (1999, 417). She claims that Chicago's black ghettos are more severely dilapidated than New York City's because the white-controlled, Democratic machine in Chicago prevents African-Americans residents from gaining tangible political power. The works of Wilson and Abu-Lughod suggest that macro- and micro-level variables interact to shape conditions of inner city communities. Thus, it's critical to explore macrostructures, such as global and federal-level processes, and equally important to understand how particular contexts at the city and community levels mediate and interact with other forces to modify the urban landscape.

Global Processes

A burgeoning literature has explored the relationship between global dynamics and neighborhood revitalization. Despite globalization scholars' claim that international processes dominate the urban landscape, several authors note the importance of local city actions in the development of global structures and processes, and in ensuring neighborhood gentrification (Brenner and Theodore 2002; Cox 1997; Sites 2003; Smith [1996] 2000; Swyngedouw 1997). Erik Swyngedouw describes the complex, reciprocal nature of local and global dynamics: "local actions shape global money flows, while global processes, in turn, affect local actions" (1997, 137). For example, a municipality may foster the emergence of global forces by giving tax breaks that allow multinational firms low-cost access to the central business district, which may in turn promote increased land value and facilitate redevelopment in adjacent neighborhoods. This study seeks to pinpoint specific linkages between global and more local processes promoting gentrification.

National Legislation

Several studies stress the importance of national policies in generating and subsequently ameliorating concentrated neighborhood poverty. In *Making the Second Ghetto* ([1983] 1998), Arnold Hirsch shows that the Federal Housing Act of 1949 had a direct impact on the creation of impoverished black ghettos by providing large amounts of money to cities for the construction of public housing. The concentration of public housing in particular minority communities contributed to the downfall of black inner city areas (Massey and Kanaiaupuni 1993). Since the 1960s, cities have relied on federal funding through a variety of programs such as Community Action Agencies, Model Cities, Urban Development Action Grants, and Community Development Block Grants to promote neighborhood redevelopment. Today, three important components of federal legislation, the Housing Opportunities for People Everyone (HOPE VI) program, the Empowerment Zone (EZ) Initiative, and the public housing guidelines in the Quality Housing and Work Responsibility Act of 1998 are associated with the redevelopment of inner city neighborhoods (Bennett and Reed 1999; Goetz 2003; Turbov and Piper 2005; Wyly and Hammel 1999; Zielenbach 2003).

Federal policies are mediated by distinct municipal circumstances. While the same federal policies apply to New York City and Chicago, the programs are implemented quite differently. In Chicago, Bronzeville's public housing high-rises are being torn down, while public housing projects remain in Harlem. Further, the New York City EZ has $300 million in assets, including additional state and city funds, while the Chicago EZ has substantially fewer resources. I investigate how distinct political contexts reconstitute broader federal development processes and describe mechanisms each city and community employs to alter the effects of these national policies.

City Structures and Action

The ability of city governments to promote urban neighborhood development and economic growth has been well documented. Cities decide how and where public resources from the federal, state, and city level will be spent, which in turn can facilitate the development of a particular neighborhood (Logan and Molotch 1987). The city politics literature, exemplified by the work of Robert Dahl (1961), Clarence Stone (1989), and Paul

Peterson (1981), is concerned with the connection between neighborhood conditions and who governs, how they govern, and to what extent the broader political economic environment affects local governing decisions. This literature can be used to investigate how cities can promote community development with federal and city resources while controlling dissent or opposition arising from neighborhood gentrification.

Comparative studies suggest that a city's political landscape affects aspects of economic development, policy implementation, and the management of community dissent (Ferman 1996; Fuchs 1992). In her study of New York City and Chicago, Ester Fuchs claims that distinct political structures influence the effectiveness of interest groups to obtain scarce city resources. Regarding interest-group participation, she notes, "Chicago and New York are at the opposite ends of the [political] spectrum" (251). New York City's system is pluralistic, open to various interest group demands, while Chicago is a closed structure run by a one-party, hegemonic political machine. She argues that Chicago's machine-dominated system is more capable of denying funding demands; therefore the city is less prone to financial problems. Fuchs's work suggests that it is not who governs, but within what structure they govern, that may affect urban neighborhoods.

The structure of a city's political system can influence the implementation of federal policies in poor black communities. Barbara Ferman's investigation of Chicago and Pittsburgh shows that various political climates affect the likelihood of successful progressive movements and policy outcomes related to minority neighborhoods. Her study examines how city-level institutional arrangements are associated with the allocation of the federal Community Development Block Grant (CDBG). She claims that Chicago's hegemonic Democratic machine ignores neighborhood-based grassroots requests for resource allocation, while Pittsburgh's political landscape is more attentive to neighborhood demands. According to Ferman, Pittsburgh's funding structure operates outside the "old machine structure" and helps establish trusting, collectively organized efforts, while Chicago's centralized, ward-based politics facilitate individualistic pleas for funding, cynicism, and mistrust. The difference in the political climates explains why neighborhood groups in Chicago receive a much lower percent of the CDBG compared to those in Pittsburgh. Ferman argues that distinct local political cultures and institutional arrangements lead to vastly different CDBG policy implementation outcomes. While national trends affect urban development, citywide political circumstances, such as unique institutional arrangements and their connections with neighborhood activism, can affect how federal policies are implemented locally.

The citywide political landscape might explain differences concerning Harlem and Bronzeville's redevelopment. In this book, political landscape is defined as the structures and norms that set the political "rules of the game" (Clark and Inglehart 1998, 12), or as Ferman puts it, "the collective expectations of the population about the roles and behaviors of their government and political system" (1996, 8). In Chicago the political structure approximates a one-party system with strong central control, while New York City's political landscape is more diffuse, fragmented, and decentralized—a difference repeatedly noted for the past fifty years (Fuchs 1992; Greenstone and Peterson [1973] 1976; Kantor 2002; Mollenkopf 1991; Simpson, Adeoye, Feliciano, and Howard 2002; Thompson 2006; Wilson 1960). My study explores whether the difference in political structures and norms influences the implementation of federal policies and the extent of displacement protest politics.

Cities often attempt to promote place-based growth through targeted housing and business incentives. In the cases of Harlem and Bronzeville, the New York City and Chicago governments have implemented several growth initiatives. To attract businesses, Chicago uses Tax Increment Financing Districts, and New York City uses Business Improvement Districts. Additionally, the New York City Housing Authority and the Chicago Housing Authority are implementing city-generated housing plans. These housing strategies are quite different. New York is rehabilitating its public housing, while Chicago is tearing down all of its high-rise developments. In Chicago, this is having a tremendous impact on the development of Bronzeville, since the community contains numerous public housing high-rise projects that are slated for demolition. I explore how the unique political structures in these cities relate to the drastically different approaches to public housing, and how this affects redevelopment outcomes.

Community Organizational Structure

In addition to external factors, internal neighborhood organizations and structures may exert local control affecting neighborhood conditions. Of particular interest is the extent to which formal community organizations such as established block clubs, community development corporations, and tenant advocacy organizations promote or inhibit economic development. Although studies by Robert Putnam (1993) and Robert Sampson, Stephen Raudenbush and Felton Earls (1997) suggest that informal groups and community norms of trust are more important than formal neighborhood organizations, other scholars present evidence that formal, community-based organizations remain critical factors in determining neighborhood conditions (Crenson 1983; Freeman 2006; Medoff and Sklar 1994; Taub, Taylor, and Dunham 1984).

Matthew Crenson's study of twenty-one communities in Baltimore finds that only 10 percent of the 1,637 individuals interviewed said that entities other than formal community organizations affected neighborhood issues: "In all the neighborhoods studied...the institutions most frequently mentioned as mechanisms for dealing with local matters were organizations that not only were formal, but had been established for specific purposes of handling neighborhood business" (1983, 207). Further, in *Paths of Neighborhood Change*, Richard Taub, Garth Taylor, and Jan Dunham find that elite community organizations greatly contribute to property value escalation in transitioning Chicago neighborhoods. Thus studies focusing solely on informal groups and norms as explanations of community change, as suggested by concepts such as social capital and collective efficacy, has limited usefulness. Recognizing this limitation does not deny or dismiss the importance of norms of engagement, trust, cohesion, and informal neighborhood groups, but we must understand the specific mechanisms by which norms are translated into local action and control. According to Crenson and Taub and colleagues, community transformation can be explored through an analysis of formal organizations.

Robert Putnam's 1993 study of social capital implies that common neighborhood goals, solidarity, and trust among neighborhood organizations make it more likely that collective action will emerge. However, in economically transitioning communities, as noted by Lance Freeman in *There Goes the 'Hood* (2006), collective interests are often hard to maintain, and residents seldom agree on collective goals. Generally, homeowners view development trends as a blessing, while others fear unrestricted development will drive rents soaring beyond their reach. Competing factions, who often form formal organizations, must decide on a tolerable level of displacement and the place for affordable housing in the midst of rapidly increasing property values. In Harlem and Bronzeville, community leaders representing different resident constituencies debate these questions.

Competing groups, distinguished by income and education, collectively act to promote or limit development in Harlem and Bronzeville.

Class distinction within black America is a critical area of research and its importance can be traced back to two classics, W. E. B. Du Bois's community study *The Philadelphia Negro* (1899) and E. Franklin Frazier's 1957 book *Black Bourgeoisie*. More contemporary scholars such as Michael Dawson (1994) and Manning Marable (2002) have continued to focus keenly on the political implications of class conflict among African Americans.[3] Recent studies of Harlem and Bronzeville suggest that intra-racial class differences play a critical role in the economic redevelopment of these communities (Boyd 2000; Taylor 2002). I explore whether the type of city regime and level of intra-racial class conflict inhibit or facilitate contested politics at the community level and if protest relates to community conditions. Contested politics refers to political actions of organizations that advocate for residents and small businesses threatened by displacement.

The organizational structure of these communities represents aspects of black civil society. By black civil society, I mean "institutions and social networks formed by individuals who participate . . . in some type of public-oriented collective action" within African-American communities (Dawson 2000, 3). By investigating the actions of competing factions in Harlem and Bronzeville, I assess aspects of black civil society and attempt to uncover whether black-led institutions affect the process of transformation.

The heuristic framework in figure 2.1 displays the variables and relationships investigated. Starting at the top of the figure, the broader political and economic context consists of forces that originate at the global and national level, as both New York City and Chicago operate as "command and control centers" within the global economic system and have specific national policies such as the EZ Initiative. I assume that "general forces generated at the level of the global" affect these cities (Abu-Lughod 1999, 406). Global structures and forces are illustrated by new social phenomena and infrastructure developments that are seen as critical components to participation in a worldwide economic network. Examples include the proliferation of a bifurcated labor market of high-wage and low-wage positions, widening income inequality and centralization within the central business district by increasing population, service sector employment, and property values. I investigate whether these macro forces are indirectly connected to community redevelopment and gentrification patterns.

Global and national forces are mediated by city political structures before they influence these communities. Some suggest that these broader forces shape community conditions or a community's organizational

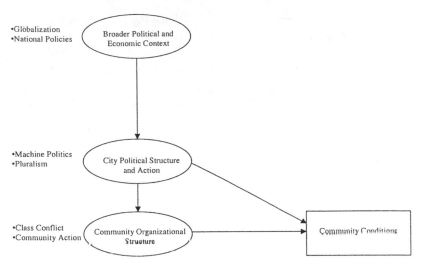

•Globalization
•National Policies

Broader Political and
Economic Context

•Machine Politics
•Pluralism

City Political Structure
and Action

•Class Conflict
•Community Action

Community Organizational
Structure

Community Conditions

Figure 2.1 A theoretical framework.

structure directly, as when large groups of immigrants flock to a particular area (Portes and Rumbaut 1996). However, this is not currently occurring in either Harlem or Bronzeville. Some argue that a direct path leading from the broader political and economic context to the community's organizational structure exists. For instance, William Julius Wilson (1996) claims that the changing global/national economy is directly tied to organizational infrastructure of low-income black areas through employment. While I agree, I want to add to Wilson's work by illustrating alternate or indirect paths through which both global and national processes have effects. Direct federal influences might have occurred during the 1960s, when large amounts of federal dollars went straight from the national government to community-based organizations. However, today most federal community development funds filter through city control, as is the case with the CDBG, the HOPE VI program and the EZ Initiative. Hence, I investigate how external factors have indirect affects on community development.

The political regimes and respective structures in New York City and Chicago are distinct. New York City is a pluralist system and Chicago is a city entrenched in machine politics. These unique regimes facilitate or inhibit contested politics stemming from the organizational structure at the community level. Moreover, specific city policies, such as Tax Increment Financing Districts and Business Improvement Districts, facilitate the development of infrastructure required to participate effectively in the global economy. Therefore, I investigate the ways in which common forces originating from the global and national level are mediated by unique pre-existing political structures and reconstituted at the community level. Theoretically, it is possible that the relationship between the broader political and economic context and the city is bi-directional. For instance, mayors advocate for favorable federal legislation through lobbying organizations, such as the National League of Cities. However, I am concerned with understanding how cities mediate global and national processes, not how they alter them. As Janet Abu-Lughod notes, "The present fates of the urbanized regions of New York [and] Chicago ... are linked to a changing geography of power, and thus, ultimately, to the shape of the larger system" (1999, 405).

The communities' organizational structures are made up of the institutions, agencies, and associations within these communities, and the relationships and actions deriving from these groups. Class divisions among and within groups in these communities are an important feature of their internal organizational structures. Through tracking black-led elite organizations, as well as smaller social service agencies and activist groups that represent low-income residents, I explore the role that intra-racial class antagonism plays in the redevelopment process. I investigate how city political structures influence contested politics at the community level, and whether internal community debate and action affect patterns of development and gentrification.

Community conditions include the physical, social, and economic features of Harlem and Bronzeville. These community characteristics are assessed over time by measuring changing racial and socioeconomic population patterns, including community investment trends and property value escalation. Lastly, this study will assess how the redevelopment process affects the extent of residential and business displacement, that is, forced removal from the community.

The multiple-level framework is different from past analytic paradigms and theories of community change because it stresses the importance of interactions among factors that originate at various levels. It also recognizes that community action may influence altering neighborhood conditions. In the next chapter, I explore the relationship between global and local processes and how these dynamics interplay to affect the redevelopment of both Harlem and Bronzeville.

3

What's Globalization Got to Do with It?

Most Starbucks coffee shops are located in middle-class communities; however, one recently opened across the street from Cabrini-Green, an infamous public housing project on the Near North Side of Chicago. The large windows of the coffee shop face out upon two, sixteen-story, gray concrete public housing high-rises. During a visit, I notice groups of people, mostly white, sitting at tables conducting business meetings. They all have PDAs, laptops, and cell phones. One group works on marketing strategies while another focuses on real estate transactions. They are, in a sense, the workers of the information age and the global economy. As I turn to look at the high-rises, I cannot help but think that the high-wage service employees of the global economy and the lives of the Cabrini-Green residents, mostly low-income African Americans, are connected. I suspect that the high-wage workers, who possibly live in the new $400,000 townhomes replacing the projects, are connected to the new Starbucks. As I sit in the coffee shop, watching business consultants order their grande mocha lattes against the backdrop of the demolition of public housing and construction of luxury townhomes in their place, I realize the international economy influences the redevelopment of poor urban communities.

Three scholars suggest that the global economy influences Bronzeville and Harlem's redevelopment. In *Global Decisions, Local Collisions* (2003),

David Ranney argues that globally traded real estate finance products help produce gentrification on the South Side of Chicago. He asserts that bonds and mortgages, which are eventually securitized and traded on the secondary market, drive up property values. He suggests that opening these financial markets to international investors frees a tremendous amount of capital that is rapidly flowing to inner city real estate markets. Mamadou Chinyelu's slightly different view is that global capital, represented by multinational corporations, such as Disney, JPMorgan Chase, and Old Navy, are emerging in Harlem, which he claims destroys indigenous "mom and pop" businesses (1999). Lastly, Lily Hoffman (2000, 2003) posits that the New York City government is investing in Harlem because of its draw as an international tourist destination.

While these global processes may contribute to neighborhood gentrification, they cannot sufficiently explain community change. First, global capital, in the form of mortgage-backed securities, has been available for some time now, yet failed to produce substantial changes in urban black communities during the 1980s. Secondly, global corporations, as well as tourists, have, until the 1990s, avoided inner city environments. We need a better explanation why global investors such as "big box" chain stores and companies deploying mortgage or commercial financing now perceive certain low-income areas as emerging markets. Further, what has altered the preferences of international tourists who find certain inner city areas top destinations? Increased market pressures for properties in the central business district—a dynamic associated with the global economy—encourages real estate developers to build in Harlem and Bronzeville.

In some cities global forces are major contributors to inner city redevelopment. High-wage global economy workers are coming back to the central city from the suburbs. This dynamic puts new market forces in play in areas surrounding the central business district (CBD). The population influx to the city center raises real estate values in once economically abandoned African-American communities. CBD expansion also encourages city governments to allocate public resources toward redeveloping nearby inner city communities, which attracts private capital and makes these areas more desirable places to live and visit.

Although an emerging line of scholarship investigates the relationship between aspects of economic globalization and inner city gentrification, the global economy is not the only force behind inner city redevelopment. Local governments are directing public investments to these communities. City political actions such as targeted tax incentives and local housing plans continue to be important. Inner city revitalization is a by-product of the interaction between macro global forces and more local factors, which produces CBD expansion and associated neighborhood gentrification.

The Global Economy

While a worldwide economy has existed at least since the days of the Greeks, in the last several decades, the international economy has developed a greater global reach, rapidity, and comprehensiveness than ever before. Today national economies all over the world are linked and can quickly affect one another. Economic events in Mexico, Argentina, Thailand, or Japan can have a direct and rapid effect on the United States, particularly its financial markets, since U.S. funds and direct investments are spread throughout these countries.[1] Forces stemming from this global economic system affect America's inner city areas.

This worldwide economy arises out of three interrelated circumstances: the opening of international financial markets, an increase in foreign direct investment (FDI), and the expansion of multinational corporations. In the 1970s, many foreign stock markets opened to international capital. Individuals and institutions, described by Thomas Friedman in *The Lexus and the Olive Tree* (2000) as the "electronic herd," today literally invest twenty-four hours a day through international money markets. As electronic transactions occur all over the world, investors make direct capital investments in foreign countries by financing the development of manufacturing plants and other production-related infrastructure. A United Nations report indicates that the world's stock of foreign direct investment skyrocketed from $213 billion to $4.1 trillion between 1972 and 1998 (Sassen [1991] 2001).

FDI sets the stage for the proliferation of multinational companies. Multinational, U.S.-based corporations such as Nike, Wal-Mart, Disney, General Motors, IBM, Intel, and Cisco manufacture and assemble their products all over the world to achieve the lowest production costs. In 1970 there were approximately 7,000 transnational corporations; today that number reaches nearly 60,000 with 800,000 subsidiaries scattered throughout the world (Ranney 2003). The magnitude of these investments leads to increased interdependency among national economies, which in turn affect communities at the local level.

World Cities Hypothesis and Inner Cities

Saskia Sassen's "world cities hypothesis" provides a useful theoretical lens to investigate global phenomena, particularly the relationships among deindustrialization, centralization, and inner city gentrification. An important component of the world cities hypothesis is the notion that the decentralized manufacturing process is coupled with "a new geography of centrality" (Sassen [1991] 2001). As the country became less industrial, companies have closed factories in the United States and transferred manufacturing to developing countries where labor costs are cheaper. As a result, inner city ghettos and communities lost crucial manufacturing jobs during the 1960s, '70s, and '80s (Wilson 1996, 1999). Decentralization, the tandem force to deindustrialization, creates the need for transnational firms to locate in strategic places to finance, coordinate, and manage their global activities. Large companies that manufacture and assemble products in different countries spanning several continents need a primary space for global coordination.

Lawyers, investment bankers, insurers, marketing specialists, and others are needed to help multinational firms expand and merge globally (Fainstein [1994] 2001). These transactions usually occur within global cities, the "command and control centers," of the international economy.[2] Thus, the central business districts of global cities are flooded with high-wage jobs in fields such as law, advertising, finance, and accounting, which in a post-Fordist era of production help multinational companies perform global coordination and mergers. In addition, smaller service-based companies that perform the outsourced work of the large transnational firms flock to the central city. Thus, the downtowns of global cities experience employment and population growth in service sector occupations.

The new centrality, based on command and control functions, has two important consequences for world cities: rising income inequality and neighborhood gentrification. The world cities hypothesis predicts that global cities will proliferate with high-wage and low-wage laborers. Since world cities are no longer sites for manufacturing, they become major markets for the production of knowledge or nonmaterial products, such as business plans, marketing strategies, or financial tools. In short, they become places that draw white-collar workers, like the customers in the Starbucks. As Sassen puts it, world cities experience "a demand for highly specialized and educated workers alongside a demand for basically unskilled workers" (1998, 146). Low-wage jobs are created in supportive businesses, such as restaurants, hotels, and cleaning services that maintain the lifestyle of the high-wage workers. The simultaneous need for high-wage and low-wage jobs leads to a bifurcated labor market and growing income inequality.

As the CBD expands, neighborhood gentrification occurs in response to the increased demand for high cost housing close to the CBD. Sassen states that, "Central to the development of this core in these cities [is] ... high income commercial and residential gentrification" (1999, 6). In *The City Builders*, a comparative study of real estate development in New York City and London that supports Sassen's theory, Susan Fainstein writes, "Central business district (CBD) expansion has increased property values in areas of low-income occupancy, forcing out residents, raising their living expenses, and breaking up communities" ([1994] 2001, 5). The central business districts of New York City and Chicago in the 1980s and 1990s attracted the well-to-do, resulting in the subsequent economic revitalization and gentrification of Harlem and Bronzeville.

New York and Chicago as Global Cities

By most standards, New York City and Chicago are global cities. During the 1980s, the amount of foreign direct investment in the New York/New Jersey area increased 198 percent, while in Illinois it skyrocketed 245 percent (Abu-Lughod 1999). With an increasing amount of foreign direct investment, processes originating from the international economy affect these metropolitan areas. Specifically, deindustrialization and new forms of centralization, related to command and control functions, affect the central business districts of these two major cities. As manufacturing flees these metropolitan regions, their central business districts grow with increasing service sector employment, middle-class population, and high-priced real estate.

Since the 1980s, New York and Chicago have experienced an expansion of their service sector economy with a simultaneous decline in the percent of workers employed in manufacturing. Table 3.1 displays the changing percent of this sector in New York and Chicago from 1981 to 1996. In this same period, New York manufacturing plummeted 50 percent while in Chicago it decreased by 35 percent. As the percentage of manufacturing declined, the services and financial, insurance, and real estate (FIRE) sectors increased. The service sector grew from 23 to 44 percent in New York and from 21 to 37 percent in Chicago. The FIRE sector in both cities nearly doubled. Additionally, the absolute number of jobs

Table 3.1   New York and Chicago: Percentage employed in select industries, 1981–96

	1981		1985		1996	
Sector	New York	Chicago	New York	Chicago	New York	Chicago
Manufacturing	16.0	28.4	14.0	20.9	8.1	17.6
TCU*	6.5	5.4	6.5	5.8	6.2	7.0
FIRE**	11.5	6.1	12.4	7.4	23.2	10.3
Services	23.3	21.2	26.5	24.6	43.5	37.1

Source: A version of this table appears in Sassen [1991] 2001.
* Transportation, Communications, and Utilities.
** Finance, Insurance, and Real Estate.

Table 3.2   Changing employment opportunities in New York and Chicago

Place	1980	1990	1998	Total jobs added
NYC*	3,302,000	3,595,000	3,524,000	222,000
	1981	1987	1997	
Chicago**	2,247,119	2,213,434	2,395,111	147,992
	1981–1987	1987–1993	1993–1996	
U.S.**	85,483,800	94,789,444	102,198,864	1,6715,064

*Source: Fainstein [1994] 2001.   ** Source: Sassen [1991] 2001.

increased, as the regional economies of these cities became dominated by service employment. As shown in table 3.2, in New York City 222,000 jobs were added to the economy between 1980 and 1998, and in Chicago 147,992 were added between 1981 and 1997.

As the number of employment opportunities climbed, the population, after decades of decline, began to increase in these cities, especially within their central business districts. The populations in New York City and Chicago increased 9 and 4 percent respectively between 1990 and 2000 (table 3.3). Although these percentages might seem small, in the 1970s, these cities lost 10 percent of their population (U.S. Department of Housing and Urban Development 2000). Moreover, much of this new population lives within and near the central area of business activity in these cities, but as mentioned above, income inequality rises with growth. The gap between the rich and the poor grew by 6 percent in New York and

Table 3.3 Population flows in New York and Chicago

Place	1980	1990	2000	% Change 1990–2000
NYC*	7,072,000	7,323,000	8,008,000	9
Manhattan*	1,428,000	1,456,000	1,537,000	6
Chicago**	3,005,072	2,783,726	2,896,016	4
Loop**	6,462	11,954	16,388	37

*Source: Fainstein [1994] 2001.   **Source: Census data.

3 percent in Chicago between 1990 and 2000.[3] Consonant with a population influx, growing income inequality, and downtown expansion, Harlem and Bronzeville, which occupy spaces in close proximity to their respective CBDs, began to gentrify in the late 1990s.

New York as a Global City

Any analysis of world cities ranks New York as a preeminent powerhouse on the global scene. Today, New York City's top ten banks maintain approximately $1.2 trillion in assets (Gladstone and Fainstein 2003). New York is home to two major international exchanges, the New York Stock Exchange (NYSE) and the National Association of Securities Dealers Automated Quotations stock market (NASDAQ). Additionally, the city and its suburban ring are home to the corporate headquarters of sixty-five large firms, including those in the financial and media sectors (Fainstein [1994] 2001). New York is truly a cosmopolitan city where people from all over the world come to visit and do business. In 2000, 6.8 million (37 percent) of the 18.4 million tourists visiting New York City were international tourists (Gladstone and Fainstein 2003).

In the 1990s, New York City prospered. Commenting on the fiscal health and growth of New York City in the 1990s, William Sites, who studies the redevelopment of New York's Lower East Side, states, "Soaring employment growth in the service sector, fueled by job increases in business services, was finally helping to diminish the city's high unemployment rate to its lowest level since 1980s. Wall Street enjoyed profits of $16.3 billion in 1999, up more than one third from the record of $12.2 billion registered two years earlier. The commercial real-estate market was also operating at record levels, driven in part by leasing activity from the high-flying Internet, news-media, and high technology firms in the business-service sector" (2003, 63). Sites's remarks effectively illustrate the relationships among the stock market, the high-tech industry, and rising real estate boom in the city.

To fully understand the connection between the centralization process and neighborhood gentrification, it is important to sketch out the spatial geography of New York City and its five boroughs, Manhattan, the Bronx, Queens, Brooklyn, and Staten Island. Manhattan is the principal borough, surrounded by the other four, and is composed of twelve community districts, and most commercial and financial activity occurs in Lower and Midtown Manhattan. While wealthier than the other boroughs, Manhattan does have concentrated poverty in three areas: the Lower East Side, Hell's Kitchen, and the areas north of 110th Street. In contrast, the rest of Manhattan contains some of the most expensive real estate in the world. Figure 3.1 displays Central Harlem's location in relation to other areas in Manhattan.

While employment prospects increase throughout the city, the centralization process disproportionately affects Manhattan. In the early 1990s, Manhattan's population rose as the populations in other boroughs declined. According to the 1996 New York City Housing and Vacancy Survey (HVS), Manhattan experienced the largest percentage (7 percent) of population influx compared to the other four boroughs (Schill and Scafidi 1999). Additionally, vacancy rates for both residential and commercial spaces decreased in the 1990s. According to the HVS, between 1993 and 1996, the vacancy rate of residential rental units in Manhattan remained virtually the same at 3.5 percent, while all other boroughs experienced a slight increase (Schill and Scafidi 1999). In Lower and Midtown Manhattan, commercial space tightened as vacancy rates declined from 17.6 and 14.5 percent in 1990 to 4.9 and 5.0 percent in 2000, respectively (Fainstein [1994] 2001).

The economic boom, exacerbated by a bullish stock market, led to a bifurcated labor market and polarized the city's income structure. In the 1990s the FIRE sectors accounted for 57 percent of the wage growth in Manhattan. The changing employment and compensation structure resulted in income polarization; both the number of rich and poor households grew dramatically, affecting the housing market in Manhattan (Gladstone and Fainstein 2003). Property values in Manhattan soared as the percentage of service sector employment increased and the gap between the rich and the poor widened.

Median home values grew sharply in Manhattan, from $500,000 to over $1 million between 1990 and 2000 (see appendix B). In the early

Figure 3.1 Map of select New York City neighborhoods.

1990s, many working-class neighborhoods in Lower and Midtown Manhattan, including the Lower East Side (Mele 2000; Sites 2003), Chelsea, Hell's Kitchen, and Times Square (Sagalyn 2001), turned into high-rent commercial and residential districts. As these low-rent neighborhoods developed, affordable housing in Manhattan became increasingly scant; the number of low-rent areas, as well as the percentage of affordable dwellings decreased (New York City Economic Development Corporation 2004). Sites comments, "Shifts in the city's income structure [widening inequality], coupled with the booming land economy, created growing affordability problems for New York's low-income residents" (2003, 64).

The redevelopment of neighborhoods below 110th Street had subsequent consequences for Harlem. This new housing demand eventually moved uptown to Harlem, one of the last low-rent areas in Manhattan. One expert on economic development in New York City proclaims that Harlem is gentrifying, but "all of Manhattan is gentrifying." David Patterson, former Harlem New York state senator and current lieutenant governor, during an interview explains: "Well, between October 10, 1990 and June 8, 1998, the Dow Jones on the stock market quadrupled from about 2,500 to over 10,000. In the year of 1999 the NASDAQ increased 81% by itself, there was—by 1994, 1995—big [dollar] number around, [and] nobody knew what to do with it. People started investing and their investing turned this neighborhood into a giant scaffold, which is where we are now."[4]

Harlem's recent development can only be understood within the broader context of Manhattan's real estate market. Two anecdotes from my field notes illustrate the new market pressures uptown. I attended a real estate event for those interested in buying brownstones in Harlem. The gathering took place in a private VIP room of a restaurant. The room had about seven little tables, decorated with leopard print tablecloths and votive candles. On the walls hung African masks and other artwork. A flat screen TV on the wall showed music videos from Black Entertainment Television's (BET) program *106th and Park*. The room had a full bar, and crab cake appetizers were served. Even though the restaurant was on 72nd Street in the Upper West Side, an affluent, predominantly white area, most of thirty or so people attending were African-American bankers, lawyers, doctors, and insurance agents. I got myself a beer and sat down at one of the tables. An African-American woman in her mid-forties, sitting next to me, introduced herself. She explained that she had been looking in Harlem for almost two years, but had not found anything in her price range. She was living at the time near Central Park West in a one-bedroom apartment, which she bought for $400,000 on the eighteenth floor of a condominium building. She liked her unit because of the beautiful view of Central Park, but she was looking for more space and hoped to find a Harlem brownstone with three or four levels for around the same price. I then understood why she had been looking for so long. In the early 1990s, $400,000 might have afforded a brownstone in Harlem, but by 2000 most rehabilitated brownstones cost much more. In Manhattan's high-priced real estate market, many two-bedroom condos units below 110th Street cost nearly one million dollars. As much of Manhattan has become affordable only for the very wealthy, the market price for brownstones in Harlem also accelerated.

Those looking to own a house in Manhattan for less than one million dollars must look to Harlem. I spoke with one of Harlem's black real estate developers about the conditions affecting the housing market. He mentioned that "as properties values are increased south of Harlem, there is this great desire [for] . . . the properties up here . . . because people are paying $2,500 [a month] for a one-bedroom apartment below 110th Street. So they come up here; they can afford [to rent] a brownstone for $2,500 and you have 4,000–5,000 square feet of space. So, it's just economically feasible to come here. You know, there's value." The former director of the Empowerment Zone explained, "Harlem is the only place in Manhattan where you [can] get a brownstone shell for between $300,000 and $400,000. Anywhere else in Manhattan the shell alone might cost a million."

One afternoon, I strolled along one of the beautiful brownstone-lined blocks, near Strivers Row in Harlem, and noticed a cardboard For Sale sign in the window. As I walked by, I saw that the door of the building was wide open. I approached the stoop and hollered into the house, "Hello." A woman, in her early to midfifties, with dreadlocks and a red handkerchief around her head, came out. We introduced ourselves and shook hands. "Are you interested in buying or just looking?" she asked. I told her I wasn't interested in buying, but that I lived on the block and was curious about the house and wanted to see the inside. "Sure," she replied, and she took me through the three-story structure. Although most of the brownstones on the block were rehabilitated, this house was really, as they say, a "shell." There was no running water. There were holes in the roof, and the stairs looked as if they might cave in at any point. In fact, I was a little nervous going up them. Most of the original wood had been removed, and the floors were all torn up. Even though the inside of the house was in bad shape, the front exterior was unblemished, and with a significant amount of work this home would become a stunning residence.

After the tour, Mary and I talked on her stoop. I told her I was in graduate school. "Are you in urban planning?" she asked. "No, sociology." "Who owns the place you live in?" she asked. "Ken," I said. "I know Ken. His place is beautiful, right, with all that cherry wood." I agreed. I asked her how long she'd owned the house. Mary obtained it from the city thirty-two years ago when she was attending City College and explained that she never really had the money to fix it up. When I asked her what she was selling it for, she quickly replied, "$600,000. That's how much these things are going for these days. Things around here have really changed in the last three years." "How much would you have asked for three years ago?" I asked. "$350,000." "So the market has almost doubled in three years," I said, and she replied, "Yeah, just about." Although the house was a "shell," in need of much repair, brownstones in Harlem were now commanding prices between $600,000 to over $1,000,000, depending on their condition and location. Three days later the sign was removed; renovations began within a month.

Soaring property values lead to increased threats of gentrification and displacement in Harlem. A staff member from one of Harlem's leading political officials, declared, "We have a big problem of displacement here. There are many land speculators out there ... and very little vacant land so there is nowhere to put people who are displaced. The gentrification in Harlem has two sides to it, one is the small businesses and the other is the resident population." When asked about whether recent economic development in Harlem would lead to displacement, Terry Lane, the former head of the Upper Manhattan Empowerment Zone, bluntly stated, "Displacement is a by-product of development." Favorable market pressures lead to the rehabilitation of many brownstones. Once improvements are made, the landlords either raise rents or sell the entire building as a single family home. This forces renters who cannot afford the increases to look for housing elsewhere.[5] While living in Harlem and working for one of Harlem's high raking politicians, I witnessed several low-income residents and small businesses being forced out as a result of mounting market pressures and rising real estate prices (see chapter 5).

Affordable housing activists are especially concerned with rising real estate values. When discussing the current housing circumstance, one of the organizers declares, "There are many people who are being displaced here with the improvements. ... Rents at $1,000 a month are not affordable to many people here." When asked where people are going, one explained that some people are heading back down South, while another told me people are moving to parts of the Bronx and New Jersey. A similar process of centralization and neighborhood gentrification affects Chicago.

Chicago as a Global City

The international processes of deindustrilaization and centralization affect the metropolitan landscape in Chicago. However, Chicago is not on the same global scale as New York City. It has a smaller population and is less recognized as an international tourist destination. Yet, Chicago has certain qualities of a global city, such as its financial capacity. Chicago has 130 domestic and 70 international banks and two major exchange markets (the Chicago Board of Trade [CBOT] and the Chicago Mercantile Exchange [MERC]). The CBOT and the MERC are international exchanges where agriculture and debt futures and options are traded. Although Chicago is known for regional and domestic interactions, it exports to and imports from all over the world. According to a report by the Chicago Department of Development and Planning (1993), the value of exports to Japan is approximately $2 billion, while imports are $6 billion. Chicago is the fourth largest advertising market in the world with sales of approximately $11.2 billion (Short and Kim 1999). Foreign direct investment is prevalent, as there are over 1,600 foreign-owned enterprises in Illinois, mostly in Chicago. Chicago's metropolitan region also has approximately fifty-five Fortune 500 companies (Feagin 1998). With multinational firms such as Motorola and the Boeing Company headquartered in and around Chicago, "the old 'city of the big shoulders' is being remade into the global city capital of the Midwest" (Simpson 2001, 289).

Chicago's transition from an industrial center to a more service oriented high-tech economy has had repercussions for its central business district and the low-income, black neighborhoods south of the Loop. Chicago comprises seventy-seven community districts that radiate to the north, south, and west around the Loop, Chicago's central business district.[6] Lake Michigan prevents any eastward expansion. In Chicago, the community areas just north of the Loop (i.e., the Gold Coast, Lincoln Park) are primarily white and wealthy, while the Near West and South Sides mostly house low-income African Americans. Figure 3.2 shows Bronzeville's location in relation to the Loop.

In Chicago, new forms of centralization have followed deindustrialization. Data from the 1980s and 1990s show that that the growth in Chicago's Loop, or CBD, has had a subsequent impact on the real estate values and population demographics in contiguous South Side neighborhoods. Between 1972 and 1982, the number of employment opportunities increased in the CBD by 8 percent, while the rest of the city lost 17 percent of their jobs (Squires, Bennett, McCourt, and Nyden 1987). Between 1980 and 1990, the CBD had an 85 percent increase in population, the highest of all community areas in the city (Chicago Planning and Development 1997). The Loop's median home value during this time soared nearly 300 percent from $55,250 to $218,182 (see appendix B). In

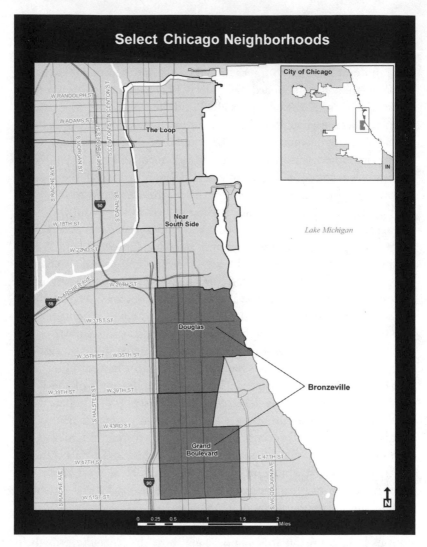

Figure 3.2 Map of select Chicago neighborhoods.

the 1990s, as the CBD's property values stabilized, the population influx continued, increasing by 40 percent.

This process of centralization is accompanied by job growth and labor market wage polarization. Federal Reserve Bank economists Douglas Evanoff, Philip Israilevich, and Graham Schindler (1997) indicate that Chicago's financial markets are leading the area's transformation from a manufacturing hub to a service center by adding jobs to the local economy. However, these employment opportunities are not producing benefits for all Chicago residents. According to Janet Abu-Lughod, "becoming a 'global city' via the MERC has not contributed general prosperity to the region's population; indeed, if anything, it has widened the gap between the 'haves' and the 'have nots'" (1999, 329).

After the reemergence of the Loop in the 1980s, gentrification began in many nearby low-income, black neighborhoods in the 1990s. After forty years of population decline, the Near South Side, directly south of the Loop and north of Bronzeville, had a nearly 40 percent increase in population between 1990 and 2000. The new population inhabiting both the CBD and the Near South Side is made up of mostly high-wage earners, as evidenced by the high cost of the apartments and new commercial spaces being built.

The Near South Side has been transformed from a decaying industrial center to a chic professional neighborhood. The Near South Side was once considered part of Bronzeville; in the 1960s it was rezoned as an industrial area and became sparely populated, but it remains primarily African American. In the 1980s, the area contained several single room occupancy (SRO) buildings for the homeless and those of modest income. However, most of these units have recently been demolished or converted to pricey condominium and rental units. One SRO building that housed a check-cashing outlet has been converted into an expensive rental building with a trendy breakfast eatery on the first floor. Across the street, another SRO footprint now houses a large chain grocery store, a Starbucks and a dry cleaner. The neighborhood now contains many luxury high-rises, stylish bars, and upscale restaurants.

As commercial and residential investments are made in this area, home values escalate. Recently constructed loft-style units command prices from $500,000 to $800,000. In 1990, Near South Side median household income was $6,804, well below the poverty line. By 2000 the household income had jumped over 400 percent to $34,329, a clear sign of the Loop's southern expansion and gentrification. As the Loop and Near South Side develop, the market pressure mounts in Bronzeville, directly to the south.

During the 1990s, Bronzeville had large increases in its home values. Between 1990 and 2000, real estate prices in Douglas and Grand Boulevard, the two contiguous districts that make up Bronzeville, rose 67 and 192 percent, respectively. Many vacant lots in the community display

Figure 3.3 Bronzeville's graystones.

large signs illustrating newly planned construction, with units ranging between $350,000 and $600,000. On Martin Luther King Jr. Drive, the community's main thoroughfare, graystones once split into smaller one-room kitchenettes, are rehabilitated into beautiful single-family homes.

Downtown centralization is associated with the increased market demand for housing in Bronzeville. During an interview a foundation program officer who has lived on Chicago's south side for many years, explains:

> Affordability has to be a real issue because the Near North Side is so unaffordable. So even with the near south developments, where ... [people] come up pretty quickly with $300,000 to $500,000 to buy some little postage stamp size condominium with a black wrought iron patio, stapled into the side of the building, it still works, it's still a draw. I worked in the South Loop when Printers Row and Dearborn Park were all getting built next to the financial district. ... So I think it is a natural pattern, although I haven't studied this, that cities sort of revitalize around the core. ... We are in that kind of pattern, and the mid-south side [i.e., Bronzeville] has just been an undiscovered jewel for lots of people who were looking for new housing. Now, [they] see it and find that the city is really making it a safer place to live and understand the inevitability of the private market in making this place unaffordable for those who aren't like them.

He outlines the relationship between the development of the South Loop, a middle-class enclave, the subsequent development of the Near South Side, and the gentrification process in Bronzeville. The areas in the South Loop that were first developed are located directly adjacent to the financial district.[7] Dearborn Park, Printers Row, and now the Near South Side house high-wage service workers, some of whom surely work at the nearby Chicago Board of Trade.

The increased presence of high-wage individuals near the "inner core" is associated with a new demand for properties in Bronzeville. Middle-income African Americans, both young professionals and retired couples, are moving to the community. The program officer continues, "We know that there is interest in returning to urban centers from people who fled the same centers to the suburbs when they were raising children. They are now returning to [these] mixed-income communities." He points out that those moving to the community are not stereotypical gentrifiers in that "they are not returning to be [urban] pioneers." They are established middle- and upper-income households. As these households purchase in Bronzeville, property values skyrocket. A leader of a resident-driven neighborhood association comments on the rising property values in the Gap, a middle-class and professional enclave in Bronzeville:

It's been remarkable what has occurred on a scale when you look at property values and some people, seventeen years ago, paid $15,000 for a house. That same house with nothing done to it, can sell for anywhere up to $250,000. There is one house that is on ... Calumet. That house has been boarded up [for years]; it's on the market for $360,000. Someone is going to come in and put another $100,000 [in repairs], so it's a $400,000 house. Someone [else] just built a house in the 3400 block of Calumet and the house is ... just shy of $500,000. I remember talking to one of my neighbors, and we were saying, we're not going to move out until we can sell our house for half a million dollars. That was seventeen years ago, that's not far from being off. Would we have ever thought that [our] houses would have increased in value in that amount of time? No.

As property values in the Loop and in Bronzeville increase, the link between downtown centralization and neighborhood gentrification becomes evident to community activist Ron Carter. Carter is a former merchant association leader and community newspaper editor who grew up in the Robert Taylor Homes, a public housing project in Bronzeville; he asserts,

The Loop can only grow so much without expanding. So Bronzeville, which is really next door to the Loop, is getting that attention. It's just, to me, a normal pattern of a city development when you're close to the Loop. You can look at what contributes to that idea, as the Loop or the surrounding Loop [area] develops, those people of affluent financial status do not want to be next door to people in public housing. So in order to attract those people of affluent financial status, you're going to have to get rid of the public housing or the menace that would not attract new buyers. So those folks of lower income had to go.

Though Carter calls the development of the Loop and its surrounding neighborhoods part of a "normal pattern," consistent with how most cities attempt to develop their downtowns, Chicago's Loop and its adjacent South Side neighborhoods have been experiencing population loss and economic decline for so long that the Loop's reemergence is far from the norm. Although Carter does not use terminology of economic globalization, clearly he perceives that market forces affecting the downtown are affecting the redevelopment of Bronzeville.

As luxury homes are constructed, large high-rise public housing complexes scattered throughout the community are coming down (see chapter 5), and their tenants are relocating to more distant South Side neighborhoods and inner suburbs (Fischer 2003; Venkatesh, Celimli, Miller, Murphy, and Turner 2004). Displacement is also occurring in the private housing market; several private rental units have been converted to condominiums, and tenants who are unable to buy are cleared out. In addition, landlords who once accepted Section 8 low-income housing vouchers now prefer to rent to market-rate tenants.

The data on job growth, population movement, and housing prices in New York and Chicago support a prediction of the world cities hypothesis. While the CBD expands with high-wage service workers, adjacent inner-city neighborhoods are redeveloped and gentrified. But before concluding that globalization alone is leading to the revitalization of Harlem and Bronzeville, we must consider the role of tangible city actions.

Global-Local Interaction: BIDs and New York City's Housing Plan

New York City uses a variety of local economic strategies to facilitate the development of the central business district and nearby low-income neighborhoods. One tool that has been successful in New York City is the Business Improvement District (BID). BIDs are quasi-governmental associations that require a levy from for-profit businesses in a designated district, and use those funds to develop an area (see National Council for Urban Economic Development 1988). BIDs also have the authority to issue bonds to raise capital for district improvements. Some BIDs use their money to hire security, while others employ funds to increase garbage collection services or to upgrade lighting fixtures or sidewalks. All enhancements are paid for by area establishments as a way to promote a business-friendly environment. There are forty-six active BIDs in New York City. Times Square is an example of an extremely successful BID that helped transform the area from its seedy days to its recent "Disneyfication." Many sections of Lower, Upper, and Midtown Manhattan have their own BID. The BIDs facilitate centralization and community redevelopment in Manhattan by making certain districts more attractive to investors, which can increase property values. BIDs have been very successful in Lower and Midtown Manhattan.

In Harlem, the 125th Street BID plays a modest role, but public resources, connected to the city's housing plan immensely contribute to Harlem's redevelopment. In the late 1970s, New York City became the default manager of nearly 40,000 occupied units and 60,000 vacant apartments (Branconi 1999). During this time, numerous landlords abandoned their buildings and refused to pay property taxes. The city repossessed these properties, and either boarded them up or converted them into housing stock for homeless and low-income individuals. These properties are known as "in-rem," the legal term for tax delinquent properties. Starting with Mayor Koch's administration in the mid-1980s and persisting through the Dinkins and Giuliani administrations, there was a push to return these buildings to the private market. The push to reduce the in-rem housing stock is part of the city's comprehensive Ten-Year Housing Plan (Schill, Ellen, Schwartz, and Voicu 2002). The rationale is to have developers rehabilitate these buildings, and sell them to middle- and upper-income individuals, thus generating tax revenues for the city.

The Department of Housing Preservation and Development (HPD) is implementing three strategies to rid the city of its management and ownership duties of the in rem housing stock. Under the HPD's Division of Alternative Management, the agency attempts to promote homeownership through its Tenant Interim Lease program. This program is designed to turn the management and ownership of the buildings over to the tenants. By 1996, 600 buildings had been sold to tenant co-operatives, with mixed success. Some remained viable but many went into fiscal deficits. The second approach is to sell the housing stock for a minimal price, usually a dollar, to nonprofit organizations, with the hope that they will rehabilitate the buildings and rent units out to moderate-income tenants. As of 1996, 23 percent of the dispositions were given to nonprofits. The last strategy, and most controversial, is the Neighborhood Entrepreneurial Program (NEP), which provides buildings to private, for-profit developers. After his election in 1993, Mayor Giuliani appointed a new housing commissioner, Deborah Wright, to implement this program. To the surprise of many, the initiative focuses on selling buildings to minority-owned, private developers. The move partly silences advocacy groups because of the goal to improve minority businesses, but it does little to secure affordable housing, since few income restrictions are placed on the units. Many of the newly redeveloped, high-priced brownstones and condominiums in Harlem are financed through the city's NEP.

During the 1980s, the city controlled approximately 65 percent of Harlem's residential properties (Wylde 1999). Since the city owns such a large proportion of Harlem properties, HPD action greatly accelerates the redevelopment of the community. HPD invested over $400 million in the greater Harlem area from 1994 to 2000, resulting in a 68 percent reduction of the number of city-owned vacant buildings (New York City Department of Housing Preservation and Development 2002). The city's investments are noticed by the private sector, and major banks begin financing the rehabilitation and development of newly constructed luxury condominiums and townhomes. The once red-lined areas of Harlem essentially become green-lined, as every major bank, including JPMorgan Chase, Bank of America, and Citibank, invest in residential and commercial construction. In fact, one bank alone invested approximately $400 million in Harlem between 1999 and 2004. Figure 3.4 pictures some of Harlem's new townhomes financed by JPMorgan Chase.

The head of the community real estate division of one of the large commercial banks walks through Harlem with me and describes the neighborhood as "an underserved market" compared to areas below 96th Street. The housing "demand outweighs the supply," he remarks. He then mentions how the city's actions contributed to the bank's interest in the community. In 1996 and 1997 the city put numerous subsidies into Harlem to "reduce the risk of investments," according to the banker. The city provided funds for land clearance, he explains, and the bank and city agreed that if homeownership fails, the city would turn the properties back into rentals and buy the mortgages from the bank. The initial public subsidies facilitated the bank's decision to invest in Harlem, he says, but today fewer public subsidies are available and that the bank carries

Figure 3.4 Harlem's new townhomes.

more of the risk. Therefore, the bank now supports the construction of more market-rate and luxury housing in Harlem, which provides greater returns on their investments.

The policy decision to rebuild the city's abandoned housing stock and the subsequent action of the banks to partner with the city and real estate developers to build new structures are local actions. However, the process of centralization, stemming from economic globalization, is the broader context facilitating this circumstance. Banks do not finance housing construction or rehabilitation without strong evidence that the units will sell. The rise in real estate prices in Lower and Midtown Manhattan encourages greater market demand in Harlem. This new housing demand, created by an interaction between global and local forces, helps to reduce investment risk in Harlem while increasing the threat of displacement.

Global-Local Interaction: Chicago's TIFs

In Chicago, compelling evidence suggests that the actions of the city government facilitate the processes of centralization and gentrification. A series of plans has been developed by Chicago's business elite to construct "large scale government infrastructure projects to bring the city to the level they require to do this global business profitably" (Feagin 1998, 15). To implement these plans, the city invests huge sums of public resources into commercial and residential projects to improve the downtown and its surrounding communities.

The primary tool for providing this investment is through Tax Increment Financing (TIF) districts. TIFs allow municipalities to direct local taxes toward public and private developments, usually by providing funding for land clearance.[8] In Chicago, TIFs are the mayor's primary economic development tool, and as of 2002 the city had 119 TIF districts, encompassing properties worth well over $2.6 billion (Schwartz, Leavy, Nolan, and Jones 1999).

The TIF implementation is an example of the nexus between global and local forces since local decisions channel public funds to develop critical, global infrastructure. Much of the new construction in the CBD and the Near South Side is financed through city bonds issued by local TIF authorities. TIF funds have been given to developers to improve the Loop's entertainment district and for the construction of luxury apartment buildings in the Near South Side. In fact, until recently, the mayor lived in a lavish housing development that received substantial TIF funding (Ranney 2003). The value of the TIF subsidy in the CBD is $143 million, while the private developers who receive these funds have invested $931 million (Schwartz, Leavy, Nolan, and Jones 1999). In the Near South Side, the value of the subsidy to developers is $19 million, while private investment is $118 million. At least six TIF districts, which support business and housing construction, are in Bronzeville.

TIFs exacerbate the process of gentrification by increasing property taxes. In a TIF district, property values are assessed prior to development. This measure is called the "tax increment base value." An evaluation predicts what the increase in the tax base would be if particular development projects occur. This predicted tax value is called the "tax increment." Based on the prediction of the increment, bonds are usually issued to subsidize the cost associated with development. The difference between the tax increment base value and the tax increment is the "captured assessed value," which is used to pay back the bonds. Therefore, a successful TIF raises property values. As is often the case when property values increase, residents are forced to pay higher property taxes and increased rents. Chris Schwartz and colleagues write that in Chicago, "The problem of displacement cuts to the heart of who wins and who loses as a result of the TIF program" (1999, 21).

Ron Carter comments on the TIF program and displacement in Bronzeville. He believes that the TIF is just "another funding project that's being used against the people." He declares, "I don't think TIFs are all that needed, I think they're just more of how to control the economics of a community, opposed to really benefiting it." He acknowledges that TIFs are being used to subsidize housing, which helps to "stabilize the community" but asserts that homeownership "don't produce no real economic base." According to Carter, a real economic base produces jobs. He comments that new housing makes the community "look good" and beautifies it, but it does little to stimulate "business development." Carter recognizes that higher-income households might eventually attract commercial developments that can employ low-income residents but he questions whether this population will be in the community long enough to reap those benefits: "Again, it's going back to all of these programs and funds that are supposed to benefit the people that live in the community. . . . How's it going to benefit . . . people when they don't live there anymore?"

Local political decisions are deploying public funds to entice private capital to the inner core of the city. These investments promote features of centrality, which are seen as critical to creating a global city, while at the same time assisting gentrification. Through the implementation of the TIF program, the city's actions facilitate the development of the CBD, the Near South Side, and Bronzeville. But it would be inaccurate to claim that local policy alone brings investments into these areas, since businesses and housing developers rarely relocate, expand, or build based primarily on the availability of public subsidies (Riposa 1996). A more plausible explanation is that favorable private investment conditions are created by both an increased importance of locating in the CBD and local political actions.

Discussion

Rising real estate markets in Harlem and Bronzeville are associated with the intersection of global and local forces. Recent patterns of growth and expansion, indicated by rising population, high-wage service sector employment and escalating real estate prices in New York's and Chicago's central business districts are associated with a heightened market demand for real estate in Harlem and Bronzeville. CBD expansion is associated with the global economy since new employment opportunities are disproportionately in the service sector. In conjunction with the global dynamic of centralization, evidence indicates that city actions, such as the use of various public subsidies, also facilitate the development of the CBDs and neighborhood gentrification.

Through exploring the altering conditions of Harlem and Bronzeville, we witness the complex nature of the global/local relationship. The importance of locating in the CBD and local political action (the subsidies) stimulate private capital flows that affect community conditions. My line of reasoning coincides with William Sites, who posits that "globalist approaches can overemphasize the unmediated impacts of the international economy on cities, [while] localist frameworks often fail to address the dynamic interplay between [broader forces] ... and local politics" (2003, 67). Centralization and resulting gentrification, although influenced by a global dynamic, are also associated with targeted local political actions.

My argument concerning globalization and its effect on Harlem and Bronzeville's redevelopment is quite distinct from the assessments of other scholars. Lily Hoffman, Mamadou Chinyelu and David Ranney assert that different aspects of globalization influence these communities. Hoffman claims that increased international tourism in Harlem leads the city to spend more resources for improvements to attract greater tourism revenues. Chinyelu argues that multinational companies directly target Harlem's aggregate purchasing power. Finally, Ranney posits that integrated international financial markets relate to excessive capital and credit used by housing speculators to develop inner city real estate markets. This study adds another layer of complexity to these arguments by demonstrating that central city expansion is also associated with increased real estate pressures. Previously untapped housing markets in Harlem and Bronzeville, just outside of the traditional CBDs, are redeveloping as real estate prices escalate in the downtown areas of New York City and Chicago. As the inner city markets gentrify, new populations move into these neighborhoods, mainly the black middle class (see chapter 7), and the poor are displaced to other high poverty areas (see chapter 5).

One major problem with the evidence presented is the possibility that centralization and associated neighborhood gentrification is due to national instead of global or local forces. In two subsequent chapters, I deal with urban national policy and its relationship the conditions in Harlem and Bronzeville. However, another related argument must be addressed. There are accounts that empty nesters, suburban couples with adult children, are retiring to, or buying second homes in many cities throughout the United States (Tyre 2004). This phenomenon, which appears to be unrelated to the global economy, might be associated with the process of centralization and rising real estate prices in the some metropolitan areas. If this is a robust trend, we should witness a population increase in many major cities across the United States. However, centralization and associated inner city redevelopment in African-American neighborhoods seem to be occurring mostly in cities with global connections, including New York City, Chicago, Los Angeles, Boston, and Atlanta (von Hoffman 2003). The economic revitalization of the inner core is not happening in cities that lack the characteristics of a global city, such as St. Louis, Kansas City, and Detroit, which are still experiencing overall population loss (U.S. Department of Housing and Urban Development 2000).[9] Thus, something about global cities attracts a sufficient number of high-income people to stimulate inner city development.

The pattern of centralization and subsequent neighborhood gentrification has drastic repercussions for globalization and urban development theory. Some argue that globalization is a supranational force, affecting the landscape of world cities. However, the pattern of central city expansion and community development in New York and Chicago is by no means solely a supranational process. In Harlem and Bronzeville, we witness that a combination of global forces and tangible city actions structures their development. The high-wage workers of the global economy need to be housed, and they are buying homes convenient to the central business district. Although population increase seems to be associated with the role of New York City and Chicago as command and control centers, specific policy tools, such as TIFs, BIDs, and local housing initiatives, result in downtown centralization and subsequent neighborhood gentrification. Harlem and Bronzeville's redevelopment is, in part, a product of the interaction between an abstract and more macro external force and concrete city action. Thus, as processes originating from the global economy become increasingly important, city politics remain central to notions of inner city economic development.

Global and local forces are not the only dynamics connected to the redevelopment of the inner city; federal policies are also playing a major role. In the next two chapters, I explore how national community economic development and housing policies relate to inner city revitalization. In particular, I examine how national policies interact with the distinct city political systems of New York City and Chicago to produce changes in the urban landscape.

4

The New Urban Renewal, Part 1:
The Empowerment Zones

In his seminal study *City Limits* (1981), Paul Peterson argues that regardless of their internal political structures and conditions, cities tend to adopt similar policies. All cities endorse pro-growth initiatives to attract affluent individuals and businesses to increase land values and the city's tax base. Written at the nadir of twentieth-century urban development, his study discounts distinct governance structures, altering party dominance, grassroots movements, and varying constituent demands placed on the city. Local factors are insignificant, he argues, and "powerful forces external to the city carry great weight in local policymaking" (64). He sees dynamics beyond the city, "not the internal struggles for power within cities," as determining city policies (4). For Peterson local politics do not explain policy outcomes.

Although most scholars agree that external circumstances, such as intercity competition for industries and affluent populations, are important in shaping city policies, many consider internal political circumstances central to a city's policy choices. For example, theoretical and empirical studies of machine politics (Gosnell 1937), elitism (Mills [1956] 2000), pluralism (Dahl 1961), urban regimes (Stone 1989), and the growth machine (Logan and Moloch 1987) stress the importance of municipal politics on local policy outcomes. These works consider both informal and formal governance structures and examine who governs, how they govern, and how governance affects who benefits in the city. In contrast to Peterson, these studies claim local politics matter for resource distribution and urban development.

It is worth revisiting the debate between the "city limits" and the "city choices" perspective for two reasons (Wong 1990). First, the economic context of certain cities has changed since Peterson presented his argument in 1981. Much of the literature supporting the city limits paradigm dates to the 1970s and early 1980s when cities were on the decline, losing core industries and middle-class populations. As industries and more affluent populations left for the suburbs, cities experienced rising unemployment and financial distress, forcing almost all city mayors to make economic development strategies top priorities. But in the 1990s, as thriving international and U.S. economies attracted new businesses and high-wage earners to the downtowns of both Chicago and New York, the cities' fiscal constraints eased. This relative economic prosperity lessened the influence of fiscal concerns on municipal decision making.

Second, there is a growing need to examine the mechanisms and consequences of federal power devolution. Before the 1970s many federal programs had specific criteria limiting the types of programs cities implemented. However, since the Nixon years, the federal government has increasingly used block grants, a funding structure that provides states and cities more flexibility and autonomy. Block grants operate under the assumption that there is no one-size-fits-all program, and that cities need to tailor their urban development initiatives to their particular contexts. Currently, the federal government annually allocates $90 billion in noncategorical block grants for education, transportation, social services, welfare, housing, and economic development.[1] Today's proliferation of block grants allows states and cities to implement a variety of strategies to reach nationally determined objectives (Leland 2001; Oates 1999; Rich 1989; Wong and Peterson 1986).[2] The move to devolution enhances the potential that city political circumstances influence the direction of federal funding.

A city's particular form of government influences national policy implementation and outcomes at the local level. Barbara Ferman's (1996) examination of Chicago and Pittsburgh demonstrates that various political climates and city-level institutional arrangements influence how federal policy affects neighborhoods. She claims that Chicago's centralized Democratic machine ignores neighborhood-based grassroots' requests for resource allocation, and that Pittsburgh's political landscape is more tolerant of neighborhood demands. Pittsburgh's funding structure engenders cooperative organizing efforts, while Chicago's centralized ward-based politics deters collective demands placed on the city. The difference in the political climates, according to Ferman, explains why Chicago's neighborhood groups receive a much lower percent of the Community Development Block Grant (CDBG) compared to Pittsburgh's.

Kenneth Wong and Paul Peterson (1986) assess the implementation and distribution of the CDBG between 1975 and 1981 in two other cities, Baltimore and Milwaukee. Baltimore's political culture is in some ways similar to Chicago, while Milwaukee has been shaped by Progressive Era reforms. Unlike Ferman, they argue that the city's political structure matters less than broader economic influences and mayoral preferences. They claim that city mayors "allocated block grant resources in such a manner as to benefit themselves politically without sacrificing the communities' long-term economic interests" (294). Wong and Peterson posit that both local economic development and political concerns simultaneously influence the deployment of the block grant. They move further away from Peterson's original 1981 thesis of economic determinism but avoid espousing Ferman's institutional/cultural theory. Wong and Peterson see key institutional actors, such as the mayor, and their dual preferences for re-election and economic growth as driving local funding decisions. In my assessment of New York City and Chicago, I suggest, as Ferman does, that the structure of the local political environment is critical to understanding policy implementation.

New York City and Chicago Politics: Pluralism and the Machine

New York City's and Chicago's political environments are at opposite ends of the political continuum. Chicago is a one-party political system, while New York City has a two-party structure (fig. 4.1). In Chicago, Mayor Richard M. Daley rules over a democratic political machine. Daley is the key to understanding how resources are distributed throughout the city. In New York City no central figure controls the distribution of resources. Influential political figures in both political parties determine where funding is allocated. For instance, Democrats such as Congressman Charles Rangel and Manhattan County leader Herman "Denny" Farrell, Jr., and Republicans such as Mayor Michael Bloomberg and (former) Governor George Pataki are important players determining the distribution of resources in New York City.[3] In Chicago, groups such as community-based organizations seeking funding must go through the mayor, while in New York City organizations can approach various actors.

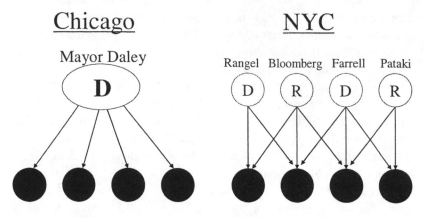

Figure 4.1 Symbolic representation of citywide political structures.

In machine cities, power is centralized and controlled by a single authority figure, like Chicago's mayor. Traditional machines are hierarchical, pyramid-like structures, with a single boss at the top, precinct or ward captains in the middle, and the voting population at the base (Meyerson and Banfield 1955). The boss, through his network of precinct captains, maintains control and secures votes. Machine governments are forms of clientalism politics where constituents vote for the machine in exchange for tangible rewards, such as municipal jobs, contracts, grants or small favors, like the elimination of parking tickets. The machine acts much like a business monopoly, consolidating power, limiting competition, and harnessing the distribution of political rewards. Machine-entrenched municipalities often attempt to use federal funding to provide civil servant employment opportunities, the traditional lifeblood of these organizations (Erie 1988).

In pluralistic municipalities like New York City, the political landscape is porous and multiple players can enter and influence the civic arena; power is diverse and diffuse, separated among different interests groups. Compared to the machine, the pluralist system has more opportunities for those seeking to influence public decisions because the power that shapes political decisions is shared among competing actors including the mayor, the city council, businesses, and grassroots interests (Dahl 1961). The distinctions between pluralist and machine cities are critical for understanding how municipalities distribute resources affecting community development.

New York City's and Chicago's political landscapes shape the spending patterns of federal economic development grants in Harlem and Bronzeville. Chicago's hierarchical Democratic machine controls the EZ funds and uses them primarily for political ends by supporting social service provision. This does little to increase job prospects for zone residents, and is associated with limited community economic development. In contrast, New York City's diverse two-party political system prevents either party from monopolizing federal funds. As a result, New York City's EZ supports mostly large-scale commercial development, producing both employment opportunities for zone residents and fear of displacement among longstanding, family-owned businesses.

In this chapter, I present a brief overview of the EZ legislation and discuss the Chicago and the New York City EZ cases in terms of political process, policy outcomes, and political history. Each subsection cumulatively builds a convincing argument that local political landscapes matter for national policy implementation and the redevelopment of Harlem and Bronzeville.

The Empowerment Zones

In 1993 President Clinton signed the Omnibus Budget Reconciliation Act, establishing the Empowerment Zone Initiative.[4] The legislation intends to moderate neighborhood poverty by opening emerging inner city markets to capital, stimulating "real opportunities for revitalization and growth" (Hebert, Vidal, Mills, James, and Gruenstein 2001, 2). The policy assumes that urban poverty exists because corporations are reluctant to locate and expand within inner city communities. Thus, as opposed to poverty legislation that focuses on social services or affordable housing, the EZ is based on the principle of place-based, supply-side economics. Businesses located in the designated zones are offered a series of tax breaks, including a $3,000 tax credit if they hire community residents and an additional tax write-off of $20,000 for depreciating property. In addition to the tax incentives, EZs receive a $100 million block grant.[5] The block grant has very few restrictions and is to be allocated by local governance structures to promote employment opportunities and economic growth. The funds can be used for a variety of purposes related to community development. For instance, social services, such as employment training, and economic development strategies, including low-interest loans and grants to for-profit corporations, are permissible.

59

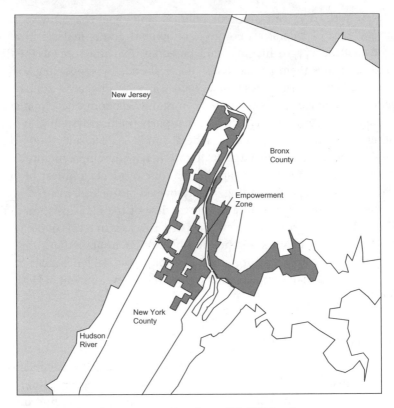

Figure 4.2 New York City's Empowerment Zone. Source: U.S. GAO (1996).

A secondary goal of the EZ legislation is to stimulate grassroots engagement in the planning and implementation process (Gittell, Newman, and Pierre-Louis 2001; Liebschutz 1995; Nathan and Wright 1996). To qualify for funding, cities submit a comprehensive strategy, based on grassroots input, to the federal government. In 1993 cities across America assembled working groups of researchers, grassroots leaders, politicians, and business owners to construct proposed plans. The federal government awarded funding based on the strength of cities' applications. On December 21, 1994, six cities, including New York and Chicago, were selected.

The New York City and Chicago EZs share one important similarity and have two key differences. Both cities submitted very similar proposals, mainly supporting social service priorities. This is critical since policy outcomes cannot be attributed to distinct local strategies. The EZs differ in the amount of total funding. New York City, because of an influx of

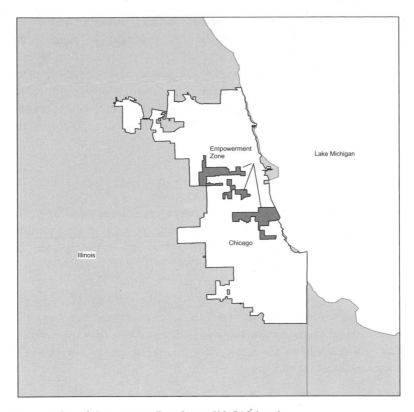

Figure 4.3 Chicago's Empowerment Zone. Source: U.S. GAO (1996).

state and city funds, has $300 million, while Chicago has only $100 million in resources. Additionally, the designated EZs in each city differ. The New York City zone focuses almost entirely on Harlem and Upper Manhattan, while Chicago's EZ is split among three noncontiguous communities including Bronzeville (see figures 4.2 and 4.3). In light of these differences, distinct policy outcomes relate almost exclusively to each city's unique political landscape.

Chicago's Empowerment Zone

Chicago's mayor Richard M. Daley directs a political machine and the funding decisions for the EZ. As a community leader in Bronzeville declares, "I know the director of the Empowerment Zone is paid by the city and that's all I need to know." Throughout most of the 1990s only one Republican alderman served on the city council, and a Republican has not been mayor since 1931. The hierarchical structure of the current Democratic machine under Richard M. Daley closely resembles the organization his father, Mayor Richard J. Daley, created during his rule over the city in the 1960s and 1970s. Richard M. Daley has centralized authority by gaining control over the city council, allowing him to use city revenues, such as the EZ funds, for political objectives. This consolidated, one-sided political context in Chicago helps to explain how the EZ is administered.

Political Process

Mayor Daley has a political monopoly over most of the city and, by extension, the EZ funds. After initial planning at the community level, funding decisions became solely the mayor's. In their review of the Chicago EZ, Douglas Gills and Wanda White explain:

> The ordinance, which was passed by City Council in late May 1995,...gave the mayor the power to appoint 37 of the 39 members of the advisory body. It reserved to city administrators the power to hire staff members to the governance body, and it made the City Council the ultimate body for determining resource allocation (1998, 65).

Having the city council determine EZ resource allocation means, for all practical purposes, that Mayor Daley is in control.

Since becoming mayor in 1989, Richard M. Daley's political skill has reduced the council to string puppets. Dick Simpson, a former alderman and professor of political science, declares, "Down on the second floor of city hall, Mayor Richard M. Daley rules over a rubber stamp city council, as his father did fifty years ago" (Simpson 2001, 289). Daley's "recommendations," or mandates to the city council, often pass without much debate or dialogue. For example, in 2003 and 2004, Mayor Daley's budget proposals were unanimously approved by city council.[6]

Daley gained control over the city council by appointing many council officials. Aldermen are publicly elected, but because of some unforeseen circumstances Daley has been able to appoint a significant number. In an interview I conducted, one Chicago political aide of a South Side alderman explained the unusual situation.

INTERVIEWEE: Yeah, his father [Richard J. Daley] basically had the committeemen, [Richard M.] Daley has the aldermen. I think that was done by design, especially if you take [into account] the African-American [aldermen]. There are nineteen of them and Daley's appointed the last thirteen. He has appointed them, so he controls them.

AUTHOR: When you say appointed, do you mean in terms of the political support, which got them in?

INTERVIEWEE: No, appointed them to be aldermen.

AUTHOR: Is that within the [city's] law?

INTERVIEWEE: Yeah, through different ways they left, through death, some of them went to jail, or whatever reason it was that the seat became vacant, until the next election it's the city council, the mayor who appoints a person to that seat until that next election. Well, he's appointed the last thirteen for different reasons, through death or through whatever reason. And those 13 owe allegiance to him. Some of them will be elected on their own. He'll make sure that they have the resources this time to get elected on their own and stay there because he basically controls them. You know, I put you here. He'll do whatever he can to keep them there, for fear a more independent type will get the job. But right now, he basically controls those aldermen.

Daley has appointed over eighteen of the fifty aldermen and has a stronghold over thirty of them (Simpson 2001). Aldermanic seats in Chicago are determined by election, but when someone dies or leaves office during their term, the mayor appoints the replacement, who must then run in the next election. Daley keeps the support of the aldermen he appoints by assisting them in their local elections. Mayor Daley is an excellent fundraiser and maintains a large political war chest, which he uses to support worthy and loyal aldermen. One alderman explains how the workings of the Chicago political machine have changed: "The machine is different. Money has replaced patronage workers as the fuel for the machine's engine. Daley can still bring out the patronage workers for some races like some aldermanic races. But, more importantly, he can drop a ton of money to fund an aldermanic candidate he favors" (Simpson 2001, 272). Appointments and "dropping the money" into local elections give Daley the majority of the votes in city council. Thus, most of his proposals pass the council without much deliberation. One Chicago newspaper reporter refers to the current city council as "world-class patsies."[7] Mayor Daley has done a superb job of intensifying his power. Rather than controlling the party and the ward committeemen (i.e., precinct captains) as his father did, Richard M. Daley rules over Chicago by directly influencing the fate of the aldermen.

Although some scholars, such as Terry Clark (2001), claim that Mayor Richard M. Daley's administration is not as heavy-handed as his father's, others argue that it contains many of the same qualities (Betancur and Gills 2004; Grimshaw 1992; Simpson 2001). The Shakman decree, a law making it illegal to fire public employees for political reasons, makes patronage positions less available today; however, Richard M. Daley quickly built a new machine by consolidating power once he was elected. According to William Grimshaw, a political scientist who specializes in Chicago politics, Daley's early actions in his administration "effectively disempowered groups that had been empowered by [Harold] Washington," Chicago's first black mayor (1992, 217).

Washington's election in 1983 broke the machine's stronghold over the city and under his rule neighborhood groups and aldermen had much more power. When Washington died early in his second term, the city shortly thereafter returned to its machine-like power structure. Grimshaw remarks that black ward leaders empowered during the Washington years, "are now [under Richard M. Daley] doing the suffering, ducking for cover, issuing private complaints, and waiting more or less patiently for happier days to arrive" (1992, 224). Strong mayoral authority in Chicago ultimately led to the EZ being another top-down initiative.

The lack of an "empowering" process in Chicago Empowerment Zone is echoed in the sentiments of community leaders and activists in Bronzeville. "When the federal government came up with the Empowerment Zone grant," states Ron Carter, "I wrote an editorial saying it was the biggest scam. It was sold as a program to promote "a bottom up process to empower the people," Carter recalls. "When the city won the Empowerment Zone funding, for the bottom up [planning] process, the first thing that happened was Mayor Daley appointed the coordinating council. How is that bottom up when you got the top making decisions on who's gonna make the [funding] decisions?" Another individual active in the planning process of the EZ explains: "Well, I think what happened was that this was not a genuine opportunity at all. It was ... another pot of money for the mayor to spend in the ways that were common to the ways he [typically] distributes public money. The charge from HUD was that there would be a bottom up involvement of citizens in the planning process. . . . The city ran roughshod over the process from its beginning ... there was never any question of who was in charge [the Mayor], so the opportunity was a very narrow one at best."

Daley uses federal funds to bolster the strength of his machine. In 1998 the EZ's coordinating council, with authority from city council, approved funding for the Chicago's Department of Housing. One employee of Chicago's EZ remarks: "[The] thing that caused a lot of people to really just walk away with disgust was [when] about $14 million [went] under the purview of the [Chicago's] Department of Housing to implement housing programs. But again, these were not unique programs, these were just different versions of the same stuff, there was nothing notable. It was like they had a single-family preservation [program] without federal [funds], now they are just going to have single family with Empowerment Zone funds, you know."

Local activists were "disgusted" by this incident because they believed money should go directly from the EZ to community groups. By funding his own city departments, Daley adds another layer of administrative management, power, and patronage. According to John Betancur and Douglas Gills, "[Daley] snatched control of the Empowerment Zone funding, using much of it for entities such as police, schools, park district, and public housing authority (CHA) and tying it to patronage and favoritism in the distribution of public resources" (2004, 103). At worst, Daley uses EZ funds to boost his patronage system and at best the federal money helps to reduce the threat of city departmental budget deficits, neither of which empowers residents.

Douglas Gills and Wanda White have made similar observations with respect to the Daley machine: "Most critics and community activists were not surprised that the current mayoral regime took this position. Community participants in the Empowerment Zone process were more disappointed in the ward aldermen, especially those representing wards in the Empowerment Zone area, for their almost reactionary rejection of the Empowerment Zone principles and for siding with the mayor against their constituents and representatives of agencies working to empower Zone residents" (1998, 65). However, what Gills and White and the grassroots leaders in the EZ areas fail to acknowledge is that Mayor Daley's machine dictates to the city council, so aldermen representing EZ areas must side with the mayor. Renegade aldermen's prospects for passing their own proposals and hopes for re-election are slim.

Policy Outcomes

Since the mayor uses resources for political motives, the EZ does little to stimulate job growth. A comprehensive, six-city study of the EZ program shows that only Chicago had no job growth. The EZs in Atlanta, Baltimore, Detroit, New York City, and Philadelphia all experienced job

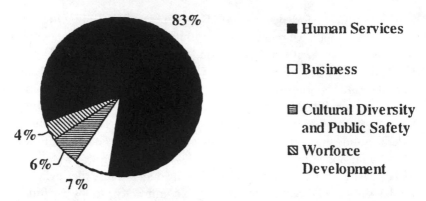

Figure 4.4 Chicago's Empowerment Zone Funding, 1994–2005, according to percentage of people served. Source: City of Chicago.

growth ranging from 9 to 51 percent between 1995 and 2000, while Chicago had a 3 percent decline in employment (Hebert, Vidal, Mills, et al. 2001). This is extremely disturbing since during the EZ implementation Chicago experienced an overall job growth of 8 percent, and, moreover, in Chicago's comparison community employment increased by 32 percent. How can the lack of performance in Chicago's EZ be explained? Evidence suggests that the money did not go toward business and job creation.

An investigation conducted by the *Chicago Reporter* newspaper argues that instead of focusing on job and business creation, much of the EZ funding went to human service agencies with strong ties to city. The Chicago EZ did little to create jobs because funds were awarded to "political allies."[8] Chicago's EZ grants were made to organizations that almost exclusively focused on social services, as opposed to economic development programs that could have created jobs (fig. 4.4). The pie chart displays the percent of people served by EZ funded programs by category between 1994 and 2005. Of the people that the EZ funding served, 83 percent were assisted through human services, while only 7 percent were served in the business category, which includes commercial and housing developments.

The focus on social services has been a disappointment to many South Side activists. One civic leader in Bronzeville laments, "The intent was to essentially use it as an incentive to attract businesses to hire local residents and it didn't do that. There maybe some examples where it did, but for the most part it didn't." According to a director of a Bronzeville nonprofit whose organization received EZ funds, "The Empowerment Zone has had a limited impact. It has been used in ways that originally I don't think it was intended to. It never was used the way we had hoped it would be."

But for Mayor Daley, a strategic allocation of the EZ funds and city resources has been useful in garnering political support from nonprofit organizations in African-American communities. The *Chicago Reporter* has highlighted a positive association between the amount of city money going to black-led churches and their increased support for Daley. According to the report, churches receive funds to run social service programs and build affordable housing.[9] In addition to funding African-American churches, a handful of black developers obtain lucrative contracts from the Chicago Housing Authority.[10]

When Daley was first elected in 1989, he had minimal support from Chicago's African-American community, but in recent years he has made gains among black voters. In the 1999 mayoral election, African-American U.S. representative Bobby Rush opposed Daley, and the mayor received nearly 45 percent of the vote in the twenty predominantly African-American wards. During his 2003 mayoral race against another African-American candidate, Daley received an endorsement from the *Chicago Defender*, a well-known African-American newspaper.[11] Daley's strategic deployment of public funds has won him ample support from the city's black middle class.

Daley rewards his supporters and crushes his opponents to maintain the strength of the machine. Mayor Daley "has developed the political capacity to co-opt community leaders, [and] intimidate potential and actual opposition" (Betancur and Gill 2004, 98). For instance, outspoken African-American Third Ward alderman Dorothy Tillman, who represents a large segment of Bronzeville, has drastically changed her tune since Daley obtained the majority in the council. When Daley first came into office, she rarely supported his proposals, yet in more recent years, her city council record agrees with him 77 percent of the time. Some speculate that her voting record is related to the amount of money Daley commits to her pet projects.[12]

The carrot (city grants and contracts) and the stick (the removal of city support) have been used to silence oppositional voices. A director of a Bronzeville organization receiving EZ funds planned to write a letter to several private foundations in Chicago outlining his disdain for how the majority of EZ funds and other city resources are distributed, but then had second thoughts. "I am going to CC [carbon copy] the letter to Jesse [Jackson] and the mayor," he says, and then half joking, adds, "Maybe not the mayor, I still want this center to exist." In Chicago, as others scholars have noted, groups aligned with the mayor receive EZ resources, while others are excluded (Gittell, Newman, and Pierre-Louis 2001).

Political History

In Chicago there is a legacy of political leaders using federal funds and political appointments to strengthen the machine. In 1955, Richard J. Daley, the current mayor's father, was elected and ruled over Chicago's Democratic machine for two decades. Known as the "American Pharaoh," his extraordinary power was rivaled by few politicians (Cohen and Taylor 2000). The elder Daley was able to build such a stronghold because he was both the leader of the Democratic Cook County Central Committee and the mayor. As is common in many cities, Chicago's elected officials often simultaneously hold public office and party positions; however, in Chicago these dual roles have increased power because of the limited strength of competing parties.

As the chairman of the reigning party, Richard J. Daley determined the fate of almost all of Chicago's political officials because his position gave him authority over the committeemen who slated officials for candidate positions. In Chicago, individuals slated by the Democratic Party are all but assured victory. Thus, during the elder Daley tenure, aldermen siding against him might get retribution in the form of omission from the Democratic ticket. Adam Cohen and Elizabeth Taylor attest that "Daley could afford to treat the City Council as little more than an advisory board.... With a few words at a slate-making meeting, Daley could end the political careers of most of them" (2000, 144).

In the 1960s, Mayor Richard J. Daley applied federal resources for Community Action Agencies (CAAs) to solidify his base among African Americans (Grimshaw 1992). Great Society legislation provided cities funding to set up CAAs, grassroots organizations designed to fight poverty. CAAs were to provide "maximum feasibility participation" for low-income and minority residents and were supposed to be run and controlled by residents of impoverished communities.

When federal antipoverty monies for the CAAs came to Chicago, Richard J. Daley made sure that the funding decisions were managed by city hall, despite the desires of black activists and D.C. bureaucrats. As Ester Fuchs notes, "Contrary to the spirit of the antipoverty legislation [of the 1960s], Chicago's program was dominated by city hall" (1992, 263).

The elder Daley recognized that if federal money went directly to community leaders, their increased autonomy could threaten his authority (Cohen and Taylor 2000). So he insisted city council give him the power to appoint the board of the CAAs.

The elder Daley used CAAs funds to create social service organizations, particularly in black wards, to lessen public dissent, protest, and conflict. Steven Erie, an expert on machine politics, declares, "Machines like the Daley organization judiciously used welfare-state programs to control the minority vote and to siphon off discontent" (1988, 166). In *Rainbow's End*, Erie shows that 54 percent of the black job gains from 1960 to 1980 in Chicago occurred in city-controlled social service agencies. Employment supported by the machine was an effective tool for "co-opting the black middle class and depoliticizing the underclass" (168).

Daley's son learned from his father's experiences. After his election in 1989, he began appointing aldermen and created a new machine. Once he consolidated his power in the city council, he was able to appoint leaders of the EZ's coordinating council and eliminate grassroots participation in the decision making process. Then he effectively used the EZ and other city funds to produce a small number of social service jobs for the black middle class, silencing protest and conflict. As black middle class voter support has increased, Richard M. Daley's power has intensified, and he has been repeatedly reelected with ease. His actions mirror his father's regime and are intimately tied to the history of the hierarchical, one-sided political structure in Chicago. In Chicago, the EZ is used to serve political objectives, not, as was its original intent, economic development. Thus, this initiative brings very little fiscal growth to Bronzeville.

New York City's Empowerment Zone

No single individual, organization, or party controls the EZ in New York City. Although some claim that the Upper Manhattan Empowerment Zone (UMEZ), the formal name for the New York City EZ, is driven by the "growth machine" (Chinyelu 1999; Davila 2004), the UMEZ is actually subject to competing party politics, and no particular interest group controls it. The UMEZ reflects the competitive, pluralistic structure of the city as a whole. Since the 1930s, New York City's political structure has been a contentious, two-party system. Republicans, although more moderate than their national party, have held the position of mayor in New York City at various times throughout the twentieth century. This competitive party governance system affects how the New York City's EZ distributes its resources.

Political Process

The instability and fragmentation of New York City's political environment affect the EZ implementation. When the EZ legislation was announced in 1993, Democrats controlled both the New York City mayoral office (David Dinkins, the only African American ever elected to this office) and the New York governor's office (Mario Cuomo). Another important player in the New York City EZ was Harlem's Democratic congressman, Charles Rangel, who introduced the EZ legislation into the U.S. House of Representatives. With Democrats in key positions, EZ funds were to be used for social services to garner political support, as in Chicago. However, the political climate in New York City and in the state of New York drastically shifted the following year. Incumbent Governor Cuomo lost to Republican George Pataki in 1994 and Republican mayoral candidate Rudolph Giuliani defeated Dinkins. These elections altered the implementation of New York City's EZ.

The New York governor's race was important because, unlike Illinois' relationship to Chicago, state government decisions are critical to New York City. Chicago historically has had immense autonomy from the state capital in Springfield, especially when compared to New York City's connections to Albany. New York City receives a large percent of its budget from the state government—50 percent of New York City's budget comes from sources outside the city, compared to 30 percent in Chicago (Fuchs 1992). This pattern of city revenue generation is illustrated with the EZ; the state of New York added $100 million, while the state of Illinois contributed nothing to Chicago's EZ coffers. This system of revenue generation often gives New York City more money to spend on social programs, but it comes at the political price of less centralized control. Thus, state politics are less influential in Chicago's EZ, but are critical in New York City.

When Democrats held the power positions in 1993, Harlem's political core, the "Famous Four"—Congressman Charles Rangel, Mayor David Dinkins, former Manhattan Borough president Percy Sutton, and former secretary of the state Basil Patterson—attempted to monopolize the EZ and capitalize politically.[13] The EZ was scheduled to fund primarily social services in Harlem. For instance, the 1994 plan submitted to HUD earmarked nearly 60 percent of the total money for social services, such as youth and substance abuse programs (Moss 1995). At that time, some feared New York City's EZ program strategy was nothing more than Democratic "political pork."

The Democrats intended to funnel the EZ through the infamous Harlem Urban Development Corporation (HUDC). Though intended to create economic development, the HUDC has a long and tumultuous history tied to party politics (see Johnson 2004). In 1967, New York's Republican governor Nelson Rockefeller decided to place a large state office high-rise in Harlem on 125th Street and 7th Avenue. Many local activists opposed the project and perceived it as a covert plan to channel white-controlled Republican money into Harlem. In 1969, protesters halted the development of the building. However, construction resumed shortly after Harlem's Democratic political leaders and activists struck a deal with representatives from Rockefeller's office. The governor agreed to award state funding to create the HUDC, which was to be a locally (i.e., Democratic) controlled economic development engine housed in the new building. Although the HUDC's mission was to revive Harlem, it quickly became a cesspool of Democratic patronage. Political scientist Kimberley Johnson notes: "For some in Harlem, the HUDC would be the realization of a goal that community development was truly in the hands of the community. For others, especially an ambitious politician named Charles Rangel, it could be an opportunity to fuel future political ambitions" (2004, 114). In 1977, Harlem's political elites took full command of the HUDC and it officially separated from state government. The initial CEO stepped down and a new leader, with strong ties to Harlem's politicians, took the helm.

In the years that followed, the HUDC became a bastion of patronage politics and was known as Harlem's gatekeeper for development. During the 1980s, the organization developed an unsavory reputation by receiving sums of public money while producing very little tangible development. Some blamed federal cutbacks of community development and affordable housing during the Reagan years, while others alleged the HUDC misappropriated funds. Johnson states, "Rather than accomplishing the goal of bottom-up comprehensive redevelopment, HUDC became largely known as a patronage machine" (121).

The HUDC and the Famous Four had a monopoly on Harlem's development. According to Tamar Jacob and Frederick Siegel, the HUDC "called all the shots" by designating "who was hired, how the deal was financed [and] which developers were involved" (1999, 24). Randy Daniels, former Republican secretary of state for New York, declares,

"Anyone who wanted to do business in Harlem had to go through them" (Jacob and Siegel 1999, 24). As strong as the HUDC was, its power did not last.

Giuliani's and Pataki's elections in 1994 destroyed the HUDC's role as the EZ fiscal agent. Pataki launched a formal investigation of the HUDC for misappropriating funds. The politically inspired investigation of the HUDC concluded that the organization squandered money on administrative operating costs (New York State Commission of Investigations 1998). The investigation tarnished the HUDC's credibility and its funding essentially disappeared. With the HUDC virtually shut down, Rangel, Pataki, and Giuliani compromised by starting a new organization to distribute the EZ funds, the Upper Manhattan Empowerment Zone (UMEZ). As the HUDC folded and the UMEZ formed, Congressman Rangel lamented the end of an era where he and the Democrats had a stronghold over Harlem's development (Chinyelu 1999).

Both Republicans and Democrats control the UMEZ. To obtain funding from the UMEZ, three independent boards must each endorse a proposal. After proposals are vetted by the first two boards, the UMEZ Board of Directors (made up of Rangel, Giuliani [later Bloomberg], Pataki, and the UMEZ CEO) gives final approval. Today, this board leans Republican, since the three elected officials, two of whom are Republican, appoint the CEO. David Patterson, Harlem's former Democratic state senator and son of Basil Patterson, explains: "When the Empowerment Zone was first created, the Governor was [Mario] Cuomo, the Mayor was David Dinkins [both Democrats]. So [when] those roles flipped [meaning they went Republican], it gave [Democratic] Congressman Rangel the biggest headache that he ever had, because now he's out voted on his own board ... Rangel had to compromise."

The compromise between Democrats and Republicans is evident in the appointment of the UMEZ's first CEO, Deborah Wright, a three-time Harvard graduate with advanced degrees in law and business. Before heading the UMEZ, she was the director of the New York City's Department of Housing Preservation and Development (HPD) under Mayor Giuliani. Ms. Wright, an African American, also previously worked for the Dinkins administration and was well known by the Harlem political elites. Her experience working with both New York City Democrats and Republicans helped her navigate the competing priorities of the UMEZ board members. As the leader of the UMEZ, she exhibited the political tendency of the Republicans by insisting that economic objectives were served over social service needs.

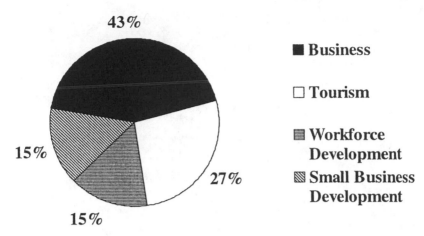

43%

■ **Business**

□ **Tourism**

▤ **Workforce Development**

15%

27%   ▨ **Small Business Development**

15%

Figure 4.5 New York City's Empowerment Zone funding, 1994–2002, according to percentage of funding spent. Source: Upper Manhattan Empowerment Zone.

With Republicans having the edge on the final UMEZ board, initial funding priorities shifted from social service programs to economic development objectives. By 1999 the UMEZ turned its focus to attracting large corporations. A Harlem resident active in redevelopment stated that the UMEZ "became an economic development...point of entry for all kinds of private sector players who were interested in coming to Harlem." The EZ, with Wright (and later Terry Lane, another Harvard Business graduate) at the helm, showed that economic development in Harlem could be accomplished without the overbearing influence of the Democratic patronage regime.

Policy Outcomes

The UMEZ mainly funds businesses and this helps to leverage private investment and create new jobs in Harlem. According to a 2002 UMEZ report, much of its funding supports economic development purposes. Figure 4.5 indicates that an overwhelming majority of EZ funds are awarded to businesses, 43 percent for large businesses and 15 percent to smaller ones. By making grants to businesses, the UMEZ serves as a catalyst for investment. Since 2002 UMEZ investments have leveraged over $250 million in private market financing. These resources attract mainstream chain stores to Harlem.

Harlem U.S.A., a sizable shopping and entertainment complex funded by the UMEZ, is one example (fig. 4.6). The site contains the Disney Store

Figure 4.6 Harlem, U.S.A.

(now a commercial bank), Modell's Sporting Goods, HMV Records, Old Navy, JPMorgan Chase Bank, a Nine West outlet, and Magic Johnson's Movie Theaters. A director of a community economic development organization explains, "Well, the one project I really give the Empowerment Zone credit for, is Harlem U.S.A. . . . They essentially put up the equity that made the project work." The EZ provided the site developer with a low-interest loan of $11 million, which helped to leverage a $50 million construction loan from JPMorgan Chase. With the UMEZ's assistance, Harlem business developments have become green-lined.

Large commercial outlets such as those in Harlem U.S.A. produce employment opportunities. According to a job growth assessment commissioned by the U.S. Department of Housing and Urban Development, New York City's Empowerment Zone experienced a 17 percent employment increase between 1995 and 2000 (Hebert, Vidal, Mills, et al. 2001). Despite the private investment and job creation associated with the EZ, people question whether Harlem's recent development is truly benefiting the majority of residents.

Some argue Harlem's Empowerment Zone is not as promising as it appears. In *Harlem Ain't Nothing but a Third World Country*, Mamadou Chinyelu writes, "The Upper Manhattan Empowerment Zone [UMEZ], with Harlem as the object of its focus, can be best characterized as a runner on a relay team, racing to disempower the African world. Having taken the relay baton firmly in its grip, UMEZ gallops through Harlem like the Trojan horse that it is. When all of the occupants of the hollow horse finally disembark, Harlem will have much more glitter, but Harlemites will have much less gold" (1999, 47). Chinyelu describes how the EZ subsidizes the entrance of glittering multinational retail corporations to Harlem, which then destroy indigenous businesses: "UMEZ is little more than a 'foreign' aid program for Harlem, designated to create a few jobs for African Americans, while simultaneously creating profit for corporate America" (47). Anthropologist Arlene Davila also articulates the false promise of local development in Harlem through the EZ programs: "The EZ's underlying premises of entrepreneurship and profits hurt most of Central and West Harelm's small businesses. . . . The largest economic loans and incentives were given to large corporations and developers, who in turn displaced local merchants through high rents and stiff competition from retail chains" (2004, 57).

Some Harlemites have echoed these criticisms against outside developers reaping the benefits from EZ, claiming that the UMEZ did little to protect small businesses. An elderly Harlem businessman declares that the EZ "did not take care of the mom and pops; it did not take care of the local businesses as it should have. . . . I mean, if you are an Empowerment Zone, my understanding is that you empower the people that are in the community." Another local entrepreneur in Harlem pronounces, "The Empowerment Zone is not empowering people, it is permitting them to be clerks." While discussing the arrival of chain stores, Harlem's former Democratic state senator David Patterson says, "There's been a real controversy over whether that's development or whether that's turning 125th Street into 34th Street. . . . I think that the community has very negative [feelings] about the Empowerment Zone. People got rejected by the Empowerment Zone; they can get rejected by a bank. They didn't need to get a new Empowerment Zone to create hope and then get rejected on the same criteria as they were rejected by the bank."

The UMEZ board members strongly defend funding large corporations. According to one former UMEZ board member, "Mom and pop stores will not provide enough job opportunities to reduce the massive amount of unemployed in the Harlem area." He claims that Harlem residents desire improved community services and says, "They want to be able to go out to dinner in their community and then be able to rent a movie at Blockbuster and go home to watch it."

One way to interpret the tension between the desire to fund "corporate America" versus "mom and pops" is to see it as a battle between

Republicans and Democrats. Republicans typically fund business interests or seek to ameliorate poverty through private market strategies, while Democrats usually support social service agencies and advocate for public sector solutions (Moynihan 1973). Initially, the New York City EZ was going to support new nonprofits and social service organizations. Once the Republicans took control, however, the money primarily went to corporate America.

Because neither political party completely dominated New York City's EZ, Democrats and Republicans compromised by funding some black-led nonprofits and small businesses. For instance, the UMEZ granted $1.5 million to Harlem Dowling Center, a social service organization. Moreover, some Harlem-based churches, such as Harlem Congregations for Community Improvement and Abyssinian Baptist Church's Development Corporation, are partnering in the large-scale commercial developments supported by the UMEZ. These small religiously affiliated, nonprofit development corporations are teaming up with larger white developers, who shoulder most of the capital risk. In these partnerships, the nonprofits often receive a fee for marketing the commercial space. Additionally, a few prominent African-American real estate developers who own and manage property throughout Harlem are making millions of dollars off the rising land values, in part brought on by UMEZ investments.

While the two political parties compete to control the funding process of the UMEZ, local residents who were involved in creating the initial plans are left out of the funding decisions. One individual heavily involved with the UMEZ and a longtime resident of Harlem first described the EZ as a "tremendous success," but then she continued,

> I think there was local disappointment. . . . For the planning process, it did require community input so there were several hundred Harlem residents that participated in committees early on. . . . Often their dreams were about owning their own business or developing a nonprofit. The focus really turned more to assisting economic development projects that would both have physical presence years after the money was spent as well as attract more of corporate America. To community residents this was disheartening because it was the community residents who sat on every one of these task force meetings. You know some meetings [were at] 7:30 a.m., others at 8 p.m. Many of the things that could have happened to bring more support directly to grassroots people were not done.

As in Chicago, the residents that created the initial plans had very little input into how the funds were distributed (Gittell, Newman, and Pierre-Louis 2001). However, in contrast to Chicago, two political parties compete to control the New York City EZ process, which has prevented the Democrats from using the funds primarily for social services and patronage.

Political History

The funding choices made by the UMEZ can be explained by the history of fragmented city politics in New York City. In 1898, following the consolidation of the boroughs, the city created the Board of Estimate to establish the city's budget (see Fuchs 1992). The board is composed of eight publicly elected officials: five borough presidents, the mayor, the city's comptroller, and the speaker of the city council. The mayor, comptroller, and speaker each have two votes and the borough presidents each have one vote. A majority must be reached to approve the budget. This structure disperses the budget authority throughout the city and opens the process up to many interest groups. Interest groups can work through the mayor or they can lobby their borough president. In Chicago, the budget process is controlled by one person, the mayor.

When the Board of Estimate was first formed, the Democrats (i.e., Tammany Hall) ruled over New York City. However, in the 1920s and 1930s, the party began to lose its strength. In New York City, the reform movement, initiated to rid the city of the corruption and nepotism associated with machine politics, built momentum. The power of the reform movement was displayed in 1934 with the election of a reform-minded, Republican mayor, Fiorello H. La Guardia. His election was a major blow to the Democratic Party and permanently changed the political landscape in New York City. Since his election, the two political parties have shared power, albeit weakly, much like children riding a seesaw.

The structure of the Board of Estimate and the election of a Republican mayor forced New York City into a fragmented, competitive two-party political system. This diffuse political landscape continues to prevent any one political party or interest group from dominating the city. "The Board of Estimate ... can effectively check the mayor's policy. ... The borough presidents, moreover, have certain powers, which enable them to sustain party organizations even in the moments of reform glory. This fragmentation of power at the very top levels of government as well as the division of electoral strength between the Democratic organization and the reform coalition frees city agencies from close central direction" (Greenstone and Peterson [1973] 1976, 40). This structure is completely different from that in Chicago where the mayor has autocratic power and city agencies are under his tight supervision. The contentious, fragmented political system in New York City explains why no person, party or interest group can monopolize federal money that comes into the city.[14]

The political fragmentation of New York City was evident during the implementation of the Community Action Agencies (CAAs), under Republican mayor John Lindsay in the late 1960s. Unlike Chicago's first Mayor Daley, Mayor Lindsay was unable to control the funding decisions of the CAAs because the structure of New York City's political environment made it difficult for any unilateral decisions on resource allocation. According to Ester Fuchs, "Lindsay could not simply implement his neighborhood plan.... He had to create a workable coalition with institutional antagonists and powerful interest groups. The mayor was forced to bargain initially with comptroller Beame, City Council president Sanford Garelik, Albert Shanker and the United Federation of Teachers (UFT), Alex Rose and the Liberal party, David Rockefeller and the banking interest, the uniformed service unions and the City Council, not to mention the three thousand community groups for which two hundred meetings were held" (1992, 267). The money for the CAAs in New York City came from diverse places, including $1 million from the city's general fund, $1 million from the private sector, and $3 million from the city's capital budget. With Lindsay controlling only the $3 million from the city capital budget, Fuchs argues, he could not monopolize the funding for his political purposes.

In contrast to Chicago, New York City has a history of weak mayoral control. "Mayors in New York cannot rely on the party to assist in the process of governing.... Without a strong, citywide party, mayors in New York have had no choice but to share power." New York City's political structure, "A weak and fragmented party organization, for[ces] mayors to forge winning electoral coalitions on their own" (Fuchs 1992, 247, 99). Therefore, mayors in New York City often accept funds from outside the city's revenue streams. Further, city programs and departments are often funded from sources not under the direct authority of the mayor, an intolerable situation for machine bosses in Chicago, since it can lead to the decentralization of political power.

Consider, for example, the resources added to the New York City's EZ by the state of New York: $100 million from the state is under the control of the governor, while the $100 million from the city is the mayor's and the rest is under the direction of Congressman Rangel. In comparison to Chicago, this pluralism effectively prevents one particular entity, interest group or party from having centralized control. In Chicago, fewer state and private funds are infused into the city's budget because it might weaken the authority of the mayor. Therefore, Chicago's EZ is much smaller and remains under the management of the mayor. The New York Democrats took a gamble by accepting state dollars, hoping key state and city positions would remain under their party's control; but as history has shown, in New York City party rule continually changes. In short, the city's unstable and fragmented political structure explains why New York City's EZ is not used for social service patronage.

Discussion

Distinct metropolitan political landscapes are critical to understanding how federal policies that affect neighborhood development are implemented. Chicago's centralized, machine-driven politics dominate its EZ, while New York City's fragmented two-party system prevents a consolidation of power. In Chicago, Daley's hegemonic control over resource allocation allows him to fund political allies and co-opt others, such as social service groups and black churches. This strategy helps the mayor politically but is less beneficial to Bronzeville's employment rate. In Harlem, dual-party control leads to the funding of large-scale projects over local mom and pop businesses and social services. New York City's EZ creates low-paying jobs but resentment among Harlem's longstanding businesses. These distinct policy outcomes strongly suggest that local politics matter for the implementation of nationally directed community economic development programs.

This finding has major implications for theories of federalism, urban politics, and neighborhood development. It suggests that Peterson's "city limits" perspective is overstated and outdated. In an era of devolution and urban fiscal strength, city politics are not limited politics. The claim that cities always focus on similar developmental policies, regardless of their internal political circumstances, is misguided. If economic growth strategies drove local politics, Daley's strategy would have looked like New York City's EZ. However, the lack of competitive party politics in Chicago allows the Daley machine to use EZ funds for noneconomic purposes. While economic constraints are not irrelevant, local political circumstances are critical factors to understanding the choices cities make.

While some results support Wong and Peterson's 1986 argument, the structural thesis discussed by Ferman (1996) is stronger. Clearly mayoral preferences, closely aligned with party affiliation, affected the implementation of both EZs. Democratic mayors (Dinkins and Daley) supported social services, while Republicans (Giuliani and Bloomberg) steered funding toward economic development. However, the political structure of these cities helps to explain which party controlled the mayoral position. In Chicago, the one-sided, consolidated system makes the election of a Republican mayor unlikely and ensures that Democratic mayors have strongholds over city resources. In New York City, the fragmented, dual party system prevents one party from dominating city politics. Thus, the structure of the political system is a primary determinant of resource deployment patterns and policy outcomes.

Alternative Explanations

At least four alternatives might explain the difference in EZ implementation. First, the amount of money New York City had at its disposal might have attracted more businesses and created more jobs. Although likely true, the historic differences between New York City's and Chicago's relationships to their state governments relate to this circumstance. New York City has more money precisely because of its fragmented and interdependent political system. New York City's mayors must rely on outside funding to forge winning coalitions. Second, some might argue local parties may be of paramount importance. In Chicago, the structure and party are indistinguishable and the centralized political structure helps to maintain the Democratic Party's power. In New York, the diffuse political structure explains why political party holdings flip-flop back and forth. So political party is not irrelevant; it is central. However, the structure helps determine which party is in control.

Third, some skeptics may claim that an elite growth machine, independent of party politics, guides the implementation of New York City's EZ. Although the dominance of the growth machine is quite plausible, pro-growth policies do not always emerge from New York City. For instance, as I will discuss in the next chapter, New York City is not removing public housing high-rises to make room for luxury condominiums, though Chicago is. Therefore, growth propensities do not always dominate urban politics. Lastly, some might argue that Harlem's higher aggregate income explains its increased business emergence compared to Bronzeville. Harlem has approximately $6 billion in aggregate-household income compared to Bronzeville's $2 billion.[15] Although vast, this difference fails to explain the gap in the commercial presence in Harlem and Bronzeville, since cost of living adjustments reduce Harlem's income edge to about $2.5 billion.[16] New York City's focus on business development with their EZ, combined with Harlem's aggregate income, explains "big business" emergence in this community.

Even if cities want to increase their economic prosperity, varying municipal political circumstances can greatly influence the direction of federal policy making. The next chapter, which focuses on the distinction between New York City and Chicago's public housing, reinforces this point.

5

The New Urban Renewal, Part 2:
Public Housing Reforms

In the United States, the adverse conditions of inner city, black communities and the history of public housing policies are closely intertwined (Massey and Kanaiaupuni 1993; Plunz 1990). Federal policies, such as the Housing Acts of 1949 and 1954, and local political decisions led to the placement of many public housing developments in black ghettos. Moreover, in the late 1960s and early 1970s, Congress enacted the Brooke Amendments, which set a preference for extremely low-income tenants, further concentrating the poor in African-American neighborhoods.[1]

While much of the past national housing and urban renewal legislation is coupled with the demise of urban black communities, recent public housing reforms are connected with the process of revitalization. In the 1990s federal policymakers passed a series of housing reforms in an attempt to alleviate concentrated neighborhood poverty. In 1992 the U.S. Department of Housing and Urban Development (HUD) began the Housing Opportunities for People Everywhere (HOPE VI) program (Popkin, Levy, Harris, Comey, Cunningham, and Buron 2002).[2] Between 1996 and 2003, this program provided funding for the demolition of nearly 60,000 public housing units nationwide.[3] Then in 1996 Congress ordered public housing authorities to rehabilitate or demolish buildings with excessive code violations or vacancies.[4] Lastly, to make it financially feasible for cities to facilitate the demolition process, the one-for-one replacement requirement for razed units was permanently repealed with the enactment of the Quality Housing and Work Responsibility Act of 1998 (Goetz 2003). Although there is a federal push to demolish the nation's high-rise public housing stock, not every major city follows this directive.

Harlem and Bronzeville are both revitalizing, however, the consequences of development are vastly different for public housing residents in each community. Bronzeville is experiencing massive displacement of public housing tenants; nearly 9,000 public housing units are being demolished, and roughly 17,000 people are being removed.[5] While Chicago razes a large percent of its public housing, New York City is rehabilitating their high-rise public housing, especially in Harlem. Some Harlemites claim public housing residents are less likely to be displaced than low-income renters in Harlem's private housing market. Harlem's redevelopment has much less displacement among its most vulnerable population.

Although recent federal housing reforms are important to the revitalization of disadvantaged neighborhoods, they do not completely explain community-level outcomes. Political circumstances in New York City and Chicago, both past and present, are essential to understanding how federal reforms influence Harlem and Bronzeville's redevelopment. As discussed at length in the previous chapter, distinct governance systems in New York City and Chicago yield alternate choices and actions related to the Empowerment Zone implementation. This political difference is critical to the conditions of the public housing stock in these cities: New York City sustains it, while Chicago consistently makes detrimental decisions that deplete their housing stock. The decentralized political environment in New York City results in greater tenant activism and better public housing management, which over time helps explain the city's superior public housing. This situation elucidates why the Harlem's redevelopment, compared to Bronzeville's, is associated with significantly less displacement among its low-income residents.

Considerable displacement is connected with the revival of certain inner city areas, but this second round of urban renewal differs from the urban renewal of the 1940s, '50s, and '60s, which was detrimental to urban black America. There is little doubt that whites were the primary beneficiaries of the first round of urban renewal. Institutional racism embedded in federal urban renewal legislation led to increased segregation and isolation for poor urban African Americans and preserved downtown growth in many areas (Hirsch [1983] 1998; Massey and Denton 1993; von Hoffman 2000). Today, however, certain African Americans reap benefits from the second sound of urban renewal. Black real estate developers and homeowners are experiencing direct financial gains from the current inner city redevelopment, forcing scholars to reconsider the legacy of institutional racism related to federal development initiatives.

In this chapter I discuss the differences between Chicago and New York City's public housing and present the Bronzeville and Harlem cases.[6] Both cases illustrate how federal public housing relates to the current redevelopment and how this is important for understanding who is being left out and who is benefiting. I then discuss how past city-level political circumstances surrounding public housing are critical for understanding the present community situations.

Public Housing: Chicago and New York Style

Public housing is often seen as a harbinger of crime, drugs, teen pregnancy, laziness, mismanagement, and corruption, but conditions in public housing vary greatly from city to city. Overall, New York City's and Chicago's public housing are at the extremes of a continuum; the New York City Housing Authority (NYCHA) manages some of the best (Thompson 1999), while the Chicago Housing Authority (CHA) has some of the worst projects in the country (Schill 1997).

The public housing conditions in Bronzeville and Harlem are strikingly different. Most Bronzeville projects are isolated from the rest of the community (see figs. 5.1 and 5.2). For instance, large highways and railroad tracks segregate public housing buildings from the rest of the community. Moreover, the buildings are stepped back from the street and appear as if they were dropped out of the sky onto land more desolate and empty than a ghost town. Few businesses and homes are nearby most of the large-scale projects.

Bronzeville's public housing is extremely dilapidated and controlled by gangs. Entering public housing means stepping into the middle of the drug trade. Gang members monitor the outside of the buildings and sell illicit substances, calling out drug code phrases like "ghost face" and "dog face" from first-floor hallways. The unlawful activity makes public housing quite intimidating and dangerous, especially when turf wars, which often involve gunfire, break out. After negotiating the daily drug activity, residents typically take stairs to their apartments because elevators are often broken. The stairwells are dark, since light fixtures frequently do not work, are covered with graffiti and reek of urine and marijuana. Many apartments suffer from rat and cockroach infestations. Overall,

Figure 5.1 Stateway Gardens.

Figure 5.2 The Robert Taylor Homes.

CHA buildings are in a state of disrepair. They are dingy, unsafe and un-healthy environments to raise children.

Harlem's public housing is in better shape and not isolated from the rest of the community. The sixteen- to twenty-story buildings abut the street and Harlem's apartment buildings and beautiful brownstones

Figure 5.3 The Drew-Hamilton Houses.

surround some of these high-rises (fig. 5.3). NYCHA projects are not dilapidated, but they are grimy and gritty, like much of New York City.
There is significantly less gang presence. Although some drug dealing
exists in Harlem's public housing, drug activity usually occurs in nearby
abandoned buildings and adjacent streets. Gang violence and shootings
occur in and around the projects, but less frequently than in Bronzeville.
In New York City public housing floors are cleaner, the elevators usually work and graffiti is much less common. Hallways and stairwells are
illuminated and odors are much less potent.

The difference between public housing conditions in Chicago and
New York City gives insight into the drastically different results in their
federally ordered viability tests. The CHA has the highest proportion of
failing housing units in the United States. Barely half of CHA units pass
(CHA 2000), while nearly all of NYCHA's buildings do (Thompson 1999).

Because of the awful condition of Chicago's public housing, the CHA
receives a greater portion of urban renewal funds from the federal government. The CHA, under the HOPE VI program, has been awarded
thirty-nine grants, totaling $340 million, from the U.S. Department of
Housing and Urban Development for public housing demolition and the
construction of mixed-income replacement housing.[7] The NYCHA, a
much larger public housing system (see appendix C), has received only
four HOPE VI grants totaling $90 million. Of the $90 million, only one

Figure 5.4 Demolition of the Robert Taylor Homes.

grant is specifically for the demolition of 102 units, while thirty-one grants are awarded to Chicago for the razing of 12,500 units.[8] As the city of Chicago destroys a vast portion of its subsidized housing stock, New York City puts funds toward rehabilitation, setting the context for public housing resident displacement from Bronzeville and not Harlem.

Bronzeville's Redevelopment and Public Housing Reforms

The CHA's Plan for Transformation

In 1999 Mayor Richard M. Daley convinced the U.S. Department of Housing and Urban Development (HUD) to return the management of the CHA to the city after a four-year period of HUD receivership.[9] Shortly after, the CHA announced a monumental $1.6 billion "Plan for Transformation." The plan is one of the largest and most ambitious urban redevelopment initiatives to emerge since the 1960s. Chicago proposed to raze nearly all high-rise public housing buildings and redevelop 25,000 units, resulting in a loss of approximately 13,000 apartments (CHA 2000). According to the plan, 6,000 families would be relocated to private housing with Section 8 vouchers.[10] To end their reputation for the worst public housing in the country, Chicago intends to eliminate their dilapidated stock (see figure 5.4).

In 1999, Bronzeville had the highest concentration of high-rise public housing in the city. Most line the State Street Corridor, a three-mile stretch that runs parallel to the Dan Ryan Expressway and spans from 22nd Street to 55th Street. Some speculated that this area contained the highest concentration of public housing in the world. South State Street had five major housing projects—Raymond Hilliard Homes, Harold Ickes, Dearborn Homes, Stateway Gardens, and the Robert Taylor Homes. Of these projects, the Robert Taylor Homes, comprising twenty-eight sixteen-story high-rises, was the largest and most daunting. In addition to these housing developments, other large-scale, public housing projects, including the Washington Park Homes, the Ida B. Wells Homes, and the Prairie Court Homes, were scattered throughout Bronzeville. While standing almost anywhere in the community, one cannot escape the sight, or weight, of Chicago's high-rise public housing.

Housing project conditions make the community, at times, unsafe and dangerous. One Bronzeville resident, who worked in public housing during the early 1990s, describes the circumstances at the projects as "frightening": "I remember when I worked in Wells [Ida B. Wells Homes]. We were doing the Wells initiative. At one point I had a girlfriend that lived in Lake Meadows and a girlfriend that lived in Hyde Park. I remember telling this girlfriend who lived in Hyde Park, 'Don't drive down Cottage Grove at night because they're shooting the cars. They were just doing random shooting between Madden Park and Abraham Lincoln Center.' For like four or five years there was gunfire where you couldn't drive down Cottage Grove at night." The harsh reality of gun violence at these developments has inhibited residential investment in the community. However, once the city declared that they were going to demolish all of the community's high-rises, totaling nearly 9,000 units, real estate developers became very interested in Bronzeville.

Bronzeville's economic development is strongly associated with the CHA's plan. A banker employed at a Bronzeville branch of a large commercial bank observes:

> Well, I've been here going on three years working for the bank. What I've seen of course is a tremendous change in housing with the increase in rehabbing. Just improving the stock of the housing, increasing the number of condos, condo conversions. . . . And I think losing the public housing is probably having the biggest effect on how the community is changing because incomes are increasing. The low to moderate-income people are leaving, so businesses find this community . . . a lot more attractive because the income is higher, the

Figure 5.5 An advertisement for "The New Homes of Bronzeville."

> housing stock is better. So I would say that's the biggest factor [leading to change], it's losing the public housing. ... When all of the public housing comes down, the impact of losing public housing in this community is going to be tremendous. Property values will skyrocket.

Although Bronzeville's property values were increasing before the CHA's Plan for Transformation, development activity and interest in the area accelerated once demolition began.[11] Large downtown real estate developers, who once overlooked Bronzeville, are now buying tracts of land directly across from lots where high-rise public housing once stood. At the same time, landlords and homeowners are rehabilitating their properties. Moreover, several large apartment complexes that once accepted Section 8 vouchers are being converted to luxury condominiums. As one longtime Bronzeville resident explains, "You are going to see this place go [development] crazy now that they've torn down Stateway and Robert Taylor."

Bronzeville's large public housing projects are being converted into "mixed-income" housing developments. These new developments, which are HOPE VI sites, will have one-third public housing units, one-third market rate rentals, and one-third market rate homeownership. At the former Stateway Gardens project, now called Park Boulevard, the high-end, market-rate homes are selling for $625,000 (Shashaty 2007).

At the former Robert Taylor Homes, renamed Legends South, prices for single-family homes start at $325,000.[12] The public investment from the federal government, and the city's decision to construct townhomes on and near former public housing lots, helps to increase property values throughout the community.

Local city decisions about where to target federal funding strongly influence Bronzeville's development. While most of Chicago's high-rises, mainly concentrated on the west and south side of the city, are slated for demolition, only certain projects receive HOPE VI funding to build mixed-income replacement housing. Mayor Daley has ensured that Bronzeville receives over half of the city's HOPE VI demolition funds, approximately $45 million. Additionally, nearly $100 million is targeted toward the construction of "mixed-income" housing developments.[13] Other public funds, generated through the use of Tax Increment Districts (TIFs), discussed in chapter 3, are also being used to subsidize the construction of mixed-income replacement housing.[14] According to a local newspaper article, "Mayor Richard Daley has flexed considerable muscle to see this area revitalized."[15]

While Bronzeville develops, an important question becomes: what is going to happen to displaced public housing residents? Theoretically, the demolition process provides an opportunity for public housing residents to find better homes. Sudhir Venkatesh, a sociologist who has done substantial fieldwork at the Robert Taylor Homes, comments, "Outright demolition of the housing developments would enable the integration of tenants into the larger (mainstream) city" (2000, 8).

Studies on public housing resident mobility stemming from the Gautreaux and the Movement to Opportunity (MTO) programs suggest relocating out of public housing and concentrated poverty to more prosperous neighborhoods may be beneficial to households (Orr, Feins, Beecroft, et al. 2003; Rubinowitz and Rosenbaum 2000). However, with Chicago's demolition and relocation most tenants end up in highly segregated, disadvantaged neighborhoods. Beside a 120-day vacate notice, a three-hour "Housing Choice" lecture about housing options, and a three-hour "Good Neighbor" session to learn how to maintain their Section 8 apartments, little guidance is given to tenants. Many of Bronzeville's community leaders are skeptical that two three-hour courses will adequately prepare CHA tenants. One woman, who had worked with residents trying to transition out of public housing before the Plan for Transformation was put in place, asserts that it will take an intensive fourteen-week program to effectively prepare longtime CHA

families to move. She calls the Good Neighbor program and the relocation process "a joke."

The Plan for Transformation's relocation strategy is severely under-
funded, making it extremely difficult for residents to find decent housing.
The CHA budgeted $6 million for relocating residents in its first imple-
mentation year, less than 1 percent of its $1.6 billion plan. Successful
relocation programs and social service mobility programs have one housing counselor for every 25 to 40 families; the CHA plan has only enough
money for one counselor for every 139 families (Synderman and Dailey
2001). Some developments have one relocation counselor for at least 500
families (Sullivan 2003).

Additionally, Chicago's housing market is incapable of accommodat-
ing so many Section 8 vouchers holders. A report commissioned by the
Metropolitan Planning Council, a citywide civic organization, indicates
that the city's private low-income rental market is extremely tight, with a
4 percent vacancy rate (Lenz and Coles 1999). "Very poor African Americans are [being] removed from their homes and given a voucher to find
housing that for the most part does not exist" (Ranney 2003, 198).

The public housing demolition in Chicago has relocated neighborhood poverty, not alleviated it. The vast majority of residents are moving to new, segregated and disadvantaged neighborhoods further from
the city center. Tom Sullivan, a consultant hired by the CHA to monitor the relocation efforts, claims, "The result has been that the vertical
ghettos...are being replaced with horizontal ghettos" (2003, 13). As of
2002, 80 percent of those relocating are residing in communities that
are over 90 percent black and nearly 70 percent of residents leaving the
high-rises with vouchers are going to neighborhoods where the poverty
rate is above 23 percent (Fischer 2003).[16] While this poverty rate is lower
than Bronzeville's once was, as more families relocate, poverty rates in
communities where former CHA tenants are clustering will likely rise.
Additionally, subsequent relocation studies that track the movement of
former CHA tenants, such as the one conducted by Venkatesh and colleagues (2004), show that nearly all tenants are ending up in segregated,
high-poverty areas. These new horizontal ghettos are forming in neighborhoods on the far south and west sides of Chicago and in the inner
south suburbs.[17]

The Chicago public housing relocation process may put former tenants in a more vulnerable situation. Many tenants are moving to neighborhoods with less formal and informal social support services and possibly higher crime rates. Low-income residents of inner city Chicago

are "closer in proximity to social service providers than poor populations living in suburban areas," where many of the voucher holders are relocating (Allard 2004, 5). Furthermore, Chicago communities with the highest concentration of Section 8 vouchers have more crime than some of the locations previously saturated with public housing (Bennett and Reed 1999). Jamie Kalvin, director of the Neighborhood Conservation Corporation (NCC), an organization that advocates for residents of Bronzeville's Stateway Gardens housing project, states, "Individuals and families are being hurt and are being rendered more vulnerable by this [relocation] process. And it's not hard to see, if you actually make yourself available to it."[18] Rather than helping public housing tenants reach mainstream society, the demolition process may be making the situation for many families and children even worse.

Illustration of Displacement

One afternoon, Jamie and I help Tony and his family, who have been squatting at Stateway for almost four years, move to another neighborhood. Tony has worked sporadically at Stateway for ten years as a janitor's assistant. The maintenance staff pays him, under the table, for the work they are supposed to do. Tony and his wife have five- and six-year-old girls. His wife works the night shift at a local fast food restaurant. Even though some reports suggest that 6 to 16 percent of the CHA tenant population is squatting, meaning they are not legal leaseholders and are living in vacant units, the CHA effectively ignores these tenants and provides little relocation support (Venkatesh 2002; Venkatesh, Celimli, Miller, et al. 2004). The NCC has made an effort to help this population at Stateway.[19]

Tony's Stateway apartment is on the fourth floor and we help him move the day before his building is to be razed. Since the elevators are broken, we walk all of Tony's family belongings, including clothing in large plastic bags, down the dark stairwells to Jamie's truck. Jamie has connected Tony's family with a housing assistance organization, which has helped Tony get a Section 8 voucher and an apartment. As we help the family leave the building, it is apparent that although Tony's children are excited about the move, Tony is extremely nervous. He has lived at Stateway for almost ten years and he and his wife have not yet visited their new community. His wife tells me that she hopes the apartment is near a grocery store.

Tony's new apartment is in a four story, red brick, horseshoe-shaped building, in an African-American neighborhood south of Bronzeville with a high concentration of Section 8 voucher holders. The apartments have little, rusty metal balconies that overlook a courtyard. The hallways are carpeted and have working light fixtures. This, however, is nobody's dream apartment. The wood floors are old and scuffed up, it needs a new paint job, and bathrooms are grimy. Regardless, this apartment is a marked improvement. Jamie jokingly asked, "So do we want to go back to Stateway?" Tony's wife and children laugh. Tony says nothing and has a look of concern.

I go outside with Tony and we start to bring in his family's belongings. While walking up the stairs, I ask him what he thinks of the new apartment. He tells me bluntly, "I don't like it. I don't know my way around here." He proclaims that he is more concerned about being robbed at this place than Stateway because he knows that people there watch his back. He is apprehensive about the new neighborhood and insists he saw street gangs as we approached his new residence. In addition, he says it will be difficult to get public transportation back to his job at Stateway. Although the new apartment is in better condition than the one they left, there is a strong possibility this neighborhood will become more impoverished as the rest of the CHA buildings come down.

The vast majority of public housing tenants will not benefit from CHA's Plan for Transformation. Possibly, a small percentage may be able to return to the community when the new mixed-income developments are completed. During the "Housing Choice" sessions, residents are asked if they want the "right of return" to the replacement mixed-income housing. However, most residents know their chances of returning to newly constructed units are slim. Tre, a Stateway Gardens resident, says to me, "Ain't no one gonna come back here. This is prime real estate." A Bronzeville's organizational leaders states, "It would be a miracle if a third of [public housing] residents moved back." Many real estate developers are setting very strict guidelines for the readmittance of public housing residents to the new mixed-income projects. This procedure, along with the limited number of available units, makes the promise of a new home an unlikely scenario for former public housing tenants.

Louanna (Lou) Jones, then the Illinois state representative from Bronzeville, explains the difficult situation: "You're between a rock and a hard place. In order to revitalize the area or rebuild the area, and advance the area, you have people getting angry because they [CHA tenants] do not have anywhere [in the community] to go." While massive amounts of low-income residents get displaced, others in Bronzeville benefit from the redevelopment.

Who's Benefiting?

Some claim that Chicago's actions are tantamount to the urban renewal of the past, which was extremely detrimental to African Americans (Bennett and Reed 1999; Popkin, Gwiasda, Olson, et al. 2000; Ranney 2003). Although there are some similarities, the current development in Bronzeville differs. Urban renewal in Chicago between 1940 and 1960 primarily benefited white real estate developers and profit-seeking corporations, while blacks remained segregated and powerless (Hirsch [1983] 1998). Today, however, certain African-American businesses are benefiting.

Although several major white construction firms, architecture companies, and real estate developers have large contracts to demolish, design, and redevelop new mixed-income developments in Bronzeville, politically well-connected, black-owned development, management and construction companies are profiting from Chicago's Plan for Transformation. Black-owned firms such as Elzie Higginbottom's East Lake Management, Allison Davis's Davis Group, Rev. Leon Finney, Jr.'s Woodlawn Development Corporation, and Paul King's UBM, Inc hold million-dollar contracts to build and manage new housing developments.[20] In a two-year span, East Lake Management received nearly $30 million to oversee thirteen of the CHA's developments.[21] Smaller black homebuilding companies also receive city funds to construct homes in the community (fig. 5.6). As Bronzeville's Alderman Dorothy Tillman insists, "We [need]...to ensure that African Americans take part in the redevelopment."

Moreover, Mayor Daley nominates respected black leaders willing to support the city's demolition and relocation efforts to high-ranking post within the CHA. In 1999, when the Plan for Transformation was announced, Mayor Daley appointed Phil Jackson, a former resident of the Robert Taylor Homes, to head the CHA, and Sharon Gilliam as chair of the CHA's Board of Commissioners. Additionally, when Jackson stepped down in 2000, Daley appointed another African American, Terry Peterson, as the executive director of the CHA. These positions are more meaningful than mere tokenism, considering black real estate developers receive substantial CHA contracts.

The public investments in Bronzeville relate to increased property values for a number of black homeowners. Middle- and upper-income families who bought houses in the area in the 1980s and early 1990s are seeing substantial increases in their home equity. Properties worth

Figure 5.6 Homes built by African-American homebuilders.

$100,000 or $200,000 ten years ago are doubling and tripling in value. In other words, the new phase of urban renewal is connected to a certain level of black prosperity.

Although Bronzeville's redevelopment is greatly influenced by new federal legislation, the legacy of Chicago's political machine and its housing management decisions have contributed to the decay and downfall of public housing through a misuse of national housing resources for local political objectives. In short, the political history of Chicago's democratic machine has driven the demolition of Bronzeville public housing.

The CHA under Mayor Richard J. Daley: Linking the Past to the Present

In an interview, a staff member for a Bronzeville alderman expressed some of the common assumptions about the residents of public housing, distinguishing between those who have left and those who have stayed, almost as if they are two classes of people—one that is responsible for poverty, and another that has managed to liberate itself from it:

> They were supposed to come in, get on their feet, get working and [then] move out and start a life, like a starter home almost. Some did that back in the 60s

and I think that kind of worked out. In fact, I know a couple of people, one or two people–there's the lady working the front desk, she lived in public housing and she eventually moved out and got moving on with her family. And there is a guy I know that lives in the Gap, [a middle and upper-class section of Bronzeville]. He grew up in Stateway and he's an architect now. There's a lot of success stories [coming] out of there.

He continues:

However, there are also a lot of bad stories that come out of [public housing]. It got to the point where people got places, they got too dependent on the government . . . and it was easy and they didn't do what the housing was supposed to do and they wound up having generation [after generation there]. I think that is why the CHA is the way it is now, where you have generations of families that kept moving in–I mean they just had their kids and the kids just moved downstairs and then their kids and they just moved to the next building and before you know it you have got a generation after generation of uneducated, poorly skilled people who are stuck, they're stuck there. And I think that's why the CHA is the way it is now.

Many like this political staffer assume Chicago's public housing residents are wholly responsible for the adverse situation in the projects. He clearly distinguishes between those who left and those who remained in public housing, and identifies the remaining families as the underclass, "uneducated," "poorly skilled," and dependent on government handouts. Unquestionably, intergenerational poverty and individual choices have, in part, led to the undesirable conditions in Chicago's public housing (Venkatesh 2000). Many people in the projects made poor choices and became involved with drugs and gang violence. However, the legacy of political corruption in the CHA, connected to Chicago's centralized political structure, has also contributed to the city's horrendous public housing.

Segregation, corruption, patronage, and mismanagement were all hallmarks of the CHA throughout Mayor Richard J. Daley's twenty-year regime. Under the leadership of the first Mayor Daley, the CHA promoted intense segregation by placing large projects exclusively in black neighborhoods: "more than 99% of the 10,256 [units] built after 1955 . . . were located in all-black neighborhoods" (Hirsch [1983] 1998, 243). Daley was responsible for the development of the notorious public housing concentration on the State Street Corridor.

But the stark segregation of Chicago's public housing cannot be placed solely on Daley's shoulders. Initial CHA site selection occurred before his tenure, and white rioting and real estate interests contributed to the placement of CHA projects in predominantly black neighborhoods (Meyerson and Banfield 1955). However, the management of the CHA housing projects was under his control.

Under Daley, the CHA became a cesspool of patronage. When elected mayor in 1955, he quickly replaced CHA staff with his political appointees, who had politics, not housing, as their primary objective. They used their power to ensure politically connected developers and construction companies, who often used "cheap slab construction, shoddy materials, and poor workmanship," received large contracts (Popkin, Gwiasda, Olson, et al. 2000, 13). Additionally, maintenance contracts went to those affiliated with Daley. In terms of politics, the CHA was a well-run organization, but it failed miserably at facilitating and maintaining quality housing.

Patronage and mismanagement persisted at the CHA because of the strength of Daley's Democratic machine. His highly centralized administration did not tolerate grassroots dissent, particularly from public housing residents, and used eviction threats to mitigate grassroots opposition to underhanded building management and maintenance procedures. Sudhir Venkatesh notes that Robert Taylor residents in the late 1960s and early 1970s often did not voice grievances about building deterioration (2000, 54). Residents may have been silent because when they met to discuss the lack of building repairs, CHA staff disrupted their meetings with threats of evictions. These interventions were not limited to the Robert Taylor Homes; residents at Bronzeville's Ida B. Wells project accused Daley's precinct captains of threatening to evict them if they expressed disloyalty to the machine (Cohen and Taylor 2000, 139).[22] This tactic prevented residents from demanding better services from the CHA.

Although the national government in the 1960s threatened Daley with the discontinuance of CHA funds if he did not increase the amount of grassroots engagement in the management process, federal directives to boost resident activism were futile. Daley, and his political appointee, CHA chairman Charles Swibel, allowed participation only from residents who followed political directives and supported their dubious management practices. In 1971 Swibel allowed general elections for the resident leadership positions. Each development would elect a Local Advisory Council (LAC) president to sit on the Central Advisory Council (CAC), a governing body of all of the LAC presidents from across the city.[23] The CAC would elect a president to sit on the CHA Board of Commissioners, a body that approved all the CHA's resource allocations. Mayor Daley and Swibel controlled the general elections; the vast majority of those elected were known Daley supporters. In fact, the first head of the CAC was one of Daley's most loyal precinct workers. As Venkatesh has noted, "The tradition of Chicago politics seemed to have quickly penetrated the new public housing management" (2000, 62). With this co-opted resident structure in place, there was no systemic deployment of resources, building repairs were minimal, and contracts went to those close to the mayor.

Corruption Continues

Even after Daley's death in 1976, the old Democratic political machine continued to influence the CHA's dismal management practices (Popkin, Gwiasda, Olson, et al. 2000). In the 1980s and 1990s the CHA was marked by political corruption. In one year, although the CHA owed $33 million to contractors, it increased administrative positions and salaries of mid-level professionals. In another year, the CHA claimed to be running a $33 million budget deficit, yet held over $50 million in a low-interest saving account (Feldman and Stall 2004). There were also accusations that the CHA pension funds were being embezzled. HUD finally forced Swibel out after extensive allegations of corruption and mismanagement.

The corruption and mismanagement persisted after the departure of Swibel, under machine-appointed Chairman Vince Lane.[24] Lane, a black real estate developer in Chicago, began a $78 million dollar initiative called "Operation Clean Sweep," setting aside approximately $175,000 per building for extra security personnel. Unfortunately, Lane allegedly channeled security contracts to his former business partners. Under Lane the CHA neglected to perform essential management procedures, failing at "even basic tasks like collecting rents" (Popkin, Gwiasda, Olson, et al. 2000, 180). Without appropriate management, the CHA suffered severe budget shortfalls, and buildings deteriorated. While acknowledging federal cutbacks in public housing funds and the improper behaviors of residents, Popkin and her colleagues stress that "local politics have played an integral role in CHA's demise" (2000, 22).

HUD Takeover

In 1995, the U.S. Department of Housing and Urban Development (HUD) determined that the CHA was so corrupt it could no longer be allowed to manage the city's public housing infrastructure. That year

HUD hired Joseph Shuldiner, the former head of the New York City Housing Authority and HUD's assistant secretary of Public and Indian Housing, to take over the management of the CHA. When he did, his staff identified numerous "ghost workers," individuals on the payroll and not at work, a clear sign of Chicago's political patronage system (Popkin, Gwiasda, Olson, et al. 2000). Shuldiner served as the executive director of the CHA for four years but he did not have the resources to reverse the mismanagement and corruption that had rendered many buildings too run down for remodeling. Instead of rehabilitating buildings, the CHA, under Shuldiner, began leaving units empty, despite a growing waitlist for public housing units (Feldman and Stall 2004).[25] In 1983, 4 percent of the CHA units were vacant; in 1999 the number had increased to a staggering 35 percent (Ranney 2003). Many vacant units became controlled by the drug trade.

By the 1990s, the legacy of political corruption left the CHA developments in total disarray. As noted earlier, the CHA had the greatest proportion of units that failed the federal viability test and the city decided to raze all of its distressed high-rise public housing. In 1999, Richard M. Daley regained control of the CHA from Shuldiner and he implemented the Plan for Transformation. A combination of Chicago's continual mismanagement of public housing and recent federal housing reforms of the 1990s, the plan greatly accelerated Bronzeville's redevelopment. Bronzeville's economic transformation is a product of the interaction between federal policy and unique city circumstances.

Harlem's Redevelopment and Public Housing Reforms

By contrast, public housing in New York City is not being demolished. Instead, the NYCHA is rehabilitating its high-rise housing stock, and displacement among Harlem's low-income residents is less extensive. Many of Harlem's low-income public housing residents will have an opportunity to benefit from the improvement of their neighborhood. This circumstance is connected to the fragmented political structure in New York City, which results in superior public housing management and increased tenant activism. The New York City political system explains why public housing remains in Harlem.

Harlem has a substantial number of sizable public housing projects. The King Towers, St. Nicholas Houses, Rangel Houses, Drew-Hamilton Houses, Frederick Samuel Houses, Taft Houses, Harlem River Houses, and Polo Ground Towers house more than 20,000 Harlem residents

(NYCHA 2001). While property values are rising in Harlem, some suggest they would rise faster if public housing was torn down.[26] However, elected officials I speak with insist that razing the projects would "not be politically feasible." The tenants would not tolerate it.

Residents of the NYCHA are more active and connected to their political structure than those in Chicago. Charles Rangel, Harlem's U.S. congressman, considers public housing tenants an essential part of his constituency, and others concur. One high-level NYCHA manager says that New York City public housing residents have a "strong political network" and are important constituents of political leaders—they are politically engaged and force politicians to make public housing concerns top priorities. This level of engagement among the public housing residents with both politicians and NYCHA management at public housing meetings in Harlem has maintained the quality of NYCHA buildings. Tenant advocacy has protected public housing in Harlem from the distress and corruption endemic to public housing in Chicago.

Rehabilitation and Tenant Activism

I attend a monthly meeting of the Manhattan North Council of Presidents, a group of Northern Manhattan Public Housing Projects resident leaders. The meeting is held in the gym of West Harlem's Manhattanville Housing Project, and run by tenant leader Sandra Harper. Attending are tenant representatives, residents, building superintendents, managers, and current contractors for each public housing development. At 6:30 p.m., Ms. Harper, holding a cordless microphone, announces in her deep, gravelly voice, "Alright, let's get this started," as if she was declaring the beginning of a boxing match. She lays out the agenda for the night: NYCHA officials are to update tenants on renovations, and residents are to discuss problems with the buildings.

Ms. Harper gives the microphone to three NYCHA officials who discuss capital improvement funds available for project rehabilitation. The officials hand out an overview of scheduled improvements to be made in Harlem (NYCHA 2002a). In addition to these improvements, the NYCHA has a comprehensive plan for the continual upkeep and long-term preservation of its housing stock.[27]

After the housing officials conclude their talk, Ms. Harper announces the start of the strategy sessions. At each table, residents use easels to write down improvement ideas. I sit next to an older African-American woman from the Frederick Samuel Houses who complains about shoddy tile work recently installed in her building's entrance. I ask her if the contractor who did the work is still around. She says, "Yes, we are still working with them. It don't make no sense. They should just do it right the first time!"

After the strategy session, we socialize over a buffet style dinner. The meal helps ensure friendly negotiations between the factions. After eating, Ms. Harper asks each table to report on their major complaints. The most common concern is the need for more NYCHA inspectors to monitor the contractors working in various buildings. Other complaints include graffiti, broken elevators, and a lack of police presence. After the representatives of each project conclude their presentations, a person from the housing authority collects all written comments. Resident involvement happens not just at these monthly gatherings; it is also, and perhaps more importantly, occurs at individual housing projects.

Tenant activism ensures standards are maintained in Harlem's public housing. While working for Assemblyman Keith Wright, I receive a call from one of the resident leaders at the Drew-Hamilton Houses. One building's faulty foundation is causing small cracks in several apartments' walls. The resident leadership convenes an emergency meeting and insists that Assemblyman Wright attend to ensure that NYCHA officials repair the building. During the well-attended meeting, the resident leadership demands that NYCHA officials publicly promise to address the situation. The official agrees that regardless of cost he will have the building's structure monitored and repaired. He and the assemblyman, a member of the state Committee on Housing, agree to find the funding needed to make the building secure and safe. Tenant leadership and action explain why Harlem's public housing stock remains viable.

The viability of Harlem's public housing is critical to understanding the consequences of redevelopment. While displacement occurs among the working poor who are private market renters and those in city-owned buildings, it is not happening to public housing residents. "Public housing is the only thing preventing the total gentrification of Harlem," an individual remarks at a community forum. Viable public housing ensures that a sizable portion of Harlem's low-income population will have an opportunity to benefit from the community's revitalization.

Displacement in Harlem

Even though public housing residents are not being removed, displacement is still a major concern in Harlem. While not on the scale of displacement from dilapidated CHA buildings in Chicago, low-income residents in Harlem, as well as owners of small businesses are vulnerable. As noted in chapter 3, the city once owned a large percentage of Harlem's housing units. These units, mostly single-family homes and small apartment buildings, were repossessed in the 1970s and 1980s, when landlords failed to pay their property taxes. The city's Department of Housing Preservation and Development (HPD) is now in charge of these properties. At one point in the early 1980s, the HPD housed the homeless in many of these units. In the 1990s the city began selling these properties to nonprofit and for-profit real estate developers, and giving former tenants Section 8 vouchers. According to Harlem's affordable housing activists most of these Section 8 recipients were unable to find housing in the community and moved to other New York City boroughs, such as Brooklyn and the Bronx, and to parts of Newark, New Jersey.[28]

Many living in private market housing also face the threat of displacement. Some tenants are forced to leave properties when rental brownstones are converted to single-family homes. Further, while working for Assemblyman Wright, I met tenants in rent-controlled apartments who had been offered $10,000 to $20,000 to vacate their units.[29] Some landlords even damaged their buildings to make them temporally unsafe, forcing tenants to vacate.

On an unusually hot April morning, I witness the gentrification pressures in Harlem firsthand. As soon as I arrive in the morning at Keith's office, Mignonne, his executive assistant, tells me I need to head over to 321 St. Nicholas Avenue. She received a call from a resident saying that all the tenants were being evicted.

When I arrive over thirty people are outside the apartment building, crying, screaming, and bewildered. A few feet away from me, a teenage girl hugs her mother and says, as tears run down her face, "Mom, where are we going to go? Are we going to become homeless?" Her mother, desperately trying to hold it together, responds calmly, "Baby, we'll probably have to go to a shelter tonight." At this point I am totally confused. I need to know why these families are being evicted. I find Freddy, one of Keith's staff and we find one of the building's tenant leaders who explains that late last night the city determined that the building was "structurally unsound" and issued an emergency vacate order. The forty-eight families had to relocate immediately to shelters throughout the city.

The emergency vacate order, according to certain residents, is suspicious. Although sections of the building have been in need of repair, some community leaders and residents believe that there was no need to remove everyone from the building or in such an expeditious manner. The building is in an ideal location, just a block from 125th Street. Buildings in the area, like one just a block north, have been recently been rehabilitated and converted to luxury apartments. One tenant of the building claims, "This is criminal.... They just want us out. This is gentrification."[30] The next day, I overhear on the street two people talking about the building. One declares, "They [the city and developer] are trying to get the people out so they can charge higher rents. They used to burn the roof to get the people out, now they say it's structurally unsound. It's a fraud." Two years after the initial vacate order, the building has not yet been rehabilitated. When the building reopens, it is likely that many of the original tenants will not return, and rental prices will be higher than before the abrupt shutdown.

Several small businesses are also facing the prospects of removal. For instance, small mom and pop businesses along the major streets, such as Adam Clayton Powell Jr. Boulevard, Malcolm X Boulevard, 125th Street, and, more recently, 135th Street are feeling the squeeze as rental prices continue to rise. Small businesses contend not only with rising commercial rents, but with competition from arriving chain stores. A small optometry business on 125th Street was forced out of Harlem when Sterling Optical opened up a franchise in the community.[31] Local coffee shops are also finding it hard to compete with mainstream outlets like Starbucks as landlords seek to increase rents (fig. 5.7). Donna Lewis, owner of Home Sweet Harlem Café, attests, "Landlords are increasingly using legal tactics to push out community businesses all around Harlem in order to make room for investors with deeper pockets."[32] The encroachment of chain stores and increasing commercial rents threaten the viability of indigenous businesses.

Studies conducted in the early 1990s predicted displacement in Harlem (see Smith [1996] 2000), and others document it vividly (Davila 2004; Taylor 2002); however, a recent study suggests displacement is not as much of a pressing concern in Harlem as it is in other New York City neighborhoods. Using the New York City's Housing and Vacancy Survey, Lance Freeman and Frank Braconi demonstrate that displacement rates are lower in gentrifying New York City neighborhoods, such as Harlem, than those with more stable real estate markets (2004). Unfortunately, they assume only low-income households or those without college degrees face the threat of displacement, and they do not account for the removal of those above the federal poverty line or those with a college degree.

Figure 5.7 Starbucks on 125th Street and Malcolm X Boulevard.

While many low-income residents are safe because Harlem's public housing remains, moderate-income renters, whose income likely exceeds the poverty rate, and small businesses remain vulnerable to displacement from the community. Therefore, Freeman and Braconi's study underestimates the percent of displacement in Harlem.[33] While displacement is less visible in Harlem, than Bronzeville, it is occurring and is a major concern.[34]

Who's Benefiting?

Several black real estate developers, who occasionally partner with white investors, are making millions from the redevelopment of Harlem. Just as in Bronzeville, some of Harlem's African-American businessmen are capitalizing from the escalating property values. For instance, Full Spectrum of New York LLC, formed by Walter Edwards and Carlton Brown, has developed a $40 million luxury condominium building in Harlem. Uptown Partners, another black-led real estate team, has collaborated with a white-controlled firm to produce two posh, high-rise projects.[35] Another Harlem-based real estate company, Webb and Brooker Real Estate Inc., is benefiting as well. This company, which was founded in 1968, manages many residential and commercial spaces throughout Harlem.

With the recent redevelopment, their portfolio has expanded considerably, from managing subsidized properties to partnering in the development of private residential projects such as the $63 million Harlem Renaissance Plaza, and commercial spaces such as the 125th Street retail outlet Mart 125. Webb and Brooker are also the leasing agent for Harlem Park, a new $200 million mixed-use building expected to feature Marriott as its anchor tenant.[36] For-profit black-owned businesses involved with the real estate market, are generating huge profits from Harlem's revitalization.

Smaller players are also engaged in real estate development activities. For instance, several prominent church-based nonprofit development teams are participating in construction projects. Abyssinian Baptist Church and Harlem Congregations for Community Improvement each have development arms that are directing the construction and rehabilitation of residential units throughout Harlem. In addition, these churches are participating in large commercial developments. Abyssinian has partnered with a for-profit company to build Harlem Center, a huge commercial space on 125th Street containing CVS, Staples, Marshalls, and H&M clothing.[37]

Political Decentralization and NYCHA's Tenant Activism: Linking the Past to the Present

Known as the "Housing Czar" and "Power Broker" of New York City, Robert Moses was New York City's Richard J. Daley. He ruled over the city's public housing development from approximately 1940 to 1965 (Caro 1975). Moses's political skill and the valuable land resources he controlled as the New York City Park Commissioner enabled him to become the city's most powerful urban renewal player. Moses convinced Mayor La Guardia that he had more financial and political insight concerning housing than the appointed heads of the NYCHA (Schwartz 1993). Moses displaced people from their communities to make room for new buildings and highways and often used public housing to accommodate displaced tenants (Marcuse, Burney, and Tsitiridis 1994).

Although Moses had great power over the NYCHA, his overall authority was quite limited compared to Mayor Daley's. Moses was not mayor, and did not head any centralized political machine or party. He did not have the influence to sanction protesters by cutting resources to individuals, organizations, or city agencies as Mayor Daley did. As a result, Moses's redevelopment plans faced greater protest and the legacy

of tenant activism, which reflects the city's fragmented political structure, continues to affect the conditions of public housing in New York
City.

Many of Moses's urban renewal projects were confronted with extensive opposition, and although protest did not halt development, displaced tenants, who ended up in public housing, insisted that standards
were maintained. For instance, in 1949, to protect Columbia University
and Riverside Church from the encroachment of blacks from Harlem,
Moses planned to displace numerous low-income residents to make
room for two "superblock" buffers of six high-rise middle-income cooperative apartment buildings. Residents threatened with the prospects of
displacement organized, protested, and interrupted several city hearings
(Schwartz 1986a). Activists secured over 5,000 signatures from site residents opposing the project, and were able to organize 250 protesters to
attend city hearings. Consistent advocacy delayed the project for several
years.

In 1953, despite intense resident protest, the project was approved.
Many displaced residents were relocated to the newly constructed Manhattanville public housing project, a few blocks north of 125th Street. Although Moses's plan eventually prevailed, the prolonged protest showed
him and the city that displaced tenants would not acquiesce easily. Tenant activism persisted at other urban renewal sites, and displaced residents, who eventually ended up in NYCHA buildings, used the power of
protest to insist standards were maintained in public housing developments.

The tenant engagement of the 1950s and 1960s has continued to shape
the management of Harlem's public housing. Terry Williams and William
Kornblum's study of Harlem's public housing projects in the 1990s argues
the degree of tenant involvement in planning and maintenance is extraordinary compared to other large housing authorities. One NYCHA architect interviewed by Williams and Kornblum attests that "nothing can be
done [to the buildings] without meeting with the tenants" (1994, 242).
This architect says that residents are also vigilant against drug and gangs.
He notes that "some [tenant leaders] have been killed for their activism,
and when they are, despite the danger, others step forward to fill their
places" (242). This activism has played an important role in the superior
conditions in New York City's public housing.

Additionally, the NYCHA's internal governance structure, to some extent, mimics the structure of the citywide political landscape. Management of the projects is more decentralized than the CHA.[38] The control

over resources is dispersed in New York City, and the NYCHA has a good deal of autonomy from the mayor. One of the NYCHA submanagers who examined the CHA in the 1990s says, "There seems to be less nepotism in NYC. We have very few political appointments and there are exams and standards that lead to more accountability." The standards of New York City's public housing are higher than Chicago's because funding decisions are decentralized and not based on political considerations. In New York City, he says, middle-level housing managers have relatively greater control of their resources. This level of fragmentation prevents the housing authority from becoming the mayor's political vehicle and keeps NYCHA's focus on providing quality housing.

In the 1980s and 1990s, while Chicago's public housing deteriorated because of continued corrupt management practices, the NYCHA aggressively modernized and rehabilitated its housing stock. Between 1982 and 1994, while the federal government made severe cuts in public housing programs,[39] the NYCHA increased its modernization funds from $82 million to $435 million. The NYCHA also kept its commitment to social programs, operating 479 community facilities throughout the developments. These city decisions to preserve the public housing stock are linked with aggressive and sustained tenant activism, which stems from the city's fragmented political structure.

Discussion

The citywide environments surrounding Bronzeville and Harlem greatly affect their redevelopment and its consequences. Chicago's centralized Democratic machine allowed, if not encouraged, the CHA to become a bastion of political corruption and mismanagement, ultimately leading to intolerable public housing conditions. The New York City political landscape is fragmented and more open to dissent and activism, which is associated with better public housing management.

Thus, when the federal government mandated that local housing authorities demolish or rehabilitate their distressed housing stock in the 1990s, it differentially affected these two cities. Because Chicago had so much distressed public housing, the only fiscally sound plan was to raze its high-rise public housing. This action has led to the displacement of nearly 17,000 low-income residents in Bronzeville and triggered an economic boom as real estate speculators and developers rush to invest in the community. In New York City, superior management and tenant activism, associated with the city's open political system, ensured that standards were consistently maintained in NYCHA buildings. As a result, the public housing in Harlem has remained viable, and current redevelopment persists without extensive public housing tenant displacement.

The clear difference in public housing between Bronzeville and Harlem has forced a reexamination of the role federal policy has in redeveloping inner city areas. While most agree that past urban renewal was linked to the demise of the inner city, the current round of urban renewal, promoted by the HOPE VI program and the Quality Housing and Work Responsibility Act, contributes to, but is not the sole cause of, urban community revitalization. The national priority to demolish distressed public housing is a major factor leading to Bronzeville's redevelopment, while it has little effect on Harlem's development. Federal housing legislation is being mediated by unique city contexts. Distinct political conditions in these cities greatly affect redevelopment patterns in Harlem and Bronzeville. Political decisions to manage or mismanage, rehabilitate or ignore the public housing in New York City and Chicago relate to how current federal public housing reforms impact the redevelopment of these inner city areas. To fully understand community development, interactions among larger political economic forces and more local political circumstances must be considered.

The current round of urban renewal is unlike the past. African Americans are being differentially affected: many are being displaced, while others are prospering. Federal housing reforms are facilitating the demolition of public housing and forcing residents to relocate to other impoverished and segregated communities. At the same time, black real estate owners in redeveloping areas are profiting from constructing new commercial spaces, townhomes, and apartment buildings. Additionally, property owners in revitalizing areas are benefiting through the appreciation of home values. The intersection of race and class affects who is benefiting and who is not in today's urban renewal.

Some might argue that the residents of the Harlem projects are more active because, when compared to Bronzeville residents, they have more income, which is a strong predictor of rates of civic participation. The average household income in the NYCHA is $15,000; in the CHA it is $7,000 (see appendix C). However, when cost of living adjustments are made, the difference between these figures is reduced to $3,000.[40] Therefore, income may not be the key factor explaining the difference in levels of engagement between Harlem and Bronzeville public housing residents.

Others may argue that a greater liberal tradition of activism, dating back to the early 1900s, exists in New York City (see McNickle 1993; Schwartz 1986b; Schwartz 1993), and that this culture of liberalism explains the public housing situation. But the activist tradition in New York City is in part due to the diverse political structure, which dates back to 1898 with the formation of the Board of Estimate. A diffuse political structure, once in place, is associated with more activism, which results in better public housing management and conditions.

Notably, New York City's and Chicago's public housing differs considerably in racial composition. Today, African Americans make up 94 percent of Chicago's public housing population but only 54 percent of New York City's (see appendix C). The citywide public housing racial difference may relate to better subsidized housing in New York City in general and in Harlem specifically. Racial differences and racist beliefs towards African Americans, might, in part, account for why less attention was given to the upkeep of CHA housing stock. However, in Harlem and Bronzeville most of the public housing has remained predominantly African American, minimizing to some extent concerns of racial differences. If racial attitudes were the sole determiner of housing maintenance quality, Harlem's stock should have looked more similar to Bronzeville's.

Despite racial and income differences, distinct conditions in public housing have more to do with the political structures and related housing management practices in these two cities. For instance, while rent collection in Chicago is often overlooked, it provides half of the operating budget for the NYCHA (Thompson 1999). Additionally, the percent of working families is higher in New York City developments (35 versus 15 percent, see appendix C). Phillip Thompson, an expert on New York City public housing, comments, "[The] NYCHA [has] historically maintained a mix of families on welfare, working families, and retirees–one-third each–in public housing. ... NYCHA's tenant mix has been widely credited for the unparalleled success of public housing in New York" (1999, 131). Rent collection and tenant building composition, although constrained by federal government to some extent, are local managerial decisions. Distinct political environments best explain local managerial and resident activism differences, which engender vastly dissimilar public housing conditions. The distinct condition of public housing in these two cities ultimately elucidates the displacement consequences in

Harlem's and Bronzeville's current redevelopment. The focus until now has been primarily on how external forces at the global, federal, and city levels interact to shape Harlem and Bronzeville's redevelopment. In the next two chapters, internal community actions are thoroughly investigated.

Figure 6.1 Harlem mural with St. Nicholas Houses in the background.

6

City Politics and Black Protest

Much of the literature on black politics claims that African Americans are the most politically uniform group in the United States. According to Dianne Pinderhughes, a leading expert on black politics, "The African-American population consistently displays the clearest signs of...political cohesion; their homogeneous behavior arises out of distinctive historical experiences" (1997, 77). If this were true, we might expect similar political behaviors surrounding the economic redevelopment and gentrification of Harlem and Bronzeville, but as we've seen, this is not the case. Harlem has a strong activist tradition and more protest politics related to its revitalization. But in Bronzeville, oppositional voices are muted, despite the extensive and ill-managed displacement. Moreover, these communities have very similar racial and socioeconomic characteristics.[1] The most significant difference, as we've seen, is that these two neighborhoods are embedded in cities with drastically different political landscapes. Do the unique citywide political landscapes in New York City and Chicago influence internal community debates?

Exploring the dynamics associated with civic engagement and public dissent within black communities is particularly important since African

Americans, compared to whites, are more likely to participate in non-traditional political action (Verba and Nie 1972). For instance, African Americans are more likely to affect their community through civic group participation than by voting. Engagement may alter local redevelopment policies, such as reducing the income qualifications for newly built subsidized homes, which might increase the chances for equitable development. Although many survey studies investigate individual and community-level determinates of black political action (e.g., Cohen and Dawson 1993; Marschall 2001), few explore how conditions beyond the community affect informal political engagement. By comparing the extent of protest politics related to Harlem and Bronzeville's redevelopment, we can see how the structure of citywide political environments affect contested politics at the community level.

While numerous African-American Bronzeville and Harlem residents are elated by the economic revitalization, several organizations attempt to preserve a place for the 45 percent of households that are low-income.[2] Since these communities are similar on many levels, one might expect equivalent levels of support and opposition from residents and black-led organizations in both neighborhoods. However, the degree of "contested politics" or "black activism" (Jennings 1992) associated with the redevelopment processes is drastically different. Harlem is full of public dissent, while activists in Bronzeville are reluctant to challenge the development process.

Unfortunately, civic engagement studies of African-American communities have been markedly limited. In his book *Black Visions* (2001), Michael Dawson comments that we know little about how structural considerations affect the black political ideologies of civic action. Further, in *Black Corona*, Steven Gregory criticizes the urban community change literature because little of it has "been devoted to [the] social and institutional structure(s) of urban black communities" (1998, 10). By exploring how metropolitan political contexts influence the organizational structure of two important African-American communities, this research can respond to Dawson and Gregory's concerns.

Ample research suggests that a city's political structure matters for several important outcomes. For instance, district elections, compared to citywide council elections, lead to larger overall voter turnout (Bridges 1997). Additionally, more centralized city political systems facilitate less public dissent and smaller budget deficits (Fuchs 1992). Lastly, strong machine systems, compared to weak party city governments, limit contested politics in low-income neighborhoods (Wilson 1960). Since the structure of a city's political system influences several outcomes, we can expect the normative and structural differences in city-level politics to also influence levels of activism and resistance within black communities.

Comparative studies suggest a link between citywide political environments and African-American community politics. For instance, Barbara Ferman (1996) posits that alternate political climates affect the likelihood of successful progressive movements stemming from minority neighborhoods. Further, in their study of the implementation of Great Society programs in five cities, David Greenstone and Paul Peterson note the importance of a city's political landscape on progressive black institutions. They argue that compared to NAACP chapters in other large municipalities, Chicago's is one of the least militant because of the local political climate ([1973] 1976).

Political differences between New York City and Chicago affect the context surrounding the redevelopment of Harlem and Bronzeville. Municipal political climates, in particular distinct structures and norms for political engagement, influence the implementation of federal policies and public debates connected to the redevelopment. New York City's diverse political system helps to facilitate public dissent, while Chicago's one-party, centralized structure inhibits it. The unique political context of each city is an important explanatory variable for understanding the extent of black-led protest politics and the redevelopment process in these communities.

Concept of Protest Politics

Protest politics and opposition are public and private acts of informal collective actions taken by organizations and individuals to contest economic development. My notion of protest moves away from nonspecific and abstract forms of resistance discussed by historian Robin Kelley. His definition of resistance, such as alternative "dress codes," is too broad for the politics of community development. Powerful forces are escalating the real estate markets and only concrete acts of opposition, such as protest at public meetings, are likely to alter the development process. I do agree with Kelley, however, that community organizations are important mechanisms in "black working-class political struggles" (1994, 38). Here I examine actions taken by organizational leaders and everyday individuals in civic forums attempting to directly impact public redevelopment decisions.

Political Contrasts

Harlem residents are very vocal and almost unruly at public meetings; they are willing to denounce their local politicians' actions. Despite likely criticism, politicians regularly attend public meetings where these exchanges take place. After a local political official presents at a community forum, a woman concerned about rising rents stands and shouts, "The elected officials here in Harlem are part of the problem. If I vote for you and you can't help me, you don't get my vote the next time." In Harlem the presence of a competing party facilitates civic dissent.

An excerpt from my field notes shows how the existence of a rival party in New York City has at least some effect on the political environment in Harlem.

> I am getting my hair cut in Jackson's Barbershop on 135th Street. This is the second time I have been there and the barber, Joe, remembers that I live on 137th Street. As he cuts my hair the other barber in the shop asks if we know if there are term limits for the governor. I say, "I don't think so, but I'm not exactly sure." He replies, "I'll tell you what, Pataki [the Republican governor at the time] is going to win." Joe, who has lived in Harlem for thirty-six years, responds, "After all the money he's invested in Harlem, I'm going to vote for him." He then stops cutting my hair and says, "I'm a Democrat, but if I like the other candidate I'll vote for him." The other barber in the shop calls out, "Me too." Joe continues to cut my hair and says, "I am what you call a smart voter; I go by the candidate not the party."

Joe's perception that a Republican official is investing in the community suggests one party does not dominate Harlem politics. In addition, the lack of loyalty the barbers express toward the Democratic Party is an example of the diversity of New York City politics.

In contrast, the Democratic Party dominates Chicago politics. During my time in Bronzeville, rarely does a political discussion center on a Republican candidate. Often in local elections in Chicago, Republicans don't even run for office. People in Bronzeville commonly refer to this one-sided, Democrat government system as "the Party" or "the Machine." Simply put, "In Chicago [the] party and government [are] indistinguishable" (Ferman 1996, 138).

In *Mayors and Money*, Ester Fuchs discusses how the diversity in New York City's political system compared to Chicago's monolithic Democratic machine has consequences for fiscal stability. She argues that during the 1970s fiscal crisis, Chicago weathered the predicament because of "the mayor's ability to control," while New York City's deficit spun out of control because of its decentralized and fragmented political system (1992, 16). Fuchs describes Chicago's political system as a hierarchical political machine, while New York City has a diffuse power structure with extensive interest group competition. She contends that this structural difference relates to the proliferation of protest politics and requests for funding. In New York City the fragmented system facilitates constituent demands, while the machine dictates the terms of budget negotiations. These differences at the city level affect community structures and norms, influencing internal political debates and actions.

Structural and Normative Differences

The structural differences between New York City's and Chicago's political landscape are evident at the community level. In New York City the five boroughs are divided into fifty-nine community districts, each with its own community board. The New York City community boards began in 1947 and officially became part of the City Charter in 1961.[3] They originated as part of a governmental reform strategy by creating "competing legitimate entities to neighborhood party organizations" (Katznelson 1981, 142). The boards function as local planning bodies and vote on community development projects in their districts. Real estate developers who receive city funds are required to present at these meetings. The community boards are official components of the political system in New York City, but they have an advisory role—board members vote on development plans, however official approval comes from the city council. But the community has some say, as area councilmen attend these board meetings, giving members and residents the opportunity to influence the decisions made by their local politicians.

Community Board 10 presides over Central Harlem. Their meetings are open to the general public and give residents and organizational leaders an opportunity to voice their opinions about redevelopment. Every month the board, consisting of approximately forty politically appointed residents, meets, debates, and votes on community planning proposals in their district.

Chicago has no structural equivalent to the New York City community boards.[4] No regularly occurring public forums or gatherings exist for political leaders and developers to report their activities to residents. In Bronzeville, public meetings, where residents are updated on community issues, are held by community-based organizations such as the Mid-South Planning and Development Commission, the Grand Boulevard Federation, and the Gap Community Organization.[5] These gatherings are not formally connected to the city's political structure. Real estate developers are not required to attend, and when they choose to present their plans, they do not seek resident input. And when political leaders visit, they are greeted with cordial, almost reverent exchanges.

New York and Chicago have different expectations and norms for political engagement. In Chicago, city officials are confident in the power of the machine, and interact with residents in a commanding and almost patronizing manner. As one community leader in Bronzeville puts it, "[Chicago] is the most unusual city in the country. No other city functions like this. I've lived in Cincinnati, in New York City, and in Boston. ... In these places your representatives actually ... sit down [with you] and act like they work for you. Here nobody works for you, you work for them, you know, so that's the way it is. Maybe that's only in the black community but that has been my experience here. I work for the alderman, you know, she doesn't work for me." Another community leader in Bronzeville comments, "The aldermen have a tradition of being sort of autocratic powers in their wards for the most part and they tend to run things according to their own terms and according to their own interests." In Bronzeville, when elected officials speak, people usually praise them or stay silent, while in Harlem residents and organizational leaders often raise their voices and publicly castigate their political leaders. Distinct party strength, community structures, and expectations for citizen engagement within the political systems of these two cities help explain the extent of community-level protest politics.

Debates in Bronzeville

In Bronzeville I regularly attend the biweekly meetings of the South Side Partnership, an organizational membership group that discusses and acts on community issues.[6] The partnership consists of approximately fifteen organizations including a major commercial bank, several local social service agencies, a neighborhood block group, a neighborhood planning organization, two local advocacy organizations, two major educational institutions, and several area hospitals. Many partnership members are themselves groupings of smaller block clubs and other service organizations in the community, making the membership of the South Side Partnership quite diverse.

The city's plan for public housing transformation is debated constantly during this period. The plan, as discussed in chapter 5, calls for the demolition of the majority of high-rise public housing buildings in Bronzeville and will displace a significant percent of residents. Many social service organizations in the partnership express concerns about displacement because a large percent of their clients live in public housing. Other organizations in the partnership, such as the block group association, want the public housing removed as quickly as possible. After considerable internal debate, the partnership agrees to try to influence the relocation and displacement aspects of the plan. They collectively declare, as stated in their meeting minutes, "We need to make a deliberate effort to ensure the current residents are able to remain in the community and that redevelopment can and should be done without massive displacement." Toward this end, the partnership decides to invite the head of the Chicago Housing Authority (CHA) to discuss how the partnership can help guide the implementation of the CHA plan. Although the director of the CHA is formally invited, the chief officer for CHA's development division is sent instead.

The interactions during this meeting illustrate how the political climate in Chicago typically differs from New York City. At this gathering, the CHA officer discusses the transformation plan in detail. His presentation emphasizes that community groups and other institutions are eligible for both social service money and management contracts for some of the remaining CHA buildings, and only touches upon the consequences for public housing residents. Even though, at previous meetings, the members discuss and fiercely debate the issue of displacement, not one of the social service agencies questions the CHA representative about relocation or displacement. Immediately after the meeting, a social service agency director shows me a report, which indicates the extent of displacement outlined in the CHA plan.

The lack of debate concerning displacement in Bronzeville and its relationship to the Chicago political structure is evident. One organizational leader of the South Side Partnership states, "In terms of Chicago politics, there is this thing where you have the strong mayor and the weak aldermanic system. So there is the movement afoot to not really challenge the mayor because it wouldn't be politically astute to really fight [since] ... the mayor has the resources." He continues, "Some people will always say, 'Well, who's speaking up for CHA residents?' You know, who's taking a lead on these things and you look at these organizations [in Bronzeville] and some of them, us included, are laid back and part of the reason why you're laid back is because you don't want to upset the pot, because your livelihood depends on it. So in a lot of ways people are co-opted through the structure of the way their funding works, through the local government, through the whole CDBG [community development block grant] process."

Fear of direct reprisals, such as the elimination of community organization funding by the reigning political machine, in part, influences the lack of opposition at the South Side Partnership meeting. Mayor Daley fully supports the CHA plan. It originated from his office and, furthermore, he appoints the CHA's director. Therefore, some of the social services agencies and housing advocates do not challenge the CHA plan for fear of retaliation from the mayor. Many of the social service agencies receive grants and contracts from the city government.

The ability to administer direct sanctions is associated with Chicago's centralized, Democratic political system. As a current alderman in Bronzeville explains, "Chicago politics is like a feudal system, where Mayor Daley is king and the aldermen are the lords and ladies of their ward." This level of political centralization and control inhibits public debate around issues such as displacement in Bronzeville. One community activist in Chicago insists that public dialogue and debate on displacement and redevelopment in Bronzeville is virtually absent. When speaking about the massive demolition of CHA high-rises in the community, he rhetorically asks, "How can this be happening ... with so little public discussion, public challenge, [and] public scrutiny?" He continues, "There is no public discourse remotely commensurate with the gravity and scale of what's happening."

Sudhir Venkatesh also notes a lack of political engagement by longstanding social service organizations in the Robert Taylor Homes project: "Only three agencies [of the many that surround the housing project] saw the need to intervene on the behalf of Robert Taylor tenants in politicized matters" (2000, 201). One resident, interviewed by Venkatesh, comments, "They [social service organizations] all just say they got to protect themselves...against what?" But political consequences are one reason why many of these institutions are not more politically involved. While the political environment in Chicago is hierarchical and residents and organizational leaders in Bronzeville are, at times, intimidated by public officials, in Harlem residents and politicians are on more equal footing.

Debates in Harlem

The open political environment in New York City allows Harlem community leaders and residents to publicly attack and question their political leaders and real estate developers. After a developer presents his proposal for a new market-rate housing project at a Community Board 10 meeting, a resident asks, "What is the price for a 2-bedroom?" The developer responds, "It will cost between $250,000 and $300,000." A woman sitting next to me stands up and shouts, "Families for these units ain't coming from Harlem!" She then turns to a city housing department employee and explains that it angers her that developers are receiving city funds to build housing beyond the means of many current residents.

In Harlem, numerous community meetings, forums, and conferences focus on gentrification. The Harlem Tenants Council, an association that advocates for affordable housing and tenants rights, sponsors several of these gatherings. When local political figures attend, residents and community leaders air their redevelopment concerns. As documented in my field notes, during one session a local housing activist describes to a group of concerned residents how Harlem's economic development threatens its cultural integrity.

> The activist tells the residents that many black landlords are renting to whites and not blacks. One woman in the crowd shouts out, "It's disgusting." The activist follows this by saying, "The elected officials, they know about it." She speaks about how the local politicians engage in symbolic politics by changing the signs of the streets, like Lenox to Malcolm X but that, "If Malcolm knew what was happening on 125th and Lenox he'd be turning over in his grave." Lenox Avenue at 125th now has a Starbucks, McDonalds, and an AT&T cell phone store, and there are plans to build a Gap clothing store across the

street. She says how some people think "The Gap" mural on 125th, which is up on President Clinton's office building, looks nice because it has Danny Glover on it wearing a Gap button-down shirt, but she shouts, "I don't see anything around there looking African." She then says, "We have a managerial class [of African Americans] in Harlem from places like Harvard and Yale," who are orchestrating the redevelopment for "outside wealthy white folks." She continues, "You know what [the director of the Upper Manhattan Empowerment Zone (UMEZ)] does with plans that come from the community. This is what he does," as she vigorously tears up a piece of paper and throws into a nearby garbage can. She explains that she has been trying to get the attention of the chairman of the board of directors for UMEZ to have the director removed.

While this excerpt indicates that intra-racial class conflict and the interracial divide are perceived as critical factors in the redevelopment process, my central point is to demonstrate that public displays of dissent, especially ones directed at local officials, are far more common in Harlem.

New York City, David Greenstone and Paul Peterson note, is "the pluralist's dream" ([1973] 1976, 39). Others describe New York City's political landscape as "an ethnic 'poker game' in which no single group commands most of the chips and when the politically federated system provides numerous entry points" for contested politics (Abu-Lughod 1999, 417). Community groups in Harlem are able to obtain resources from a variety of places, allowing them more latitude to be vocal on development issues. In fact many community organizations receive funds controlled by both Democrats and Republicans. With local structures such as the community boards and more importantly a weak party system, no person or group controls the political process.

The Palm Tavern versus Smalls Paradise

The redevelopment of two historic businesses, the Palm Tavern in Bronzeville and Smalls Paradise in Harlem, illustrates how the different "rules of the game" are played out in Chicago and New York. The redevelopment of these properties shows how the local political context, structures, and norms for political engagement, facilitates contested dialogue in Harlem and inhibits it in Bronzeville.

The Palm Tavern is a bar and night club in Bronzeville where many jazz greats of the 1930s, '40s '50s, and 60s played. It is located on 47th

Street, just a few blocks east of Martin Luther King Jr. Drive. In the 1940s, 47th Street was the social center of Bronzeville (Drake and Cayton [1945] 1993). Today, 47th Street still has some viable businesses but, as a whole, is run-down. To stimulate development the city designated the street a Redevelopment Area and a Tax Increment Financing District and then condemned and seized certain structures along 47th Street. In 2001 the Palm Tavern, which was operating at that time, was shut down. Many leaders in Bronzeville claim that the closing of the tavern occurred without sufficient public input.

In an article on the closing of the Palm Tavern, Harold Lucas, a long-time resident and preservationist who heads the Bronzeville Tourism Council, states,

> I don't know of any community participation [concerning the tavern], and I've lived around the corner [from 47th and King] for 15 years. What we're talking about is maximum feasibility participation and citizen involvement. ... Do political agendas supercede the will of the people? In this case, I guess they do. It's absolute demagoguery. ... The city wants [development] on their terms—that's the problem. ... They [local officials] should represent the entire community, not just represent your own fiefdom and act like lord over the people and violate the public trust.[7]

Lucas is not the only person concerned by the way the Palm Tavern was closed. In the same article, Ron Carter states, "Bottom line, there has been no business and community participation. ... There was no opportunity to take part." He recounts that when he was head of the 47th Street Merchants Association, city plans to seize the land for redevelopment were being made; according to Carter, however, city officials were constantly proclaiming that such plans did not exist. The lack of information regarding city development proposals in Bronzeville is not isolated to this event. During an interview one community leader comments that trying to find clear and accurate information on city redevelopment blueprints is like mission impossible. The city's lack of clear communication with business owners and residents inhibits citizens' ability to act.

There is very little community dialogue and protest concerning the takeover of this site. The local alderman, Dorothy Tillman, is virtually silent. Alleged handouts or payoffs by the city surrounding this situation have been reported. Some speculate that "the flow of money into the neighborhoods has effectively muzzled former critics such as Ald.

Tillman," who has "benefited from major projects" in her ward "partly funded by the city."[8] Further, the owner of the tavern, who rents the property, receives $100,000 from the city for the memorabilia in the bar.[9] The tavern is now boarded up while infrastructure improvements are made in the area. At this point, the city has not announced the future use of the tavern. However, there are plans to redevelop 47th Street and make it into a touristy blues district.

Like the Palm Tavern, Smalls Paradise in Harlem showcased many famous jazz musicians and big-bands in the 1930s and '40s. The building where Smalls once operated is located on the southwest corner of 135th Street and Adam Clayton Powell Jr. Boulevard and has been abandoned and boarded up for several years. When residents became aware that Abyssinian Baptist Church's Development Corporation plans to redevelop the site with the use of public funds, opinions were mixed. The point of contention is the church's plan to include an International House of Pancakes on the ground floor. In comparison to the Palm Tavern, the redevelopment process of Smalls is more open and transparent.

Activists publicly oppose Abyssinian's plan and take their concerns to Harlem's Community Board 10. At one meeting, Henry Michael Adams, a local historic preservationist, seeks the board's support to obtain an emergency city landmark designation for Smalls Paradise. If enacted it may prevent the pancake restaurant from being built on what Adams considers a historic site. During the meeting Adams explains the issues to the board and the seventy attending residents: "There is a law called the Historical Housing Preservation Act, which prohibits landmarks from being impaired with federal and state funding, and since we have the Empowerment Zone in our area, and since they have ignored this act. ... It seems to me very important for this board ... to identify [and preserve] all of the historically significant, architecturally significant and culturally significant structures in Harlem that make up the African-American cultural capital."

The board, by majority vote, approves to support the emergency landmark designation for Smalls. However, the city's landmark commission ignores the community board vote and Abyssinian continues with their initial plans. At the redevelopment groundbreaking ceremony, Adams and his small group of activists protest the event, shouting repeatedly, "Save Paradise, Save Harlem."[10] Over the chanting, Reverend Calvin Butts of Abyssinian speaks: "Our goal here today is economic revitalization. Now, you hear some people … say they want to save Harlem. Save Harlem. Sure. But you know what wise men say. They say, 'Money on the wood makes the game go good.' And so I need the money to save Harlem. So I went to the politicians with my hat in hand … [and] these people came through." Throughout the ceremony, Adams continues shouting, "Save Harlem now! Save Harlem from pancakes!" Speaking to reporters shortly after the event, Butts says, "The issue is economic. Landmarking, preservation-those things cost money. Maybe they add twenty percent to your costs. If you're waiting on the money to do preservation work, that retards your progress. And Mr. Adams, much as I respect his position and appreciate him as an individual, a person—I don't think he's got any money."

The protest at the community board and outside of the groundbreaking ceremony does little to affect the original plans for Smalls, but Adams's voice and others are heard. Importantly, it is a relatively open process in comparison to the Palm Tavern. Few opponents in New York City complain of covert development plans. Abyssinian's Development Corporation regularly presents at the Community Board 10 meetings, and residents are aware of their plans. The redevelopment of Smalls is an open public process, unlike the Palm Tavern, where city authority is used to acquire properties and viable establishments, while residents and business leaders are shut out of the planning process.

Discussion

The political contrast between New York City and Chicago is important for understanding the role of black organizations in Harlem's and Bronzeville's redevelopment. Chicago's monolithic structure inhibits debate concerning displacement, while New York City's decentralized, fragmented, and diverse political system facilitates it. This result bolsters Fuchs's claim that the structure of the Democratic machine in Chicago enables the mayor "to control the demands of neighborhood groups" (1992, 270). Although Harlem and Bronzeville are very similar, different levels of political discourse surrounding redevelopment result from distinct city-level political circumstances, strongly suggesting that citywide political structures affect black protest.[11]

Often research on black civil society involves large-scale survey research of individuals, which sometimes fails to capture key variables affecting black organizations. Although past research has suggested that black political attitudes often appear identical in the aggregate, organizational behaviors can differ based on the metropolitan political climate. Political scientist Ira Katznelson asserts that when conducting urban community research "it proves necessary to comprehend how external social forces pattern and inform local events and behavior" (1981, 200). City-level political structures, "external social forces," shape behavior patterns and events related to the process of redevelopment in both Harlem and Bronzeville. Aspects of black civil society act differently based on alternative structures and norms (e.g., expectations for political consequences) in these two communities. These findings reinforce a critical point in James Q. Wilson's seminal study, *Negro Politics:* "Politics cannot be understood apart from the city in which it is found" (1960, 23). To understand the actions of black institutions, the metropolitan context in which they are embedded must be considered.

Levels of civic engagement are different in these communities. But many scholars and policymakers are concerned with whether local participation relates to community improvement or, in this case, whether it affects rates of displacement. In the case of the redevelopment of Smalls, protest was unsuccessful in facilitating historic preservation. Further, there were few instances in which public action affected major development policies. There were some victories, however, such as the arrest of a Harlem landlord who threatened tenants in rent-controlled apartments and did not address damages to encourage vacancy.[12] Moreover, as noted in chapter 5, sustained activism in New York City's public housing is associated with superior housing conditions, which may relate to why Harlem's public housing residents are not being displaced.

As Harlem and Bronzeville revitalize, large segments of their populations are fearful that they will be displaced, and their protest around this concern differs depending on the larger metropolitan political landscape. To understand the function of segments of black civil society, it is vital to examine how distinct city politics and unique political structures and norms affect the actions of black-led organizations. While noting that global and federal forces affect black communities, it is equally important to acknowledge the influence of metropolitan-level dynamics.

We can now turn to the question of how civic behaviors stemming from the black middle class are shaping changes in Bronzeville and

Harlem. The actions of this group are critical to the future of these communities, and at the same time filled with contradictions and tension; their desire for community improvement relates to the displacement of the "underclass." Is the redevelopment of these historic black communities tied to the notion of "racial uplift"?

Figure 7.1 Harlem mural depicting a middle-class lifestyle.

7

Racial Uplift? Intra-racial Class Conflict

Many studies exploring the conditions of poverty stricken, black neighborhoods focus on the influence of white society. In the most prominent book to date, *American Apartheid* (1993), Douglas Massey and Nancy Denton claim that institutional racism and residential segregation are the primary causes of the deplorable conditions in black ghettos. They leave little room for the role of African Americans in shaping black communities. In contrast, William Julius Wilson suggests that the flight of the black middle class from these neighborhoods is associated with the downward spiral of these areas. In *The Truly Disadvantaged* (1987, 56), Wilson writes that "the exodus of the kind of the middle- and working-class families from many ghetto neighborhoods removes an important 'social buffer' that could deflect the full impact of prolonged and increasing joblessness." For Wilson, the national economy and jobs are central; he maintains, however, that the movement of the black middle class weakened community organizations that had provided an important social infrastructure. According to Wilson's work, the return of the middle class to the inner city would greatly improve conditions for low-income residents.

In the 1990s several formerly low-income African-American inner city areas began to experience an influx of the black middle class. Recent studies in redeveloping black areas illuminate tensions and conflicts that emerge when such migration occurs (Boyd 2000; Freeman 2006; Moore

2005; Pattillo 2003; Taylor 2002). Intra-racial class conflict arises when competing factions, such as homeowners and renters, debate the path of neighborhood development. The black middle class fiercely wants to "restore" these communities to safe, prosperous, and tranquil places. To achieve this, they often display negative attitudes and behaviors toward the poor in their community. While a great deal of scholarship depicts inter-racial conflict in urban life (Hirsch [1983] 1998; Massey and Denton 1993; Sugrue 1996), inadequate attention is given to the role intra-racial class antagonism plays in the economic development of inner city areas.

The economic transformations of Harlem and Bronzeville illustrate the impact of black middle-class mobilization and class antagonism in shaping the landscape of today's inner cities. The "second renaissance" of these areas is marked by an influx of upper- and middle-income African Americans, threatening to displace many low-income, black residents. In these communities, low-income residents and institutions representing their interests are working to ensure a place for people of varying incomes, while more affluent residents come together to promote greater economic growth, with little concern for the black "underclass."

This raises two important questions related to the works of Massey and Denton and Wilson. First, in what ways are black organizations influencing the redevelopment of the former ghetto, and second, is the return of the black middle class assisting low-income residents? Although many scholars have discussed class differences among African Americans and its effects on general attitudes and behaviors (e.g., Cruse [1967] 1984; Du Bois [1899] 1996; Frazier 1957; Landry 1987), my point of departure is to understand how more contemporary class distinctions translate into specific political actions influencing property values in revitalizing black neighborhoods.

An investigation of Harlem and Bronzeville provides a unique opportunity to explore class relations within black America. Many revitalizing inner city areas experience an influx of white residents (Smith [1996] 2000), but Harlem and Bronzeville are revitalizing without drastic racial changeover. In the last ten years, Central Harlem's white population increased only from 1.5 to 2 percent, and the percentage of whites in Bronzeville increased from 2.5 to 4 percent (see appendix A). While remaining racially homogeneous, these communities' income structures have diversified, with an influx of black professionals, making these communities ideal for exploring issues of class.

Harlem and Bronzeville are arguably the most historic African-American neighborhoods in the country, and segments of the black middle class perceive that by relocating into these formerly impoverished, black communities they partake in "racial uplift," advancing the interests and goals of the entire race. For residents "in Bronzeville, buildings are not just pieces of individually owned property, but symbols of community spirit...the physical entities through and within which race uplift may be achieved" (Boyd 2000, 117). Similarly, according to Monique Taylor, the "black gentry" moves to Harlem "to express a larger commitment and solidarity with the race as a whole" (2002, 131).

Certain scholars contend that the black middle class is "saving" these communities from a white takeover and thus contributing to the preservation of black history in the United States. But the actions of the black middle class, with regard to racial uplift, are filled with contradictions. The movement of upper-income blacks to these areas and their political action are associated with the displacement of many low-income residents. Can racial uplift occur in the face of displacement? As one resident in Bronzeville explains: "The black middle class, [returning] from its corporate isolation and having done the integration thing, are now saying I need to get back to blackness, 'cause I'm still being discriminated against.... Now, when you get back, are you going to turn on your *brother*, or are you going to try to use your resources to help empower him?" (italics mine, Boyd 2000, 119).

In this chapter I argue that class antagonism is important to the redevelopment of these communities. The attitudes and beliefs of the black middle class translate into political actions associated with rising property values and the displacement of the black underclass. Middle-class African Americans—those who have lived in these communities for some time and new arrivals—are creating and reinvigorating institutions and organizations that make community improvements coincide with their preferences.

Middle-class interests dominate various local organizations and institutions, such as planning boards, block clubs, and religiously affiliated community development corporations, which are critical to the development process. This important finding contradicts several accounts claiming that the behaviors of whites are principal in shaping black neighborhoods (Hirsch [1983] 1998; Massey and Denton 1993). Secondly, the actions of the black middle class contradict what many researchers have described as their coming "home" to these communities to facilitate racial uplift, unity, and pride, since their actions influence the displacement of poor African Americans. In light of Wilson's work, this finding has important implications, as it suggests that the arrival of the black middle class is not clearly advantageous for the "underclass." For many in the black middle class, "coming home" refers to returning to culturally significant spaces where poor blacks are no longer welcome.

Many studies of neighborhood change, particularly in black neighborhoods, fail to focus on the active participation of the local institutional structure. Although studies demonstrate that black social networks and formal associations effectively moderate the effects of poverty, very few scholars claim that black-led organizations have the political wherewithal to alter broader conditions such as property values. For instance, sociologists Carol Stack (1974) and Sudhir Venkatesh (2000) show that informal and formal black-led associations, composed of mainly single mothers living in abject poverty, help provide a safe and manageable living environment for their children. However, as Venkatesh notes, the impoverished conditions in the Robert Taylor Homes were primarily "shaped by larger social forces" (235).

The community development literature debates whether formal, local organizations produce changes in the community landscape. Studies like Robert Putnam's work on social capital, or Robert Sampson, Stephen Raudenbush, and Felton Earls's work on collective efficacy argue that alternative internal community mechanisms of change, such as the density of informal groups and neighborhood norms, are more important than formal organizations. On the other hand, others demonstrate that certain community-based organizations are critical in determining neighborhood conditions (Crenson 1983; Gittell 1992; Taub, Taylor, and Dunham 1984). For example, Matthew Crenson's Baltimore study finds that most residents see formal community organizations as effective entities in their neighborhoods. Further, a comprehensive investigation of change in Chicago neighborhoods reveals that elite community organizations greatly contribute to property value escalation (Taub, Taylor, and Dunham 1984). Studies that solely focus on informal groups and community norms are limited in scope. We must begin to understand the specific mechanisms by which norms of collective actions translate into tangible expressions of local political action and control. According to Crenson's and Taub's work, elite formal organizations are viable agents of change.

In low-income black communities, collective action alerts city policymakers to resident concerns. In economically transitioning communities like Harlem and Bronzeville, however, collective interests are often hard to maintain and residents seldom agree on shared goals, like property values (Freeman 2006). Sociologists John Logan and Harvey Molotch distinguish between individuals who seek "use" and those who desire "exchange" value in properties. The use-value faction is composed of renters who do not put a priority on enhancing land cost since this type of development could drive rents beyond their reach. Individuals desiring exchange value, usually homeowners, encourage rising real estate prices to increase the worth of their neighborhood investment. The tension between use- and exchange-value seekers "determine[s] the patterns of neighborhood life—the ways in which people...interconnect with one another, and defend (or offend) the places in which they live" (Logan and Molotch 1987, 99). These competing interests manifest in local organizations attempting to either preserve the existing neighborhood or transform it into something new.

Is the Concept of Class Important in Black America?

Scholars dispute the value of class as a theoretical line of inquiry within black communities. In *Harlem World*, John Jackson acknowledges Harlem's current economic stratification is fueled by the influx of the middle class; but he also argues that people's lives and behaviors "don't necessarily make sense in terms of middle classes, underclasses, or even carefully measured working classes" (2001, 84). Monique Taylor claims that the lives of Harlem residents cannot be explained by "a differentiated black class structure" (2002, 176). In contrast, Mary Pattillo's ethnographic research documenting the "perils" of the black middle class in two South Side Chicago communities brings the importance of class conflict within black America to the forefront. She states, "Class, status, and lifestyle are real axes of distinction in the black community" (Pattillo-McCoy 1999, 209). In Pattillo's study of Northern Kenwood/Oakland, a redeveloping black neighborhood just east of Bronzeville, she writes, "The politics of neighborhood change...is occurring not only at the level of the city bureaucrats and developers who wield electoral or financial powers, but also among residents—new and old, formally educated and not, owners and renters, rich and poor" (2003, 64).

The black middle class has tripled since the 1960s (Gates 2004). As the black middle and upper classes expand, there is debate concerning how this affects social and political unity among African Americans. Wilson's 1987 study of the inner city suggests that the movement of the middle class to formerly low-income neighborhoods will positively affect lower-class residents. He predicts that middle-class residents will reinvigorate and strengthen community organizations and act as role models for the lower-class residents by demonstrating appropriate social behaviors, though it is not clear if the black middle class desires to take on this function.

Some researchers suggest that the persistent experience of racism binds African Americans together, regardless of income and educational background, while others contend that intra-group strife is prevalent. This dispute has important implications for economically diversifying black communities and is exemplified in the research of two influential scholars: Michael Dawson and Manning Marable. Dawson, a political scientist, sees black society as a relatively cohesive unit as compared to other ethnic groups. Although he recognizes the growing economic division within black America, he maintains that racial solidarity persists. In *Behind the Mule* (1994), Dawson analyzes the National Black Election Panel Study and concludes that most blacks believe that what helps the race also benefits their individual interests. He coins this phenomena the *black utility heuristic*. This concept, based on the idea of linked fate and identification among black individuals, suggests that African Americans will identify with their own racial group, regardless of class differences. One critique of Dawson's work is that it is mainly based on perceptions of racial solidarity rather than actual behaviors grounded in black communities.

Marable, a historian, argues that the growing economic division among blacks is leading to greater social division in America. He writes, "As the scope, complexity, and size of the black elite grew to unprecedented dimensions, the bonds that tied it to the bulk of African American majority fragmented and in many instances ceased to exist" (2002, 172). In response to recent claims of racial solidarity, he writes, "the black bourgeoisie's connections with the fates of the black working class and poor have gradually become more tenuous" (191). Marable contends that as segments of black America achieve financial success, they will become less attached to lower-class African Americans. In this study, I found that socioeconomic differences embedded within neighborhood organizations contribute to local political processes shaping emerging conditions.

Changing Class Structure

Much of the community dispute, as it relates to the redevelopment, is associated with distinct income and educational levels, which lead to different patterns of behavior and consumption among residents. Surplus income allows people to achieve distinct lifestyles, including fancy cars, private education, evenings at upscale restaurants, and most importantly the opportunity to purchase homes. Most advocates for community improvements, associated with rising real estate value, have, on average, educational and income levels that enable them to become homeowners. This more affluent group is distinctive from low-income renters who are fighting rising property values to stay within these communities. I loosely define class as a socioeconomic construct associated with distinct levels of educational attainment and income, relating to property ownership.

Black middle and upper classes are rapidly moving into these neighborhoods. From 1990 to 2000, the percentage of households earning between $25,000 and $74,999 increased by 35 percent in Harlem and 50 percent in Bronzeville. Moreover, the number of households earning $75,000 or more skyrocketed in both communities. In Harlem this population jumped from 3 to 8 percent, while in Bronzeville they climbed from 2 to 10 percent. The 2000 Census numbers also indicate that the percentage of the population with a bachelor's degree or higher increased by 50 percent in Central Harlem and by almost 40 percent in Bronzeville between 1990 and 2000. At the same time, the percent of homeowners increased from 4.6 to 7 percent and 5.5 to 10 percent, in Harlem and Bronzeville, respectively.

In addition to quantitative evidence, my field observations revealed an influx of the black middle class. For instance, the executive director of one of Harlem's largest nonprofit developers notes, "Five years ago we had to beg the young professionals to move into Harlem, but now they are begging us for brownstones." As the middle class moves in, there is a sharp decrease in the number of low-income households, yet a sizable proportion of these communities remains extremely poor. In 2000, approximately 45 percent of households in both neighborhoods earn under $15,000. While the middle class arrives and the poor exit, median home value and household income soar.

Intra-racial Class Antagonism

Class discord is ubiquitous in both communities, manifesting itself within community organizational structures. Various elite-dominated, black-led organizations are simultaneously contributing to community development and the displacement of the poor. Interest in property value escalation drives the political actions of homeowners and segments of the middle class. Upper-income residents are more concerned with "community improvements" than with mentoring and supporting members of the "underclass" in their neighborhood. The pervasiveness of this phenomenon is illustrated in a subsequent section that suggests that some religiously based organizations, once seen as critical to the civil rights movement, are serving the interests of the middle class at the expense of the poor. The culmination of evidence forces us to consider whether the revitalization of these historic black communities exemplifies racial uplift.

Property Values

One evening I attend the meeting of Community Board 10, the politically appointed resident planning board that oversees land use and housing development in Central Harlem. The gathering is on the second floor of the Harlem State Office Building at 125th Street and Adam Clayton Powell Jr. Boulevard. Two opposite entrances are used to access the large meeting room, one for the public at large and the other for community board members. Board members are mainly homeowners and are selected by the Manhattan borough president, a longtime resident of Harlem. Only board members are given a packet of detailed information concerning the evening's presenters. When I walk into the room, I first notice that the walls are covered with James Brown memorabilia: framed posters, albums covers, and gold records. The room serves as a gallery for black artists, denoting it as a space of black culture and pride. The seating in the room is assigned; approximately forty board members sit in the center of the room and the general public sits on either side. The meeting is packed with approximately two hundred people, almost all of whom are black.

The first presenter is a white developer who proposes to build a twenty-four-story luxury condominium building on the corner of a historic brownstone-lined block known as Astor Row. The corner, located at 130th Street and Lenox Avenue, is presently occupied by an abandoned building. The developer expects to sell two-bedroom units for approximately $450,000. The developer's architect, who is also white, claims the building would remove an "eyesore that had been there for years." As the architect holds up a rendering of the exclusive high-rise building, the crowd groans, shouting, "Oh no!" Then a man dressed in jeans and a worn flannel shirt, stands up from the general public section and says in a demanding tone: "It's unacceptable! I have been here for forty years…this is a beautiful block. I struggled. I am a poor man, all right? I worked my heart out to live on this block. Okay? Not for someone from Westchester to come onto my block. On my block! This [project] doesn't mean anything to anyone except the developers." He yells at the white developers that he does not want anyone from the predominantly wealthy, white suburban Westchester County living on "his" block. However, what happens next illuminates the conflict of interests between the lower income and more affluent blacks in Harlem.

After hearing objections from the general public, the architect immediately turns to the community board members in the center of the room. "The community board's own position calls for middle- and upper-income housing to be introduced in Harlem," he says. In fact, the community board's comprehensive plan specifies the need for quality middle-income housing and a "new income mix among residents" (Manhattan Community Board 10, 1999, 50). The architect tells board members that this is a "market rate project" and that a family earning $100,000 a year could afford a condo in this development. At this price tag, less than 5 percent of Central Harlem households qualify. Despite the high price and public opposition from numerous residents, the board members approve the luxury high-rise development.

The board consistently supports posh housing developments clearly beyond the means of most current residents. Although some might speculate that the board members have been co-opted by outside white interests, this is not the circumstance. Many community board members and others homeowners in Harlem want high-priced housing in the community. During an interview a person heavily involved in Harlem's economic transition reports,

> Some of the most low down, anti-poor people activity that I ever saw came from black people. I mean, I will never forget Amber's comments at the community board meeting when we were doing some [subsidized] project and she looked at me and she was like, "Damn it, I am tired of all these no rent and low rent people that y'all are bringing up here." Amber, her thing is homeownership. She wants homeowners in Harlem, because she is a homeowner. Oh yes, I understand her block has been ragged for all those years. She wants her property values to go up. She wants to leave something for her granddaughter and I completely understand. But it's definitely a class issue, and it definitely resonates in a lot of circumstances.

By consistently approving luxury, high-priced developments, the community board helps to drive up Harlem's housing market, increasing the threat of displacement.

In Bronzeville, many middle-class homeowners want their property values to increase and this relates to their political activity. In the early evening, I attend the monthly meeting of the recently formed Bronzeville Homeowners Association at the police station on 51st and Federal streets. Members of the association are interested in building a better community by increasing the number of homeowners and promoting property value escalation. One of the issues discussed is whether the group is willing to allow renters into the association. Some argue that renters would strengthen the membership base while others fear that renters may take leadership positions in the organization and alter its mission. Vera, an African-American property owner and manager in Bronzeville, fiercely opposes allowing renters. "Please, I don't want renters!" she says, explaining that she deals with low-income renters all day and that she did not help found an association to cater to the needs of people who rent. One member of the association later says, "Long-term residents, meaning people who bought into Bronzeville ten, fifteen, twenty years ago, really want to see the benefit of their investment and I've heard those folks saying, 'I'm tired of poor people, I don't care about poor people, I want some good homeowners in the community, we need more homeowners.'"

A massive amount of Bronzeville residents are being displaced as a result of the demolition of high-rise public housing in the community. Despite the abundance of vacant lots in the area, very little affordable or replacement housing is being built, reflecting the mayor's preference for the development of high-priced properties to increase the city's tax base. However, limited affordable housing construction is also related to the desire of middle-class residents to rid their community of undesirables, particularly Chicago Housing Authority (CHA) tenants.

Several homeowner-dominated block clubs in Bronzeville make it clear that creating a space in the community for low-income people is not a priority. Middle-class-led block clubs and organizations support the removal of the projects. One organizer sums up the situation: "We have had people that made public statements that they didn't want public housing residents living next door to them and I think a lot of people saw it as an opportunity for their property values to go up so they opted to just turn their backs, OK and let it happen." Another community leader comments, "the middle-income African Americans who have been in the community for a while or who are now moving into the community really want to see a community that's primarily reflective of their values and their interests." He continues, "The middle-income and upper-income African Americans who are buying these four, five, six-hundred-thousand-dollar houses and these two-hundred-thousand-dollar condos really have little interest in seeing affordable or low-income housing being built in their community. It's sad but true."

Segments of the black middle class express political behaviors consistent with the theory of exchange value (Logan and Molotch 1987). Homeowners, working through community organizations, are vigilantly ensuring that their property values are preserved, thus contributing to the redevelopment of these neighborhoods. In Harlem, upper-income residents ensure that luxury real estate developers have access to the community, while in Bronzeville some of the more affluent members of the community are advocating for the removal of the public housing projects and are not concerned with the construction of affordable replacement housing.

Mentoring the Poor?

In her investigation of Harlem, Taylor notes, "For successful black professionals, the values of middle class America—the importance of education, the ideal of home ownership, the work ethic, self initiative, and self-reliance—shape their visions of what life in the community should be" (2002, 86). While the black middle class upholds these American standards, they also carry an additional burden that the white middle class does not; they are expected to mentor lower-income individuals in their community (Wilson 1996). According to Dawson's (1994) research, this expectation arises out of a shared experience of racial discrimination. Additionally, many in the black middle class have family members that might be considered part of the "underclass" or grew up poor themselves (see Pattillo-McCoy 1999). While some among the black middle class feel sympathy for the plight of the black urban poor, others feel ambivalent or disdainful of low-income individuals.

Often community leaders have conflicting views about the ability of poor residents to meet middle-class standards. During a South Side Partnership meeting in Bronzeville, two women who head prominent community organizations argue about whether public housing residents can integrate into the surrounding community. A male member, who directs a social service agency and is a local homeowner, claims some former public housing residents are "tearing up the place" in their market rate Section 8 housing. "Well, you're going to see a lot more of that because," a woman begins, until she is interrupted by another woman who cries out, "Oh, you're stereotyping!" The first woman continues, "No, but the problem is—let me say this. I live across from scatter-site [low-rise public housing], and I've lived in this community now for about ten years. The first year I moved down here it was pretty bad, then it got increasingly better, since they have torn down the high rises."

However, she explains that many of the tenants from the high rises are moving in with relatives in scatter-site housing. "Where you [once] had a grandmother, now you have four daughters with five kids apiece," she says. The second woman responds emotionally, "I used to live in a house with twenty people. I did it and it goes back to saying how do we empower the people, how do we help them; they're our sisters and brothers. You may not like it but they're your sisters and brothers. They have the same spirit. They just have a different attitude. Now how do we help them with that attitude?" Although this woman is clearly making a call for racial solidarity, by claiming that the lower-income residents are "your sisters and brothers," the first woman, referring to public housing residents' abilities to change their attitudes and behaviors, retorts, "I don't think they can do it." Her tone rises and she repeats, "They can't do it!" The idea of actively role modeling, supporting, and mentoring the poor is not a major priority for the many middle-class residents.

Many Harlem block clubs are devoted to making the community "better," even if doing so is detrimental to disadvantaged African Americans. One night, I accompany Harlem's state assemblyman, Keith Wright, and his executive assistant, Mignonne, to the 136th Street block club association's meeting. The block club invites Keith to solicit his support against the opening of a group home for young, single mothers.

The meeting is in a small church basement, just two houses away from the proposed group home. About twenty-five African-American homeowners attend the meeting. When we arrive, the executive director of the social service agency in charge of the group home is making her case for the program. She explains that the home will teach mothers effective parenting techniques. When she completes her presentation, many of the block club members are very vocal about preventing the social service agency from accessing the area. They tell the director that they are prepared to protest outside of the home should the program move to "their" block. Their concerns center on the young men associated with these women, whom they fear will pose a threat to the block's safety. A bank executive, in his business suit, is extremely vocal about barring the group home from "his" block. He explains that he moved to Harlem two years ago and will not let a program on the block that would threaten its "safety" or the value of his property "investment." As he speaks, Mignonne looks at me with disgust.

When the banker finishes, all participants turn to Keith for his reaction. Keith begins by mentioning that there are many single mothers in Central Harlem. Speaking very deliberately, he says that he knows residents do not want the program, but that they may want to accept "the devil you know." He explains that this social service agency has a good reputation (the agency is based in Harlem) and that the church that owns the land could place another social service agency on this corner with fewer "community ties." The block club is not convinced. In fact, as Keith finishes his comments, the vice president of the block group hands out a list of all the social service agencies in the neighborhood and says, "Enough is enough!" In the end, the executive director says she will not place the mothers where they are not welcome. The banker and many others in the block association smile and nod their heads in approval, while Mignonne rolls her eyes at me.

Mignonne has lived in Harlem her entire life. She grew up in the Lincoln Houses, a public housing project, and raised two sons as a single mother. She is a frank woman who has worked for Keith for almost ten years. After the meeting she tells me this program could help some of the young, single mothers in the community. While elaborating on the program's potential, she says she hates the "implants," affluent people who move to Harlem, buy brownstones, and drive up property values without any concern for long-term, low-income residents. Mignonne is passionate about her contempt for "implants" because she closely identifies with long-term residents and despises newcomers who claim Harlem solely for themselves.

The preferences and tastes of the upper- and middle-income residents are dominant political forces in these communities. As Wilson predicted, the middle class is strengthening, to a certain extent, neighborhood organizations. Block clubs, reinvigorated in the last few years, have been very successful at keeping homeless shelters, drug treatment clinics, and other social service programs off their streets. Block club actions help maintain property values and neighborhood standards. However, the new arrivals, such as the bank executive, appear uninterested in being "role models" to the underclass and are more concerned with maintaining property values by keeping the undesirables out of the community. Not only are class tensions prevalent in block clubs, they have also become integrated into the organizational fabric of the black church.

The Black Church and Development

Black churches are seen as the pillars of strength and hope in low-income African-American communities throughout the country. Black congregations were central to the civil rights movement and the church is expected to help and support the downtrodden. However, in these historic, African-American communities several churches are promoting the interests of the upper and middle class, while neglecting, and in some instances contributing to, pressing issues facing the poor. For instance, many local churches have affiliated community development corporations that are building high-income housing and contributing to displacement.

The Harlem Congregations for Community Improvement (HCCI), a collaboration of several smaller churches, is one of Harlem's leading nonprofit property managers and housing developers. They also provide an array of social service programs in the community. In a meeting, Craig, the head of real estate development for HCCI, stands before Central Harlem's community board wearing a gray suit and announces that HCCI plans to rehabilitate several units near West 148th Street between 7th and 8th avenues. He says such development will turn the area into "a mixed-income block," with "units of low, moderate and middle-income housing." The 110-unit project will cost $17.5 million. To qualify for a one-bedroom unit, an individual needs to earn between $32,000 and $141,000 a year, while to be eligible for a three-bedroom unit a family needs a gross income ranging from $61,000 to $169,000. Most of the units are for the higher-income ranges.

After Craig presents these income levels, a man behind me calls out, "Forget about it," insinuating that few in Harlem could afford the development. Craig replies, "Again, this is our attempt to address a mixed-income community for this block. . . . Our feeling, at this point in Harlem's development, is that we need to create housing for a mixed-income community." Although these units are beyond the means of many Harlem residents, HCCI is implementing the type of housing that political leadership and the community board have requested. Virginia Fields, the former Manhattan borough president and a twenty-four-year Harlem resident, referring to the boom in housing for the middle class, explains, "This is what is needed in this community. For far too long living in Harlem was for low income [people]."[1]

HCCI is not the only nonprofit, church-based developer in Harlem constructing housing beyond the means of current residents. The famed Abyssinian Baptist Church is another major housing developer in Harlem. At one of the community board meetings, a representative from Abyssinian Baptist Church's Development Corporation responds to accusations that her organization is not helping residents in buildings that Abyssinian plans to redevelop. She states sternly, "We are not trying to remove anyone from the community. We have other units in this community that are vacant, that may be of less quality, but we are not sending anyone to the Bronx, Brooklyn, or Staten Island. We are keeping people in the community. People will still have a home within Abyssinian."

A resident of one building slated for redevelopment stands up and yells at the Abyssinian representative and at an employee of the City Department of Housing Preservation and Department (HPD). She tells them she was never informed that residents could have collectively purchased her building through the city's Tenant Interim Lease program, an initiative that allows residents of city-owned buildings to purchase them as cooperatives below market rate. She says she was misinformed by Abyssinian and the city about her rights as a tenant. The woman from HPD begins to read documentation of Abyssinian staff members' attempts to contact the resident about alternative housing options. As the representative from HPD reads out the dates, some residents start screaming that the situation is unjust and immoral.

Eventually, three different factions all begin shouting at once. A third of the audience blames HPD, a third blames Abyssinian, and a third blames the woman with the complaint. For example, one person calls out, "We need the facts about how reliable this woman has been in paying her rent." Another says, "It's not Abyssinian's fault because they are working within the faulty framework set up by HPD and the city." Another woman sitting next to me yells out, "Abyssinian don't care nothing about you! They have sold you out. They are in the real estate business." Order is finally restored when a board member says to the Abyssinian representative, "We know the constraints you work under with dealing with the city agency [HPD], but you have to do better than what outside agencies [other real estate companies outside of Harlem] are doing in this community." Despite the concerns regarding the displacement of this family, the community board approves the project.

On the South Side of Chicago, religiously affiliated community development corporations are building housing for middle-income individuals in Bronzeville.[2] This circumstance, as in Harlem, helps to improve the economic conditions of the community, but does little to assist the poor in these areas, and in fact often contributes to their displacement. My findings coincide with other research investigating the role of churches in disadvantaged black neighborhoods. For instance, Omar McRoberts's detailed ethnographic study of Four Corners in Boston illustrates that local religious institutions rarely advocate for the residents of communities in which they are located. The twenty-nine churches McRoberts observes, as he puts it, "were not formed to serve residents and did not try to incorporate them" (2003, 143). One explanation given by McRoberts is that many African-American churches located in depressed black communities often have a substantial membership from more affluent communities. Thus, they are uninterested in helping the poor located just outside of their places of worship.

Displacement and Discord

The behaviors of black-led community institutions and organizations, such as the community board, block clubs, and nonprofit developers, are leading to the direct and indirect displacement of low- and moderate-income tenants. The political leadership speaks about the issue but little concrete action is taken. "Everyone is concerned about gentrification— I'm not. As I see it, most of the people moving into Harlem are black," declares one political leader in Harlem. Howard Dotson, the executive director of the Harlem's Schomburg Center for Research in Black Culture, explains, "You can't have it both ways, you can't have development and have no displacement." Others feel the same way. A Harlem resident and employee of New York City's Department of Housing Preservation and Development explains that people who cannot afford to stay in the community are "a casualty of development." Florence Forbes, an economic development specialist for the Manhattan borough president states: "I think the class [conflict] thing has to happen. My big argument is that if you don't do that Harlem is going to remain a ghetto. Not that it still isn't, but that it would remain one if you don't attract people that make $50,000 and above." Leaders in Bronzeville articulate similar sentiments. Several proclaim that the conditions in public housing are so deplorable that demolition and ensuing displacement are worthy trade-offs.

However, others perceive individuals promoting the redevelopment as "sell outs," "race traitors," and "Uncle Toms." During a community meeting on gentrification in Harlem, one activist declares, "The Empowerment Zone wasn't created to help us...those bullshit artists, selling out the community....The community boards, it's the same thing. I've never seen such a bunch of Uncle Toms in my life...Community Board 10, they're selling us out!" Some public housing residents in Bronzeville refer to their local politicians as "poli-trick-ans." In their view, the current leadership makes claims of racial solidarity by supporting national issues like reparations, yet turns its back on low-income members of the community. "So this makes reparations a big contradiction," declares a former public housing resident, "You got...vacant land on 47th Street right now....You don't have to go about reparations....You got the power to actually empower the people, but you put the people on hold for your personal political agenda." As Harlem and Bronzeville redevelop, a vulnerable segment of the black population is pushed out, leading to the question of whether the "second renaissance" of these areas can be considered symbols of racial advancement.

Racial Uplift?

Some consider the redevelopment of Harlem and Bronzeville a form of racial uplift. Michelle Boyd discusses how a segment of Bronzeville sees the restoration of historic buildings as preserving the "history of the race" (2000, 116). Further, Monique Taylor notes, "Out of its symbolic meanings, Harlem gives forth an ideology of race consciousness, racial pride, and collective strength" (2002, 82). In *Black Metropolis*, St. Clair Drake and Horace Cayton define racial uplift, or "advancing the race" in this way:[3] "When Negros speak of 'advancing the race' they may be referring to either of two things: (1) individual achievement which 'reflects credit on the race,' or (2) organized social activities which are consciously designed to raise the status of the group as a whole" ([1945] 1993, 716). Undoubtedly, how these communities are characterized will disproportionately represent black America. The redevelopment of these two historic communities is racial uplift in one sense—the achievement of the black middle class is saving these culturally significant areas from a sizeable white influx. Preserving these communities' historic legacies helps to maintain an important aspect of black history and culture.

However, applying the concept of racial uplift to the development in Harlem and Bronzeville is problematic. Symbolically, the economic re-emergence of these areas will "reflect credit on the race," but it does little for "the group as a whole." In fact, I would argue that for these communities to achieve their redevelopment, conscious political decisions are made to exclude the most disadvantaged segment of the black population. While portions of the black middle class and white society might claim that the redevelopment of these communities, based on their historic past, is part of racial uplift, Boyd points out that this rhetoric "gloss(es) over intra-racial difference and construct(s) the redevelopment as a goal of the entire racial community" (2000, 116). The paradox of these communities, in regard to racial uplift, is that individual success and achievement by the black middle class have made the redevelopment possible, but as a consequence the most vulnerable members of the race are displaced to other high-poverty localities.

The meaning of black middle-class behaviors cannot be fully understood without addressing their vulnerability. Mary Pattillo-McCoy's ethnography of an African-American, mixed-income community on the South Side of Chicago, points out the economic, social and spatial susceptibility of the black middle class: "The ecological context of black middle-class families is a basic feature of difference between the white and the black middle class" (1999, 211). The black middle class, on average, lives closer to poor neighbors than their white counterparts (Adelman 2004). A recent Chicago report, using 2000 Census data, indicates that 78 percent of black middle-class blocks are within a half mile of blocks with at least a 33 percent poverty rate, while only 25 percent of middle-class white blocks are in the same spatial circumstance.[4] Many middle-class enclaves in both Harlem and Bronzeville are near public housing and known drug activity areas. Living in close proximity to the poor presents a heightened risk of coming into contact with crime. In addition to being more susceptible to crime, the black middle class is economically vulnerable. While earning comparable income, the black middle class has much less wealth compared to whites (Oliver and Shapiro 1995). Thus, by protecting property investments the black middle class may be creating safe and prosperous communities, building household wealth, and sustaining their tenuous class status.

Discussion

Intra-racial class conflict plays an important role in neighborhood development. Community organizations, dominated by middle class interests, contribute to rising property values at the expense of the poor. This important finding has major implications for theorizing neighborhood change and notions of racial solidarity.

Formal community organizational structures are critical to understanding the political dynamics of community change and local economic development. The last few years have seen an increasing focus on nonspecific informal neighborhood groups and community norms as facilitators of community improvement (see Putnam 1993; Sampson, Raudenbush, and Earls 1997). However, this line of research lacks a clear and tangible mechanism for change. I am not saying that norms of collective action and general community participation are unimportant. They may be antecedents or indicators of more specific forms of concrete political action, such as alerting a politician that certain groups will not be tolerated. My research, as well as that of others (Crenson 1983; Gregory 1998; Pattillo 2003; Taub, Taylor, and Dunham 1984), suggests that formal organizations, dominated by elite interests, must be incorporated into theories of neighborhood change.

I have argued that certain black-led organizations contribute to neighborhood conditions. Although past studies suggest that black social networks and formal organizations moderate harsh living circumstances (Stack 1974; Venkatesh 2000), their role in altering property values has not been thoroughly discussed. In the urban development literature, African-American organizations are virtually ignored as agents in the process of community change. Massey and Denton's work claims that white-dominated institutions are the only entities central to the development of the inner city. Hirsch's historical account of the altering conditions of Bronzeville in the 1940s, '50s, and '60s focuses exclusively on elite white actors, downtown real estate, and commercial interests: "Primary attention is devoted to whites," he explains, "that is where the power was" ([1983] 1998, xvi). Since the 1960s, we have witnessed a bourgeoning black middle class in the United States and this group has gained the economic and political capital to alter the urban landscape. This is not to say that white-dominated organizations such as major banks, certain government institutions, and real estate companies are not heavily influencing the redevelopment processes in these communities; they are. However, elite-led black organizations also contribute to this process. Social scientists employing concepts of "exchange value" and the "growth machine" to explain urban development need to incorporate a new constituency— the black middle class.

Although middle-class populations are important to the revitalization process in low-income neighborhoods, they might not have the effect predicted by previous works. Wilson's studies suggest that more affluent residents will strengthen neighborhood organizations benefiting the whole community. However, the positive effects he assumes are based on a time when upper, middle, and lower classes of African Americans were forced to live together under state-sanctioned segregation. Once these restrictions were lifted, those who could afford to fled the ghettos to get away from the lower classes. Now that the inner city is perceived as valuable, the black middle class is returning. But rather than acting as a support mechanism to the poor; they instead use their heightened political power to remove the undesirables. As a result, scholars and policymakers must question the presumed positive effect for the poor brought on by a return of the black middle class.

While in Harlem and Bronzeville, I found very little evidence that black middle class residents voluntarily assisted or mentored those considered part of the underclass. This does not mean that the movement of the black middle class to these areas will not have any positive impact on the poor. Some middle class residents volunteer and tutor low-income students, raise funding to strengthen public schools, and organize residents into housing cooperatives, but this is not the norm (Freeman 2006). On average, the black middle class moving into these communities does not put the concerns of the poor over the goal of protecting their property values, though this does not mean that they do not have some positive impact on the poor that remain. An influx of the black middle class brings improved amenities and may influence the behaviors of the poor through modeling certain pro-social behaviors. Despite these potentially advantageous neighborhood effects, the return of the black middle class is not a panacea for alleviating the ills associated with black urban poverty.

In terms of race theory, my data support Manning Marable's notion of class heterogeneity within black America. Harlem and Bronzeville residents have very different attitudes and actions concerning the redevelopment of their community based on differentiated attachments to distinct socioeconomic status groups. The more affluent residents advocate for "community improvements" and the removal of the poor, while lower-income residents fight to remain in the neighborhood. However, "race consciousness," "black solidarity," and Michael Dawson's black utility heuristic remain important concepts. In her study of "black gentrification," Mary Pattillo finds that while intra-racial conflict persists over who is allowed to remain in the community, there is a strong tendency for residents, regardless of class, to collectively resist the movement of whites into the neighborhood. Additionally, some black professionals see these communities as important black symbols. Therefore, black solidarity exists in particular spheres but becomes less important in others (Reed 1999). Certain African Americans desire to live in historic black communities, but they want these areas to meet their standards of middle-class urban living, even if it means organizing and advocating for the displacement of low-income individuals of their own race. Thus, we need to think more deeply about the specific circumstances when race trumps class and vice versa.

Intra-racial class conflict is essential to understanding community change and black civil society. While several outside forces, ranging from government policy to white real estate investors, influence the redevelopment of Harlem and Bronzeville, it is undisputable that the black middle class and their preferences for "community improvement" are associated with rising property values and the displacement of the poor. It is difficult to determine whether the economic re-emergence of these neighborhoods can be associated with racial uplift. Nonetheless, socioeconomic stratification within black America is extremely important in shaping social and political action related to neighborhood transformation.

8

Conclusion: A Revisit of Urban Theory and Policy

Disadvantaged, black urban neighborhoods were a dominant subject in urban sociology in the 1990s. Today, several inner city communities, once mired in poverty, are experiencing an economic transformation that scholars now need to explain. The international economy, federal policies, city initiatives, and actions within the communities themselves are associated with this urban renaissance. Community revitalization can only be understood by acknowledging the interactions among these different levels of analysis. This concluding chapter includes a summary of the substantive findings and their implications for urban development and race theory, an account of the study's limitations and suggestions for further research, and finally a forecast of Harlem and Bronzeville's future and a discussion of the symbolic meaning of their redevelopment. Lastly, I offer policy recommendations to minimize the consequences of displacement and ensure that low-income residents have greater opportunities to prosper from the transition of their neighborhoods.

Implications of Findings for Urban and Race Theories

This study has important implications for the fields of urban sociology. The cases of Bronzeville and Harlem provide little evidence for the ecological approach and mainly confirm aspects of the political economy and global perspectives. However, to deploy one of the latter two perspectives without incorporating certain ideas from all three is extremely limiting and will lead to an incomplete understanding of the forces influencing community change.

The ecological model's primary assumption concerning "natural" development is completely unfounded. Evidence strongly suggests that concrete political decisions largely determine development patterns. The massive demolition of public housing, the selling of city-owned buildings to private developers, and the use of federal money to attract businesses are altering individual preferences for these neighborhoods.

One claim of the ecological paradigm remains relevant: the importance of a community's structural location and its relationship to other city areas.[1] The geographic proximity of inner city areas to their central business districts is an important structural variable contributing to neighborhood conditions. Harlem and Bronzeville are developing, in part, because of an increased market demand for properties near the CBD. Although the assumption of natural development is misguided and outdated, the ecological paradigm pinpoints a key premise that a community's development is understood by assessing its relation to the rest of the city.

This notion is particularly relevant when considering that the economic transformation of Harlem and Bronzeville leads to the relocation of low-income populations. As public housing comes down in the inner city, Chicago's neighborhood poverty is moving into communities farther from the central business district (Alexander 1998; Venkatesh, Celimli, Miller, et al. 2004). In New York City, poverty once concentrated in Upper Manhattan appears to be moving to the outer boroughs. Development in one community can affect the entire metropolitan region.

To understand the forces and outcomes associated with inner city development, we must account for the interactions, and the culmination, of factors at multiple levels. The function of New York City and Chicago as command and control centers within the international economy relates to population increase and CBD expansion, heightening housing market pressures in nearby low-income communities. To conclude that centralization is primarily a global force, however, would be inaccurate. City-level political decisions affect centralization around and in the CBD, contributing to increased property values in Harlem and Bronzeville. Local housing plans and policy tools, such as TIF districts, allocate critical resources that ensure development occurs in particular communities. To understand the reconfiguration of urban space, particularly in revitalizing ghettos, the interactions among abstract global dynamics and concrete local political action must be considered.

Federal policies contribute to neighborhood change, but local city politics remain a critical mediating factor. Distinct political structures and internal city politics have important repercussions for the implementation of federal policies. Although the Empowerment Zone Initiative and public housing reforms pump millions of dollars into Harlem and Bronzeville, these initiatives have different effects in different contexts. The pluralist, two-party system in New York City enables the EZ monies to facilitate business creation and job opportunities in Harlem, while Chicago's Democratic machine drives EZ resources to be used for political purposes rather than economic development in Bronzeville.

Municipal circumstances have critical effects on the stock of affordable housing and development consequences for public housing tenants. New York City's fragmented political structure and associated legacy of activism ensured that the NYCHA maintained its public housing system, while Chicago's consolidated machine repressed CHA tenant participation and poorly managed their housing. Accordingly, in 1996, when the federal government ordered local housing authorities to raze distressed housing stocks, Chicago destroyed nearly half of its housing. New York City's superior public housing was basically unaffected. Thus, in the midst of redevelopment, public housing residents remain in Harlem, while they are displaced from Bronzeville.

The citywide political context influences the degree of resistance to community redevelopment and gentrification. Although a substantial percent of Bronzeville's low-income residents are displaced, public protest is virtually absent under the rule of Chicago's political machine, while public dissent is extensive in Harlem. During my time in Harlem, protest did not affect any major policies; however it should not be discounted since, over time, protest and activism within Harlem's public housing projects relate to why these residents are currently not being displaced. Distinct city political structures and actions matter for patterns and consequences of redevelopment in low-income communities.

This study speaks directly to the effect of community action on neighborhood conditions. While the broader political and economic context surrounding inner cities is important, attention must also center on actions originating from the community. The contours of impoverished

African-American communities are being altered by segments of the black middle class. Their behaviors, moving into low-income communities and becoming politically active, are associated with the revitalization of the urban core.

That black-led community organizations make a difference in community conditions is an extremely important finding related to theories of community change and race. Most research in black areas suggests that outside white influences have structured community conditions. While white-dominated institutions continue to shape black neighborhoods, the circumstances for segments of the African-American population have changed. A bourgeoning black middle class has developed and their political power has manifested in community organizations an important dynamic in the process of neighborhood change. While the flight of the black middle class in the 1960s, '70s, and '80s, led to the demise of the dark ghetto, the return of this population is turning these areas into prosperous mixed-income communities.

Class conflict is critical to transitioning black communities. While Wilson has argued that the arrival of the black middle class would benefit all residents, this has not turned out to be the case. The black middle class desires community improvements and advocates for changes directly associated with the removal of the underclass. Rather than acting as role models to lower-income members of their community, many black middle-class residents are more concerned with increasing their property values. Income differences within this racial group lead to profound differences in political action at the community level. As certain African Americans make economic gains, political polarization will likely increase. This is not to say that bonds of racial solidarity will dissipate, but that the significance of class divisions within black America is increasing.

The findings of this study enhance prior knowledge gained from case studies of Harlem and Bronzeville's redevelopment. While previous case studies focus on one or two levels of analysis with a single setting (e.g., Boyd 2000; Hoffman 2000), this study applies a vertical, comparative method (see appendix D). By assessing various levels, in particular the interactions among external and internal community forces, my study presents a more comprehensive depiction of inner city economic transformation. Simultaneously investigating similar communities in two different cities, this study demonstrates the influence of the political context as a powerful mediating factor. Furthermore, the comparative approach allows for more reliable findings than single case studies.

Limitations and Further Research

There are limits to this study. Because I am interested in various levels of analysis, and the interaction among these forces, some might be unsatisfied with the depth I probed each level. In the context of my overall research purpose, it was necessary to pay equal attention to each level. To do this, I had to limit the scope of inquiry into each level. I chose comprehensiveness over a more acute understanding of any particular level of analysis.

On a related note, I limited the description of particular actors within these communities. Many ethnographies detail the lives of the individuals (e.g., Duneier 1992; Newman 1999), however, this study focused of on the communities and the dynamics affecting them. Therefore, I was more attentive to collective action processes than to specific individuals. This presentation style keeps the focus on the dynamics of community change but deviates from more traditional ethnographies.

Even though I spent sufficient time in both neighborhoods, my data are a small sample of meetings, organizations and individuals. To compensate for this limitation, I focused on well-known community organizations that represent different factions, such as anti-growth and pro-growth interests. My sample is representative; after presenting various community leaders with a list of the meetings attended and people contacted, I was often told that I had spoken with the main players.

However, a few important actors, like universities, were not thoroughly discussed. Numerous newspaper articles and scholarly studies have explored the role of universities in the redevelopment of inner city areas (e.g., Hirsch [1983] 1998). For instance, some real estate policies stemming from the University of Pennsylvania, such as down payment grants to faculty and staff, have been credited with stimulating the redevelopment of Philadelphia's west side neighborhoods (Maurrasse 2001). Columbia University is extending its campus into Harlem. In addition, the Illinois Institute of Technology has invested millions of dollars in Bronzeville through its campus expansion. I did not focus extensively on the role of these universities because their decisions to expand followed an ongoing pattern of investment from real estate developers and the city; however, it's possible that the interests of these institutions helped facilitate city and commercial bank investment. Further research is needed to better distinguish the contributions of major universities to the process of community development.

Some might claim that I have underestimated the impact of the global economy on the development of the inner city. For instance, certain scholars posit that federal policies, such as the Empowerment Zones and recent public housing reforms, are connected with the global economy (Brenner and Theodore 2002; Small 1999). I do not make this claim since I see the HOPE VI program and Empowerment Zone Initiative to be hybrids of neoliberal and more traditional forms of liberalism. These policies were not fiscally conservative; large amounts of money were spent in the inner city. However, this does not mean that concerns of the global economy have not influenced national policies affecting inner city areas. A more in-depth investigation of the role of the international economy and its relationship to federal policies affecting the inner city should be explored.

I have argued that New York City and Chicago have remained at the opposite ends of the political spectrum, with power being more diffuse in New York City and more centralized in Chicago. Having stable, opposing political structures helps me methodologically situate the political structure as an important mediating variable leading to different community development outcomes. However, this stringent assertion fails to acknowledge that the political structures and landscapes in these cities may be more fluid than I have depicted (e.g., see Clark 2001; McNickle 1993; Mollenkopf 1994; Simpson 2001). Both cities have had brief periods that deviate from their norm, for instance less centralization in Chicago under Harold Washington and more centralized in New York City during the rule of Robert Moses. Also, some might argue that New York City has been more centralized ever since the elimination of the Board of Estimate in 1989 (Thompson 2006). Even with these slight variations over the course of the twentieth and twenty-first centuries, New York City and Chicago remain very different political systems.

Distinct economic and social circumstances at the community level might also be related to alternative patterns of development. I make some sweeping generalizations about the similarities of these communities to better isolate the local political environment. Despite many striking similarities between these two communities, there are some important differences. First, Harlem's reputation as the "capital of black America" is stronger than Bronzeville's. Harlem's symbolic meaning as the most important black community in the country might make its redevelopment more controversial. The extent of resistance to Harlem's revitalization might be associated with its heightened symbolic meaning (Firey 1945). Second, there are more people in Harlem. This demographic difference may lead to higher levels of progressive politics in Harlem simply because of a larger population. However, I am confident that if I incorporate parts of other African-American areas surrounding Bronzeville my results concerning limited contested politics would remain stable.

Third, the distinct type of displacement occurring in the two communities might affect the level of protest politics. In Harlem, displacement occurs more among those residing in the private housing market, while in Bronzeville the majority of those being removed live in public housing. Private market renters often have more financial resources and thus may have greater levels of political participation. Lastly, Harlem has more aggregate income, and a stronger reputation as a tourist destination than Bronzeville and, thus it attracts more businesses. Given these potentially confounding variables, my argument concerning the relationship between the contrasting political contexts and alternative behaviors and development patterns might be overstated. Some level of difference in Harlem and Bronzeville's redevelopment may be related to distinct pre-existing community conditions.

Harlem and Bronzeville's Future

There are many unanswered questions related to the future of Harlem and Bronzeville. Perhaps foremost, how will these communities continue to develop, and will they remain predominantly black communities? It is possible that the housing bubble brought on by low interest rates affected development. Many real estate analysts predict that as national interest rates rise, hot housing markets will cool down (Fratantoni, Duncan, Brinkmann, and Velz 2007). Will this affect Harlem and Bronzeville? I expect that it will not. Much of the development in these communities relates to government interventions, and these subsidies will continue to boost their housing markets. Further, compared to other areas throughout their cities, Harlem and Bronzeville remain undervalued. As Smith might say, there continues to be a "rent gap" ([1996] 2000). Thus, development will continue and those looking for relative value close to the CBD will come to these communities.

Given the findings of this work, I expect that Bronzeville and Harlem will remain predominantly African-American communities while becoming more racially diverse. In Chicago, the area just north of Bronzeville, the Near South Side, has already seen a tremendous increase in the number of whites. As this area expands south, whites will move to the outer northern edges of Bronzeville. East Harlem and West Harlem have experienced white influx and it will only be a matter of time before whites move into Central Harlem. However, it is unlikely that the movement of whites will diminish the importance of these communities as iconic black spaces.

Much of the redevelopment is geared toward linking Harlem and Bronzeville's past, as the centers of black life in New York and Chicago, to their futures. For instance, many of the upper-income housing developments and commercial spaces are named after African-American icons, like Maya Angelou, Duke Ellington, Rosa Parks, Harriet Tubman, and Harold Washington. In addition, these communities continue to be the home of important African-American institutions, such as the Urban League, the Wabash YMCA, the Harlem YMCA, the Schomburg Center for Research in Black Culture, and the South Side Community Art Center. Reintroducing jazz and blues districts are also part of the revitalization effort. Even the coffeehouses call for notions of racial solidarity, with names like "Some Like It Black" and "Home Sweet Harlem." The sentiments of Henry Louis Gates, Jr., a preeminent African-American scholar, are echoed by a generation of successful African Americans who wish to make Harlem and Bronzeville thriving black communities again. In discussing whether he will buy property in Harlem, he says, "I missed out on the first Harlem Renaissance and I do not want to miss out on the second." Harlem and Bronzeville are attracting a new generation of African Americans who want to preserve them as rich resources of black culture.

Race Relations

Prior studies conducted in Harlem and Bronzeville see these areas as appropriate locations to understand black/white relations in America. The current redevelopment of these communities provides an opportunity to reexamine the state of race relations, however this was not the focus of this book. My project set out to highlight the factors influencing the changing conditions in black inner cities. Having said that, the following section is designed to spark future analyses on what the new phase of urban renewal means for race relations in America.

Some evidence suggests that black/white relations may have not improved. First, the black middle class may move to areas like Harlem and Bronzeville because of persistent racism in corporate America. Monique Taylor documents that many black newcomers to Harlem claim they move there because they "feel more comfortable living amongst [their] own" and dislike "feeling rejected, carrying burdens, and constantly having to prove oneself" in the white-dominated corporate world (2002, 51). African-American communities provide a haven for black professionals from racism. Thus, the influx of more affluent African Americans to these areas occurs, in part, because of continually antagonistic black/white relations. Second, the destruction of public housing, which is sponsored by the federal government, leads to the displacement of the poor from neighborhoods that are in the midst of redeveloping. This is a form of institutional racism since poor African Americans affected by this policy are being relocated to highly segregated and impoverished neighborhoods.

Third, Harlem and Bronzeville remain segregated. Whites, as of yet, are not moving to Harlem or Bronzeville in great numbers, despite improved conditions. This might be due to a fear of living in these environments, which could be linked to the persistence of racism. There are undoubtedly stigmas attached to these neighborhoods, some of which are based on their histories as areas with high crime and poverty. Thus, it is difficult to extract whether reluctance by whites to move to these areas is based on issues of race per se. Further, many African-American residents desire to keep these areas primarily black (Freeman 2006; Pattillo 2003). These trends suggest that race relations have not improved much.

Harlem and Bronzeville do, however, symbolize black economic progress. In the last three decades, we have witnessed a rise in the number of black middle- and upper-income families, which some argue is a legacy of affirmative action policies (Gates 2004). The increasing number of upwardly mobile African Americans, some of whom are moving to these communities, suggests that economic disparity between blacks and whites might be decreasing, one indication of racial progress. Another sign of economic progress for African Americans is that certain members of this group are benefiting from the redevelopment. In New York and Chicago, black real estate developers are financially benefiting from the redevelopment of Harlem and Bronzeville. Further, black homeowners are able to build equity with rising property values. Harlem and Bronzeville's revitalization symbolizes black economic progress more than increased racial tolerance.

The redevelopment of Harlem and Bronzeville begs a question. How do African-American communities compare to white middle-class urban communities? If we are reaching greater racial equity, both middle-class communities should be similar. Some work suggests that black middle-class communities are still relatively disadvantaged compared to their white counterparts (Adelman 2004). Black middle-class blocks are much closer to areas of concentrated poverty. Further, there remains a large gap between black income and wealth and white income and wealth (Oliver and Shapiro 1995). Less aggregate wealth in black middle-class communities may affect the type of amenities, such as quality schools or park space, and other services available in these neighborhoods. Now that more urban, middle-income black communities are emerging, there are greater opportunities to compare their circumstances to white middle-class urban communities. If black middle-class communities do not have equivalent amenities then parity between blacks and whites has not been achieved.

The Concept of the New Urban Renewal

The redevelopment of Harlem and Bronzeville represents a broader trend of inner city revitalization occurring in many U.S. cities, including Boston, Philadelphia, Washington, D.C., Charlotte, Atlanta, Minneapolis, and Los Angeles.[2] I have labeled this trend the new urban renewal because it is similar to, yet distinct from, the patterns of the past fifty years. It mirrors past urban renewal because federal resources are associated with the revitalization. Further, the consequences of this development mainly affect African Americans; however, today's urban renewal has two important distinctions.

Multiple forces are associated with the new urban renewal. In the 1940s, '50s, and '60s federal dynamics were seen as the primary drivers of community change. As I have illustrated, global, municipal and community level factors also contribute to urban transformation. Second, the effect of the new urban renewal on the black population is different. As opposed to the past urban renewal, a greater segment of the African-American population is benefiting from this revitalization process.[3] More affluent African Americans, such as real estate developers and homeowners, prosper, while those of modest income are displaced to increasingly segregated and impoverished areas. Thus, the new urban renewal is different: the intersection of race and class, as opposed to race alone, define who benefits and who does not.

Policy Implications and Recommendations

Much of the urban legislation in the 1990s was geared toward attracting economic development to the inner city. Now that certain urban communities are experiencing massive investments, we must rethink and create new policies to decrease displacement and reduce the negative consequences for those forced to relocate. My recommendations target the global, federal, city, and community levels.

Community economic development, particularly in inner city areas, is an ambiguous concept. For example, community stakeholders, such as city officials, private developers, and inner-city residents, may each define successful economic development differently. Traditional definitions of economic development are primarily concerned with increasing economic activity and enhancing fiscal stability (Riposa 1996). This definition overlooks the concept of "entitlement" as noted by Nobel Prize economist Amartya Sen, where economic development is seen "as a process of expanding the capabilities of people" (1984, 497). As sociologist Richard Taub asks, "Does neighborhood economic development mean driving out the poor and encouraging the presence of a new population or does it mean improving the life circumstances of the residents?" (1988, 10). My definition of successful development is that residents of a declining community benefit from an improved quality of life as a result of the economic revitalization of their neighborhood. This definition guides my policy recommendations.

Regulating the global economy may improve circumstances for low-income residents in redeveloping neighborhoods. Some scholars argue that the flow of international capital to the secondary housing market in the United States increases neighborhood gentrification (e.g., Ranney 2003). The secondary market pools housing mortgages to support mortgage-based securities (MBS), which are traded like stocks. Congress's creation of the Federal National Mortgage Association (Fannie Mae), General National Mortgage Association (Ginnie Mae), and the Federal Home Loan Mortgage Corporation (Freddie Mac) facilitated the secondary market. Ginnie Mae ensures that investors receive payments of principal and interest on their MBS, while Fannie Mae and Freddie Mac are conduits that buy mortgages from lenders, and sell MBS. These entities became privatized in the 1960s and 1970s are now government-sponsored enterprises (GSEs) that facilitate the availability of capital and credit in the housing market.

Today, MBS transactions generate major profits because these securities have been opened to global investors. In 2003 Fannie Mae and Freddie Mac amassed a combined earning of nearly $13 billion on secondary market transactions (Smith, Pafenberg, and Goren 2006). These two companies are able to make huge profits, in part, because it is perceived that the federal government backs and guarantees their pooled mortgages. Ironically, the very GSE system that was designed to make more capital available for affordable housing may be related to heightened real estate prices in gentrifying communities.

I recommend imposing a 5 percent levy on profits made by the GSEs.[4] The revenues generated should be used to build affordable housing. Although this new pool of funding would not overhaul affordable housing concerns, it might raise public awareness of the linkage between the global economy and housing affordability. This knowledge might help garner political support to alter other federal policies that can have a more direct impact.

My study has several important implications for current federal urban development policy affecting low-income black communities. HOPE VI and Section 8 programs aim to deconcentrate neighborhood poverty; however, these programs are failing since they are pushing poverty to other marginal pockets of the urban landscape. Evidence from a variety of sources suggests that Section 8 voucher holders are ending up in highly segregated and impoverished neighborhoods (Fischer 1999, 2003; Hartung and Henig 1997). We must reform the Section 8 program to give those displaced from razed high-rise public housing greater opportunities to find apartments in more advantageous neighborhoods.

Three recommendations might help those with Section 8 vouchers find units in better neighborhoods. First, one problem is that the vouchers only cover apartments at the "fair market rent." This level varies slightly from city to city since it is based on dwellings that fall under the fortieth percentile of available units within a given metropolitan region (Turner, Popkin, and Cunningham 1999). At this percentile, vouchers rarely cover apartments in middle-income neighborhoods. For instance, in Chicago $900 a month is the fair market rent for a three-bedroom unit. If we are serious about deconcentrating poverty, we need to raise the fair market rent to a level that allows families greater choice.[5]

Second, most voucher holders receive very little relocation support. Thus, many move into other declining neighborhoods where they have family and friendship connections, though we know that families that receive relocation counseling are more likely to end up in better neighborhoods (Turner 1998). We need to increase funding for housing counselors to work with Section 8 recipients. Lastly, landlords can legally decline applicants with vouchers. Landlords often reject voucher holders because of the additional burdens of government inspections of their properties, delayed rent payments from the state and the fear that Section 8 renters may not be responsible tenants. To alleviate these landlord concerns, we need to create economic incentives for landlords to take these tenants (Turner, Popkin, and Cunningham 1999). These recommendations may help alleviate the negative consequences for those forced to move.

The HOPE VI program subsidizes the development of "mixed-income" housing developments to replace public housing in many black communities. Several projects funded through HOPE VI are designed to be occupied by one-third market rate homeowners, one-third market rate renters, and one-third public housing tenants. While this initiative seems a viable solution to eliminating high poverty areas, my findings suggest that potential antagonism among new development residents must be addressed. If maintaining economic diversity is the goal of these programs, measures must be taken to integrate and assimilate residents of distinct social economic statuses. Otherwise, two outcomes are inevitable: either upper-income residents will become politically active and remove the lower-income population, or they will move to more class-segregated areas. To successfully integrate these new developments, one would have to employ strategies to mitigate tensions between these economically distinct populations. HOPE VI funding initiatives must require developers of mixed-income housing projects to design and implement a plan to alleviate class-based hostility.

We should also maintain the viable public housing stock. Although high-rise public housing has developed a horrible, somewhat well deserved, reputation, plenty of decent public housing developments remain. This source of affordable housing must be preserved since it maybe critical to preventing massive displacement (Freeman 2006; Newman and Wyly 2006). In recent years the public housing operating fund has failed to keep up with rising utility and energy prices (Fischer 2006). In FY 2007, it is estimated that public housing authorities will only receive 79 percent of the funding they are eligible for under HUD's operating expense formula.[6] This meager funding will further deteriorate the country's remaining public housing stock, which accommodates nearly 1.1 million families. To maintain this affordable housing, operating expense funding must keep pace with inflation and rising utility costs. While public housing was not the answer to urban ills, and in many instances contributed to them, we must conserve the viable stock that remains in place, particularly those in gentrifying and mixed-income communities.

The Community Development Block Grant is another resource pool that can be used more effectively to assist those in need of affordable housing. Since 1974 the CBDG program has allocated nearly $3.5 billion annually to numerous metropolitan areas to promote community development. The funding has very few restrictions and cities can disburse these resources in a variety of ways (Rich 1993; Wong and Peterson 1986). Cities can use the funding to promote social services, housing, sidewalk and sewer repair, and street improvements. In recent years, the program has become known for its lack of accountability (Bond 2004; GAO 2006; Rich 1993), yet current reform efforts have faltered in Congress. This money could be used more effectively if resources were targeted toward fewer economic development objectives and an appropriate monitoring system was in place. This would restrict the ability of local municipalities, like Chicago, to allocate public resources for politically advantageous rather than for critical community development needs.

Recently, there has been a federal push to increase funding for faith-based involvement in neighborhood development, but the research here shows that this is not without its own complicated limitations. There is an implicit assumption that religious institutions aspire, and are in a better position than other organizations, to help those in dire circumstances. My research, as well as McRoberts's 2003 study of churches in Boston, demonstrates that this can be a faulty assumption. I have shown some churches in low-income communities have interests that align more with their middle-class membership. Churches, like other organizations, serve their core constituents and it should not be assumed that these institutions are better positioned to assist the poor simply because they are located in the inner city.

Certain federal policies, such as the HOPE VI program, are associated with the redevelopment of inner city areas across the country. During the decade that this program was implemented, there was a 26 percent decline in the number of high-poverty areas (Jargowsky 2003). This reduction in high poverty areas might be due to the displacement of residents from the inner cities. The movement of the poor from the inner city correlates with an increase in the poverty rate in certain suburban areas (Puentes and Warren 2006). In 1999, the number of poor suburban and urban poor was almost equivalent, but in 2005 the suburban poor was greater than the inner city poor by nearly 1 million (Berube and Kneebone 2006). In the Chicago metropolitan region, some of the African-American, south suburbs already have poverty rates ranging from 30 to 40 percent (Alexander 1998). Moreover, there is some evidence that gang activity, once isolated in the Chicago's public housing projects, is moving to the suburbs (Chicago Crime Commission 2006; Venkatesh, Celimli, Miller, et al. 2004). Initial research suggests that the first suburbs, where poverty is on the rise, may not have the social service infrastructure to handle problems related to poverty (Allard 2004). New national legislation that distributes resources to suburban areas that have experienced an influx of low-income families is needed.

We, as a country, must proactively prevent the creation of high-poverty suburbs. The Suburban Core Opportunity, Restoration and Enhancement Act attempts to address this by proposing to put resources in suburban areas that have housing-cost burdens of at least 50 percent of gross income.[7] These are high cost suburbs but are not necessarily ones experiencing increasing poverty rates. We should amend this promising legislation so that it targets suburban areas facing problems associated with increased poverty. Disfranchisement can occur in suburban localities just as it once did in the 1960s, '70s, and '80s in America's central cities. We must prevent our suburbs from becoming a harbor of social unrest, as was witnessed in 2005 in the socially excluded French "Red Belt" suburbs (Haddad and Balz 2006). Although the magnitude of suburban, concentrated poverty has not yet reached the levels witnessed in the inner city, legislators and policymakers should take measures to halt the flow of poverty reconcentration in first-ring suburbs.

City-level reforms can help moderate displacement of residents from redeveloping areas. Some cities, such as Boston, San Francisco, and Denver mandate that all new large real estate developments must set aside ten percent of units for affordable housing (Brunick, Goldberg, and Levine 2003). New York City and Chicago have versions of these laws whereby developments that receive city subsidies, such as low-interest loans or grants, are required to set a percentage of housing units in these developments for affordable housing. Citywide "set-aside" programs would be helpful, but I recommend that economically transitioning neighborhoods, which are often sites of real estate speculation, high profit margins, and displacement, be designated "development zones." Within the development zone, developers must either make 20 percent of new units in developments affordable or pay a steep penalty to a local affordable housing authority. Additionally, special regulations should be put in place to prevent sharp rent increases in designated development zones. Moreover, to protect landlords, property tax increases would be staggered and phased in as well. These measures would help to slow down the displacement process in economically transitioning neighborhoods.

None of these global, federal, or city recommendations will be implemented without effective grassroots coalition pressure. Some scholars advocate for community-level interventions that build social capital or collective efficacy to increase neighborhood participation (Putnam 2000;

Sampson 2001). However, an important mechanism related to activism is the citywide political structure. Therefore, to stimulate local action I would not recommend interventions at the community level, but would instead stress a fundamental restructuring of metropolitan political land-scapes to create greater opportunities for local engagement. For instance, Chicago needs a competing political party or at least policies to decrease the amount of centralized authority held by the mayor. In New York City, the Board of Estimate, which decentralized political power, was dis-banded in 1989; so far power continues to remain diffuse. Local advocates need to ensure that mayoral centralization does not take place. This recommendation supports social movement scholars who argue that the broader political opportunity structure is one of the critical factors that relates to levels of protest (McAdam, McCarthy, and Zald 1996). Stim-ulating local activism will be critical to initiating policy reforms at any level.

Closing Thoughts

Some of the nation's most impoverished urban, black communities are transitioning from decades of isolation and despair into more mixed-income and mainstream living environments. Harlem and Bronzeville are emblematic of this pattern of inner city renewal. The transformation process in these neighborhoods highlights how global, federal, city, and community forces interact and culminate to explain why after prolonged periods of concentrated poverty these areas are turning around. While the international context is becoming increasingly important, local cir-cumstances remain critical to urban community transformation. Addi-tionally, the revitalization reveals that important factors, such as race, class, and politics, influence the landscape of urban America. As urban communities continually shift, so too do the dynamics associated with these alterations. Those interested in modern cities must strive to iden-tify the complex dynamics leading to the transformation of today's inner city environments and we, as a country, must take concrete action to en-sure that the new urban renewal does not lead to a reconcentration of poverty in other localities.

APPENDIX A

Demographic Information

Table A.1 Population by community area

	1980	1990	2000
Bronzeville	89,441	66,549	54,476
Harlem	105,641	99,519	107,109

Source: Census data.

Table A.2 Percentage of population black and white by community area

	Black 1990	White 1990	Black 2000	White 2000
Bronzeville	95.0	2.5	92.0	4.0
Harlem	88.0	1.5	77.0	2.0

Source: Census data.

Table A.3   Median household income by community area

	1980	1990	2000
Douglas	$14,377	$10,577	$24,835
Grand Boulevard	$11,640	$8,371	$14,178
Harlem	$10,872	$13,252	$19,920

Source: Census data.
Note: Bronzeville consists of the Douglas and Grand Boulevard districts.

Table A.4   Household income structure by community area

	Bronzeville		Harlem	
Income*	1990	2000	1990	2000
Low	63	45	53	42
Moderate	14	12	18	15
Middle	22	33	26	35
High	2	10	3	8

Source: Census data.
*Low = below $15,000; Moderate = $15,000–$24,999; Middle = $25,000–$74,999; High = $75,000+

Table A.5   Median home value by community area

	1980	1990	2000
Douglas	$25,900	$124,632	$208,449
Grand Boulevard	$23,400	$61,601	$179,849
Harlem	$53,873	$199,025	$250,000

Source: Census data.
Note: Bronzeville consists of the Douglas and Grand Boulevard Districts.

Table A.6   Percentage of population with BA or higher by community area

	1980	1990	2000	% change 1990–2000
Bronzeville	8	13	18	38
Harlem	5	10	15	50

Source: Census data.

Table A.7   Percentage of owner-occupied units by community area

	1980	1990	2000
Bronzeville	5.6	5.5	10.0
Harlem	3.5	4.6	7.0

Source: Census data.

APPENDIX B

Community Areas in New York City and Chicago

New York City

Table B.1 Median home values in select New York City areas, 1980–2000

Community area	1980*	1990	2000	% change 1990–2000
Lower East Side, Chinatown	$13,449	$268,750	$192,000	−27
Chelsea, Clinton, Hell's Kitchen	$78,733	$500,001	$1,000,000+	100
Midtown	$170,710	$500,001	$875,000	75
Harlem	$53,873	$199,025	$250,000	26
Manhattan, avg.	$146,731	$487,300	$1,000,000+	105
NYC, avg.	$82,894	$189,600	$211,900	12

Source: Census data.
*In 1990 constant dollars.

Table B.2   Median household income in select New York City areas, 1980–2000

Community area	1980*	1990	2000	% change 1990–2000
Lower East Side, Chinatown	$14,707	$20,007	$28,745	44
Chelsea, Clinton, Hell's Kitchen	$20,442	$30,450	$50,580	66
Midtown	$27,213	$42,050	$69,075	64
Harlem	$10,872	$13,252	$19,920	50
Manhattan, avg.	$23,305	$32,262	$47,030	46
NYC, avg.	$23,221	$29,823	$41,887	40

Source: Census data.
* In 1990 constant dollars.

Table B.3   Population in select New York City areas, 1980–2000

Community area	1980	1990	2000	% change 1990–2000
Lower East Side, Chinatown	154,848	161,617	164,407	2
Chelsea, Clinton, Hell's Kitchen	82,164	84,431	87,479	4
Midtown	39,544	43,507	44,028	1
Harlem	105,641	99,519	107,109	8

Source: Census data.

CHICAGO

Table B.4   Median home values in select Chicago areas, 1980–2000

Community area	1980	1990	2000	% change 1990–2000
Loop	$55,250	$218,182	$202,476	–7
Near South	$32,500	$283,333	$335,101	18
Douglas	$25,900	$124,632	$208,449	67
Grand Boulevard	$23,400	$61,601	$179,849	192
Chicago, avg.	$47,200	$78,700	$132,400	68

Source: Census data.
Note: Bronzeville consists of the Douglas and Grand Boulevard Districts.

Table B.5   Median household income in select Chicago areas, 1980–2000

Community area	1980	1990	2000	% change 1990–2000
Loop	$19,596	$48,331	$65,128	35
Near South	$10,197	$6,804	$34,329	405
Douglas	$14,536	$12,993	$24,835	91
Grand Boulevard	$9,092	$7,146	$14,178	98
Chicago, avg.	$25,644	$26,301	$38,625	47

Source: Census data.

Table B.6   Population in select Chicago areas, 1980–2000

Community area	1980	1990	2000	% change 1990–2000
Loop	6,462	11,954	16,388	37
Near South	7,243	6,828	9,509	39
Douglas	35,700	30,652	26,470	–14
Grand Boulevard	53,741	35,897	28,006	–22

Source: Census data.

APPENDIX C

Public Housing Data

Table C.1   Public housing (PH) statistics for New York City and Chicago*

	NYCHA	CHA
Number of units	179,000[a]	38,000[b]
Overall PH population	472,000[a]	145,000[a]
City Population in PH (%)	6.4[c]	5.2[c]
Waitlist for PH	124,320[d]	30,000[b]
Vacancy rates (%)	4[e]	35[b]
Black (%)	54[d]	93[f]
Average income	$14,800[h]	$7,000[g]
Working families (%)	35[h]	15[g]
Female headed families (%)	75[h]	94[g]
Average rent ($)	294[h]	—

* The data in this table are complied from multiple sources that correspond to different survey dates beginning in the late 1980s to the present. It is presented to give an estimation of the differences between the two housing authorities.
[a] Abu-Lughod 1999.   [b] Ranney 2003.
[c] Author's calculation: I divided the number of public housing residents by the 1990 city population.
[d] Thompson 1999.   [e] Schill and Scafidi 1999.
[f] Wallace v. CHA 2003.   [g] Popkin et al. 2000.
[h] NYCHA 2002b.

The Comparative, Vertical Ethnographic Approach

My research approach draws on Jefferey Sellers's (2005) depiction of the "de-centered analysis" and Michael Burawoy's (1998) "extended case method." The de-centered analysis is a comparative procedure where macro forces beyond the nation-state are explored while the "focus shifts to local and locally based actors and to consequences specific to a given place" (Sellers 2005, 433). The de-centered approach attempts to account for how external community forces affect and are affected by more local situational factors. While Sellers advocates for the use of this approach in cross-national urban research projects, I found aspects of it quite useful for comparing similar communities embedded in two different global cities within the same country.

The extended case method is useful for researchers who want to investigate relationships between the micro-environment and more macro-variables that extend beyond the research site. Most traditional ethnographies interpret events by centering on the immediate milieu and often pay little attention to the context in which the research site is embedded. The extended case method encourages scholars to explore the ways in which broader factors influence the micro environment. The need to better understand forces beyond the neighborhood is essential, as Janet Abu-Lughod notes, "Community studies cannot afford to be ... confined only to the neighborhood itself" (1994, 194).

I modeled my comparative framework after Abu-Lughod's (1999) multiscaled, historical analysis of New York, Chicago, and Los Angeles. In her extraordinary work, she insists that the spatial consequences of international forces on these cities manifest in particular ways based on the pre-existing urban political circumstances. My approach differed in that I used ethnography to highlight how the unique pre-existing city-wide political landscapes mediate and affect outcomes specifically at the community level.

The comparative nature of the study lends itself to the quasi-experimental design, using the scientific method; however, the ethnographic technique follows a completely different knowledge-producing logic. Although these procedures are typically at odds with one another, in this investigation, where the goal is to build on existing theories, they complement each other.

My approach is a hybrid of the extended and grounded ethnographic techniques. Compared to other ethnographic techniques, the extended case method is relatively deductive. This approach is different from ethnographies that seek to create "grounded theory," where new theories emerge from the interactions with the research site (Duneier 1999; Strauss and Corbin 1998). When I entered Bronzeville in 1999, I was interested in exploring how a comprehensive set of factors, both internal and external to the community, influenced the redevelopment taking place. This initial understanding was influenced by theories of economic globalization, city politics, and inner city economic development. After spending three years studying Bronzeville, I constructed a grounded understanding about the ways in which micro- and macro-factors were affecting its redevelopment. Consequently, when I arrived in Harlem, I had a working theoretical framework, and tested hypotheses there, based on my experiences in Bronzeville. Thus, I started with a more grounded approach in Bronzeville but moved toward the extended method, having prior theories in mind, when I began fieldwork in Harlem.

Living in the community facilitates understanding neighborhood redevelopment processes. My ethnographic method follows in the tradition of other participant-observational studies, such as Herbert Gans ([1962] 1982), Mary Pattillo-McCoy (1999), and William Whyte ([1943] 1955). The ethnographic procedure allows for in-depth knowledge of the forces that affect the community as they are perceived and acted upon by individuals during their everyday lives. It is the appropriate technique for researchers interested in documenting complex processes as they unfold in multiple settings within the natural environment (see Dommel and Hall 1984; Nathan 1983; Schatzman and Strauss 1973).

There are some critiques of this research method. First, some claim that it lacks scientific rigor and is not systematic enough. In conducting a comparative study, I addressed this issue by increasing the analytic power of this technique. My selection of Bronzeville and then Harlem was strategic. I chose similar African-American communities embedded in global cities that were targets of federal as well as city-level economic interventions. These similarities increase the power of my study because they allowed me to isolate the citywide political structure as a potentially significant independent variable. Others claim that ethnographies are impossible to generalize. This critique is not aimed so much at the ethnographic technique per se, but relate to the fact that most ethnographic studies are based on a single case design. By comparing two communities, my study has an advantage over ethnographies that look at only one community area. Another critique of ethnographic studies is that they suffer from an intrinsic bias by being too narrowly focused and overly entrenched in the community. By concentrating on multiple levels of analysis while being embedded in the community, I avoid this limitation.

Several strengths and weaknesses are associated with my comparative, vertical ethnographic method. By investigating two communities, I increase the robustness of my findings compared to the case study design. By investigating two sites, however, I limit the thick descriptions that make ethnography such a compelling research technique. This is a worthy trade-off. The insight achieved by the comparative perspective is something very few ethnographic studies possess. The multileveled analysis also added to the study's comparative value. I could have written a book that focused on the global, federal, city, or community level, and while this may have led to a more detailed study, it would have been an incomplete assessment of the various processes related to neighborhood change. Plenty of contemporary studies of Harlem and Bronzeville center on one level of analysis. My study is distinguishable precisely because I take a more comprehensive approach.

Data Preparation

I used a specific procedure to prepare my data for analysis. My field notes from each community were stored separately in large notebooks in chronological order. By the time I had finished my study, I had four notebooks

per community in addition to all taped interviews and meeting tran-
scriptions, amounting to close to 2,000 pages. Before I began writing,
I separated relevant information into separate categories for each level of
analysis. I sorted field notes, sections of interviews, newspaper articles,
and prior relevant studies into files labeled "global," "federal," "city," and
"community." After reading over the material in these larger categories,
subsections emerged, such as public housing, displacement, protest politics, city politics, and intra-racial class conflict. Some of these subcate-
gories eventually became separate chapters. I did not use any qualitative
statistical packages to assess my data. My organization and assessment of
the data were influenced by the interactions I had with theory and the
information acquired in the field.

Background and Bias

The characteristics and background of the researcher can bring potential
insight and bias to the research project. McRoberts notes that even "objective" researchers come to community settings with their personal bag-
gage, having "soiled their khakis" with preconceived perspectives prior to
entering the research site (2003, 155). When interpreting ethnographic
studies, readers should be aware of the background researcher, for this
can affect what the research is observing and his interpretation of events.

The researcher must always be aware of his own socio-economic status and the way in which others perceive him. Sometimes this is obvious,
like when my conversations with public housing residents shifted to economic issues. One day Tre asked me how much my laptop computer cost.
I told them I bought it for $2,000. Tre razzed me by jokingly responding,
"Rich motherfucker." This exchange, although minor, is important because it demonstrates how income differences affect the relationship between the researcher and those he is interacting with in the field.

One's background can also affect the research questions. Many recent
ethnographic studies of Harlem and Bronzeville have been conducted by
African Americans who use these spaces to focus on black identity. Although I address issues of identity to a certain extent, being white might
have affected why I chose to center this book on dynamics of community
change.

My experience as an athlete was critical to this research. Even though
I grew up in a predominately white suburb of New York City, I played
basketball in Harlem during high school. For two years in the early 1990s,
I was a member of a Harlem basketball team that played throughout the

area. I played at the Rucker Park on 155th Street, home to the country's most well-known outdoor summer basketball league. Although I did not speak about basketball with most people I met, my interest in and ability to play basketball assisted me with my research in both communities.

Playing basketball at Stateway Gardens in Bronzeville allowed me to gain a certain level of acceptance and legitimacy. My ability to play helped me gain access to the gang-controlled buildings at Stateway. A week after working at Stateway, Tre brought me over to some of the dealers who were playing dice to see if they wanted to play us in basketball. One of the dealers said he would if we had money to gamble. Tre suggested $5 a game, and the dealer laughed and said, "You're crazy." He wanted higher stakes: "I know this white boy has a jumper and I'll play but I want to gamble." As Tre negotiated the terms, another gang member whom I had played another time shook my hand, acknowledging to the others that he accepted my presence. My experience on the basketball court granted me access to the public housing buildings. It also enabled me to get closer to being considered an "insider" because I participated in everyday community life through activities most perceived as being unrelated to my research pursuits.

My educational background and race, in other situations, helped me gain access to elite community members. For instance, my education helped me effectively mingle at cocktail parties and political fundraisers. At these functions I was able to schedule interviewers with bankers, real estate developers, and high-level political officials. In addition, many of the black-middle class residents I spoke with were often quite candid about their desire to remove the poor from these communities, which I suspect related to my race. Some I interviewed figured I was in favor of this as well. One woman, who was black and Republican and very critical of the poor in her community, said to me, "You're Republican, right?" after our interview. My educational background and race, while inhibiting at times, were assets in other instances.

Multiple "Docs"

One source that made my research more insightful was the guidance and close relationship I had with various community members. William Whyte's *Street Corner Society* ([1943] 1955) illustrates the importance of having an "insider" from the community supporting the ethnographic research. Doc was the key figure in Cornerville that allowed Whyte access to the street gangs. "As long as I was with Doc and vouched for by him, no one asked me who I was or what I was doing," Whyte explains (300). In Harlem Assemblyman Keith Wright and in Bronzeville Tre provided me with access to parts of these communities that might have been difficult for me to enter on my own. Keith opened Harlem's political doors, while Tre granted me entry to Bronzeville's public housing. With Keith I could walk into any Harlem community meeting without question. At the same time, my friendship with Tre allowed me to enter public housing without being harassed by lookouts and drug dealers. Without these people, critical pieces of the change process might have been left uncovered. It is important for "outside" researchers to have respected community representatives bring legitimacy to their research endeavor. Because of my race, and the fact that I had to be away from one community for many months as I researched the other, having support from key residents was particularly important.

Notes

Chapter 1

1. For more on the movement of boutique shops to Harlem see Ruth Ferla, "Downtown Comes to Harlem," *New York Times*, June 22, 2006.
2. Barry Pearce, "Back to Bronzeville," *New Homes*, August, 2001.
3. See Anderson 1965; Fullilove 2004; Meyerson and Banfield 1955.
4. See Boyd 2000; Goetz 2003; Grogan and Proscio 2000; Pattillo 2007; Moore 2005; Taylor 2002; von Hoffman 2003.
5. See Gates 2004.
6. There is some controversy surrounding the present boundaries of Bronzeville. The designated Bronzeville area described in this study consists of the Douglas and Grand Boulevard districts, which is smaller than the original Bronzeville outlined by Drake and Cayton in *Black Metropolis* ([1945] 1993). Most of the community leaders I spoke with viewed this smaller area as today's Bronzeville. However, some still considered sections of adjacent districts, such as Washington Park and Northern Kenwood/Oakland part of the broader Bronzeville community.
7. See Drake and Cayton ([1945] 1993, 12).
8. See Ottley (1943, 1).
9. See Boyd 2000; Freeman 2006; Jackson 2001.
10. See Clark 1965; Drake and Cayton [1945] 1993; Hirsch [1983] 1998; Johnson [1930] 1991; Lemann 1991; Osofsky [1963] 1996; Spear 1967.
11. Though Harlem is slightly further from the CBD than Bronzeville, the commutes to their respective CBDs are quite similar. New York City's CBD officially

starts at 59th Street. To get from 125th Street in Harlem to 59th Street takes approximately fifteen minutes on the A or 2 trains. From Bronzeville at 47th Street, it is a fifteen-minute drive or ride on the elevated, green line train to the Loop.

12. See McMillen 2003; Sassen 2000.
13. See Boyd 2000; Freeman 2006; Jackson 2001; Pattillo 2007; Taylor 2002.
14. See Chinyelu 1999; Hoffman 2000; Ranney 2003; Smith [1996] 2000.
15. See Burawoy et al. 1991.
16. The sample of stakeholders was identified through asking those interviewed to recommend others. Identities of those interviewed are only revealed if explicit written and verbal permission is granted. Otherwise, pseudonyms are used to conceal their identities.
17. For a broader discussion of my research method and how my race influenced data collection procedures see appendix D.
18. See Gans ([1962] 1982, 349).

Chapter 2

1. Stone's (1989) regime theory falls under the political economic paradigm. As he sees it, the informal collaborative partnership between city-level political and economic institutional actors determine the development of the municipal landscape.
2. Other global mechanisms might influence the city such as cultural integration and global consumption patterns (Zukin 1987, 1995).
3. Other political scientists, notably Cohen (1999), Harris-Lacewell (2005), Landry (1987), and Thompson (2006) have also been attentive to the issue of class discord and various ideological perspectives within black American politics.

Chapter 3

1. Some argue that one of the largest single day point drops in the U.S. stock market, in October of 1997, is associated with the East Asian financial crisis (Rubin and Weisberg 2003).
2. Examples of global or world cities include Tokyo, Frankfurt, Sydney, Singapore, Shanghai, Hong Kong, Mumbai, Sao Paulo, Paris, Zurich, Chicago, London, and New York (Friedman 2000). For more on the worldwide geography of global cities see Beaverstock, Smith, and Taylor (2000).
3. Using 1990 and 2000 Gini coefficients, I calculated these percentages for the Metropolitan Statistical Area of NYC and Chicago. The U.S. Census provided the data.
4. Quotes without references come directly from my interviews or field notes.
5. For more details on displacement in Harlem, see Taylor (2002).
6. Chicago's CBD and the Loop are the same area. Chicago has nicknamed its downtown area because it is encircled by elevated train tracks.
7. See Wille (1997) for an excellent account of the redevelopment of the South Loop and Dearborn Park.

8. For a more detailed description of TIFs see Paetsch and Dahlstrom (1990), Ranney (2003), and Wille (1997).

9. Between 1990 and 2000, Kansas City (Kansas), Detroit, and St. Louis lost 12, 7, and 2 percent of their overall population respectively. In addition, the magnitude of their growth in income inequality was less than what was seen in New York City and Chicago.

Chapter 4

1. I've calculated this estimate using FY 2005 federal agency budgets.

2. During the time the federal government moved to devolving powers, funding for many programs was drastically reduced. Some suggest that this leaves cities with less power. This might be true, but my point is that cities now have more independence to implement the resources they receive from the national government.

3. On June 19, 2007, Bloomberg left the Republican Party and became unaffiliated. Additionally, in 2007 a Democrat, Eliot Spitzer, became New York's governor.

4. Jack Kemp, the secretary of the U.S. Department of Housing and Urban Development under George H. W. Bush's administration, originally popularized the idea for the Empowerment Zone Initiative in Washington, D.C.

5. I focus on the how the distinct citywide political systems in New York City and Chicago pattern the spending of the block grant since very few corporations in the Empowerment Zones use the tax credits (GAO 2004).

6. Cate Plys, "He Gave Them the Budget and It Was Done," *Chicago Reader,* November 28, 2003.

7. Andrew Martin, "Hizzoner's Doormat," *Chicago Tribune,* August 11, 2002.

8. Nicolette McDavid, "HUD Auditing Empowerment Zone," *Chicago Reporter,* October 1998.

9. Mick Dumke, "Black Ministers Put Faith in Daley," *Chicago Reporter,* September 2000.

10. John Bebow, "The Collector," *Chicago Tribune Magazine,* October 3, 2004.

11. "Mayor Daley is Our Man for Re-election, But. . .," *Chicago Defender*, February 24, 2003.

12. Dick Simpson, "Council Applies Fresh Ink to Its Rubber Stamp," *Chicago Journal,* December 4, 2003.

13. Some call this group the Gang of Five and include New York state assemblyman and Manhattan Democratic Party leader Herman "Denny" Farrell, Jr., as the fifth member of Harlem's political core (Jacoby and Siegel 1999). Before this group came to power, Adam Clayton Powell, Jr., and J. Raymond Jones were the dominate actors in Harlem's political scene (Walter 1989). In 1970 Rangel defeated Powell and captured his Congressional seat, setting the course for a new generation of Harlem political leadership.

14. In 1989, a revision to the city charter eliminated the Board of Estimate (Thompson 2006). The budget process, however, remains outside the formal authority of the mayor. Most of the responsibilities for the approval of the budget are in the hands of the council although the mayor proposes the initial budget. Even with

the elimination of the Board of Estimate, New York City remains a two-party town without any centralized control (see Kantor 2002).

15. Social Compact, a nonprofit research firm that conducts market analysis in inner city areas, provided this information.

16. According to www.bankrate.com, Manhattan is 74 percent more expensive than Chicago.

Chapter 5

1. The Brooke Amendments removed minimum rent requirements and increased the tenant share of rent from 20 to 25 percent (which was subsequently raised to 30 percent) of their income. This policy favored low-income households and unemployed tenants since many working residents could afford private market housing with 25 percent of their income (Popkin, Buron, Levy, and Cunningham 2000). Thus, this policy had the adverse effect of increasing poverty concentration by encouraging working tenants to move out of public housing (Spence 1993; Thompson 1999).

2. The HOPE VI program allocated over $5.5 billion within a ten-year period to demolish distressed public housing and construct "mixed-income" replacement housing.

3. U.S. Department of Housing and Urban Development's website: http://www.hud.gov/offices/pih/programs/ph/hope6/grants/demolition/.

4. Before the enactment of the HOPE VI program, Congress commissioned a national assessment of the country's distressed public housing infrastructure in 1989 (see National Commission on Severely Distressed Public Housing 1992). The findings set the context for subsequent legislation that would lead to the demolition of the country's distressed public housing stock.

5. In 1996 an estimated 25,413 people lived in Chicago Housing Authority public housing units slated for demolition in Bronzeville. Assuming one-third will return to redeveloped units in the community, approximately 17,000 will be displaced. This is probably a conservative estimate since it does not account for displacement that occurs when private market rental units are converted to condominiums. Chicago does not have strong rent control restrictions and several sizeable Bronzeville rental complexes were converted to condominiums while I conducted my research (see Barry Pearce, "Back to Bronzeville," *New Homes*, August, 2001).

6. Though there are many public housing projects in Bronzeville and Harlem, I chose to focus on Stateway Gardens in Bronzeville and the St. Nicholas Houses in Harlem. Stateway Gardens and the St. Nicholas Houses are large-scale housing developments that are typical of the high-rise housing stock managed, respectively, by the Chicago Housing Authority (CHA) in Bronzeville and the New York City Housing Authority (NYCHA) in Harlem. In addition to the case studies of the two projects, I also visited other housing projects in these communities and attended numerous meetings sponsored by the NYCHA and the CHA.

7. This information is available on the U.S. Department of Housing and Urban Development's website: http://www.hud.gov/offices/pih/programs/ph/hope6/.

8. Of the 60,000 distressed public housing units taken down nationwide, Chicago is responsible for 20 percent.

9. Because of persistent corruption at the Chicago Housing Authority, HUD managed the CHA from 1995 to 1999.

10. The voucher covers expenses beyond 30 percent of household income for a rental of a unit at the "fair market rate."

11. John Handley, "A New Age for Bronzeville," *Chicago Tribune*, December 1, 2002.

12. John Handley, "Redeveloping Public Housing," *Chicago Tribune*, August 22, 2004.

13. As of FY 2006, the city of Chicago received $340 million in HOPE VI funding for demolition and the construction of "mixed-income" housing, and 43 percent of Chicago's HOPE VI funds were spent in Bronzeville (U.S. Department of Housing and Urban Development's website: http://www.hud.gov/offices/pih/programs/ph/hope6/).

14. Jeanette Almada, "Building to Start in Summer on Stateway Redevelopment," *Chicago Tribune*, February 16, 2003. Also see Shashaty's article "Home Sales Fill Funding Gap for Mixed-Income Redevelopments" in *Affordable Housing Finance* (2007), 47–48, 74.

15. "The Bronzeville Renaissance," *New City*, August 8, 2002.

16. The CHA began its demolition and relocation process before the announcement of the "Plan for Transformation" in 1999. These figures represent residents that relocated from CHA buildings between 1995 and 2002. The data in Paul Fischer's (2003) study were used as evidence in a class action lawsuit against CHA for violating fair housing laws (see Wallace v. CHA 2003).

17. Some of Chicago's inner south suburbs have poverty rates ranging from 30 to 40 percent (Alexander 1998), and the movement of the poor from the inner city in large municipalities like Chicago, New York, Boston, and Washington, D.C., correlates with a rising suburban poverty rate (Puentes and Warren 2006).

18. At Stateway Gardens, I worked with Jamie's organization for six months. The NCC office is a hub for various programs that provide health services, individual and family counseling, employment training, and legal assistance to residents.

19. Estimating the number of squatters in CHA buildings is extremely difficult. The two works cited only document the percent of squatters existing in the Robert Taylor Homes, which may not necessarily be representative of the CHA system.

20. See Keith Robbins, *N'Digo Profiles*, 2003; Angela Rozas, "Revival of an Old Housing Complex," *Chicago Tribune*, December 5, 2003; Jeanette Almada, "Building to Start in Summer on Stateway Redevelopment," *Chicago Tribune*, February 16, 2003; Chinta Strausberg "CHA Panel OK's $10 Mil Contract to King," *Chicago Defender*, December 17, 2002.

21. John Bebow, "The Collector," *Chicago Tribune Magazine*, October 3, 2004.

22. Additionally, the Daley regime often threatened to take away welfare payments if recipients did not vote the party line (Erie 1988).

23. This body would become the present-day Local Advisory Council and Central Advisory Council (LAC-CAC) tenant oversight structure.

24. Mayor Eugene Sawyer, a machine loyalist, appointed Lane. The city council appointed Sawyer mayor following the untimely death of Mayor Harold Washington.

25. In 1980, the waitlist was 13,000; by 1984 that number had increased to 24,000 (Feldman and Stall 2004); and in the 1990s, the figure stood at approximately 30,000 (Ranney 2003).

26. Julia Vitullo-Martin, "Project Vision," *Wall Street Journal,* August 18, 2006.

27. For more on NYCHA's plan to rehabilitate public housing see their 2006 publication, "The Plan to Preserve Public Housing."

28. My analysis of neighborhood poverty between 1990 and 2000 demonstrates that there was an expansion of high-poverty areas (40+ poverty rate) in Brooklyn and in the Bronx, as well as in Newark, NJ. Another study on displacement and relocation in New York City supports this finding (Newman and Wyly 2006).

29. In rent-controlled apartments, if the original tenant moves out landlords can substantially increase the rent.

30. Michael Brick, "Tenants Evacuate Building Deemed Unsafe," *New York Times,* April 17, 2003.

31. Amy Waldman, "Where Green Trumps Black and White," *New York Times,* December 11, 1999.

32. "Assemblyman Keith Wright Holds Press Conference Blasting Happyland Slumlord," *News from Assemblyman Keith L. T. Wright,* March 23, 2006.

33. For a further critique of Freeman and Braconi's (2004) study see Newman and Wyly (2006).

34. Estimating the magnitude of displacement is an extremely difficult task. I do not have data on the level of displacement in Harlem. My point is to merely demonstrate that it is an important community concern.

35. Teri Rogers, "A Developer's Rocky Quest to Revitalize Harlem," *New York Times,* November 6, 2005.

36. Tiffany Razzano, "Harlem Pioneers Grow with the Flow," *Real Estate Weekly,* November 9, 2005.

37. David Dunlap, "The Changing Look of the New Harlem," *New York Times,* February 10, 2002.

38. Phillip Thompson has argued that the NYCHA is centralized (Thompson 2006), but in fact it is significantly less centralized than the CHA. Senior level housing managers in the NYCHA have greater autonomy over the resources that they are budgeted. Additionally, NYCHA tenants, compared to CHA residents, have more capacity to alter how these resources are spent.

39. In the 1980s President Reagan's administration cut funding for public housing by 87 percent (Feldman and Stall 2004).

40. According to www.bankrate.com, Manhattan is 74 percent more expensive than Chicago.

Chapter 6

1. Some might expect high levels of poverty and changing class structures in these communities to create intra-racial class antagonism related to the level of support or protest to redevelopment. Class conflict is discussed in the next chapter. In this

chapter class discord can be seen as a control variable since both communities are experiencing similar levels of income diversification and intra-racial class conflict.

2. I define low-income as households that earn under $15,000. These percents come from my tabulation of the 2000 Census.

3. The authority and form of the community boards have changed several times. Their present structure resembles the 1975 revision of the City Charter (Fainstein and Fainstein 1991).

4. A few communities in Chicago are designated as conservation areas and these areas have entities that function similar to the NYC community boards, but these are rare. There is no conservation area in Bronzeville. Further, the mayor is influential in appointing members to these "community boards."

5. For more information on these organizations see von Hoffman (2003).

6. The South Side Partnership was established in 1989. The participating groups came together to advocate for educational improvements in the community. Since that time the partnership has broadened its mission to include community development concerns.

7. Jeff Huebner, "Whose Blues Will They Choose?" *Chicago Reader*, December 1, 2000.

8. Andrew Martin, "Hizzoner's Doormat," *Chicago Tribune*, August 11, 2002.

9. Beverly Reed, "Palm Tavern Owner Surrenders to City's Offer," *Chicago Defender*, June 25, 2001.

10. Adam Gopnik, "Harlem for Sale," *New Yorker*, April 22–29, 2002.

11. This finding is echoed in the social movement literature (see McAdam 1982).

12. "State Assemblyman Keith Wright Applauds Recent Jailing of Harlem Slumlord," *News from Assemblyman Keith L. T. Wright*, December 29, 2004.

Chapter 7

1. Alan Wax and Tania Padgett, "Things Are Looking Uptown," *New York Newsday*, August 5, 2002.

2. Mick Dumke, "Black Ministers Put Faith in Daley," *Chicago Reporter*, September 2000.

3. For a more details on the meaning and significance of racial uplift see Gaines (1996).

4. David Mendell and Darnell Little, "Poverty, Crime Still Stalk City's Middle-Class Blacks," *Chicago Tribune*, July 27, 2003.

Chapter 8

1. The importance of location as a structural variable related to community conditions is resurfacing in the urban literature (see Pattillo-McCoy 1999; Sampson, Morenoff, and Earls 1999).

2. The concept of the new urban renewal applies to the recent redevelopment of inner city areas, but it does not necessarily imply the race of the gentrifiers. Although in Harlem and Bronzeville the gentrifiers tended to be mostly African American, in other revitalizing, black inner city communities, such as Roxbury in Boston and Shaw in Washington, D.C., middle- and upper-income whites and

blacks are moving to these areas. In each city the development forces and consequences may be slightly different. This study provides a framework to tease out
the specific development forces and their consequences based on distinct city
contexts.

3. Most argue that the past urban renewal had overwhelmingly negative repercussions for urban black Americans. The construction of highways, universities,
and commercial districts destroyed black neighborhoods and relocated people
to segregated high-rise public housing developments. While some positive benefits were obtained for black America, such as heightened political power for
a few African-American politicians as a result of the concentration of the black
vote (Thompson 2006), the lasting negative consequences of intense segregation
and concentrated black poverty were enormous.

4. Regulating the GSEs and creating an affordable housing fund has been debated
in Congress for a few years, but as of December 2007, no legislation has been
enacted.

5. HUD has increased the fair market rent (FMR). In FY 2007 Chicago's FMR for
a three-bedroom unit is $1,143 (see http://www.huduser.org/datasets/fmr/
fmrs/index.asp?data=fmr07). Whether this is high enough to enable voucher
holders greater access to better neighborhoods has yet to be determined.

6. The formula is HUD's estimate of the resources needed to keep the current housing stock viable.

7. This bill was introduced by Senator Hillary Rodham Clinton in the 109th
Congress.

References

Abu-Lughod, J. L. 1994. Diversity, Democracy, and Self-determination in an Urban Neighborhood: The East Village of Manhattan. *Social Research, 61*(1), 181–203.
———. 1999. *New York, Chicago, Los Angeles: America's Global Cities*. Minneapolis: University of Minnesota Press.

Adelman, R. M. 2004. Neighborhood Opportunities, Race, and Class: The Black Middle Class and Residential Segregation. *City and Community, 3*(1), 43–63.

Alexander, S. 1998. *Balanced Regional Growth: Strategies to Revitalize Chicago's Inner City and Inner Suburban Communities*. Chicago: Chicago Urban League.

Allard, S. W. 2004. *Access to Social Services: The Changing Urban Geography of Poverty and Social Provision*. Washington, D.C.: Brookings Institution.

Anderson, M. 1965. *The Federal Bulldozer*. Cambridge, MA: MIT Press.

Beauregard, R. A. 1995. Theorizing the Local-Global Connection. In P. L. Knox and P. J. Taylor (eds.), *World Cities in a World-System*, pp. 232–48. Cambridge, UK: Cambridge University Press.

Beaverstock, J. V., R. G. Smith and P. J. Taylor. 2000. World City Network: A New Metageography? *Annals of the Association of American Geographers, 90*(1), 123–34.

Bennett, L. and A. Reed. 1999. The New Face of Urban Renewal: The Near North Redevelopment Initiative and the Cabrini-Green Neighborhood. In A. Reed (ed.), *Without Justice for All*, pp. 175–211. Boulder, CO: Westview Press.

Berube, A. and E. Kneebone. 2006. *Two Steps Back: City and Suburban Poverty Trends 1999–2005*. Washington, D.C.: Brooking Institution.

Betancur, J. J. and D. C. Gills. 2004. Community Development in Chicago: From Harold Washington to Richard M. Daley. *ANNALS, AAPSS, 594*(1), 92–108.

Bonds, M. 2004. *Race, Politics, and Community Development Funding*. New York: Haworth Social Work Practice Press.

Boyd, M. 2000. Reconstructing Bronzeville: Racial Nostalgia and Neighborhood Redevelopment. *Journal of Urban Affairs* 22(2), 107–22.

Branconi, F. P. 1999. In Re in Rem: Innovation and Expediency in New York's Housing Policy. In M. H. Schill (ed.), *Housing and Community Development in New York City*, pp. 93–118. Albany: State University of New York Press.

Brenner, N. and N. Theodore. 2002. *Spaces of Neoliberalism*. Malden, MA: Blackwell Publishers.

Bridges, A. 1997. Textbook Municipal Reform. *Urban Affairs Review*, 33(1), 97–119.

Brunick, N., L. Goldberg, and S. Levine. 2003. *Large Cities and Inclusionary Zoning*. Chicago: Business and Professional People for the Public Interest.

Burawoy, M. 1998. The Extended Case Method. *Sociological Theory*, 16(1), 4–33.

Burawoy, M., A. Burton, A. A. Ferguson, K. J. Fox, J. Gamson, N. Gartrell, L. Hurst, C. Kurzman, L. Salzinger, J. Schiffman, and S. Ui. 1991. *Ethnography Unbound*. Berkeley: University of California Press.

Caro, R. 1975. *The Power Broker: Robert Moses and the Fall of New York*. New York: Vintage Books.

Castells, M. 2000. *The Rise of the Network Society*. Malden, MA: Blackwell Publishers.

Chicago Crime Commission. 2006. *The Chicago Crime Commission Gang Book*. Chicago: Author.

Chicago Department of Planning and Development. 1993. *Chicago Cook County: A Global Marketplace*. Chicago: Author.

Chicago Department of Planning and Development. 1997. *Population Estimates of Chicago's Community Areas by Race: 1995*. Chicago: Author.

Chicago Housing Authority. 2000. *Chicago Housing Authority: Plan for Transformation*. Chicago: Author.

Chinyelu, M. 1999. *Harlem Ain't Nothin' but a Third World Country*. New York: Mustard Seed Press.

Clark, K. B. 1965. *Dark Ghetto*. New York: Harper and Row Publishers.

Clark, T. N. 2001. *Chicago's New Political Culture: Trees and Real Violins*. Paper presented at the Semiotics: Culture in Context Workshop, University of Chicago.

Clark, T. N. 1996. Structural Realignments in American City Politics. *Urban Affairs Review*, 31(3), 367–403.

Clark, T. N. and R. Inglehart. 1998. The New Political Culture. In T.N. Clark and V. Hoffmann-Martinot. (eds.), *The New Political Culture*, pp. 9–72. Boulder, CO: Westview Press.

Cohen, C. J. 1999. *The Boundaries of Blackness: AIDS and the Breakdown of Black Politics*. Chicago: University of Chicago Press.

Cohen, A. and E. Taylor. 2000. *American Pharaoh*. New York: Little, Brown and Company.

Cohen, C. J. and M.C. Dawson. 1993. Neighborhood Poverty and African American Politics. *American Political Science Review*, 87(2), 286–302.

Cox, K. R. 1997. *Spaces of Globalization: Reasserting the Power of the Local*. New York: Guilford Press.

Crenson, M. A. 1983. *Neighborhood Politics*. Cambridge, MA: Harvard University Press.

Cruse, H. [1967] 1984. *The Crisis of the Negro Intellectual*. New York: New York Review of Books.

Dahl, R. 1961. *Who Governs?* New Haven, CT: Yale University Press.

Davila, A. 2004. Empowered Culture? New York City's Empowerment Zone and the Selling of El Barrio. *ANNALS, AAPSS, 594*(1), 49–64.

Dawson, M. C. 1994. *Behind the Mule*. Princeton, NJ: Princeton University Press.

———. 1999. Globalization, the Racial Divide, and a New Citizenship. In R. D. Torres, L. F. Miron, and J. M. Inda. (eds.), *Race, Identity, and Citizenship*, pp. 373–85. Malden, MA: Blackwell Publishers.

———. 2000. *Blacks and Civil Society / Black Civil Society Project: An Agenda for Research*. Center for the Study of Race, Politics, and Culture. Race Center, University of Chicago.

Dommel, P. A. and J. S. Hall. 1984. Field Network Research in Policy Evaluation. *Policy Studies Review, 4*(1), 49–59.

Drake, S. C. and H. R. Cayton. [1945] 1993. *Black Metropolis: A Study of Negro Life in a Northern City*. Chicago: University of Chicago Press.

Du Bois, W. E. B. [1899] 1996. *The Philadelphia Negro*. Philadelphia: University of Pennsylvania Press.

Duneier, M. 1992. *Slim's Table*. Chicago: University of Chicago Press.

———. 1999. *Sidewalk*. New York: Farrar, Straus, and Giroux.

Erie, S. P. 1988. *Rainbow's End*. Berkeley: University of California Press.

Evanoff, D. D., P. R. Israilevich and G. R. Schindler. 1997. *The Role of the Financial Services Industry in the Local Economy*. Working Papers Series, Issues in Financial Regulation, Research Department, Federal Reserve Bank of Chicago.

Fainstein, S. S. [1994] 2001. *The City Builders: Property Development in New York and London, 1980–2000*. Lawrence: University Press of Kansas.

Fainstein, S. and N. Fainstein. 1991. The Changing Character of Community Politics in New York City: 1968–1988. In J. H. Mollenkopf and M. Castells. (eds.), *Dual City*, pp. 315–32. New York: Russell Sage Foundation.

Feagin, J. R. 1998. *The New Urban Paradigm: Critical Perspectives on the City*. Lanham, MD: Rowman and Littlefield Publishers.

Feldman, R. M. and S. Stall. 2004. *The Dignity of Resistance: Woman Residents' Activism in Chicago Public Housing*. New York: Cambridge University Press.

Ferman, B. 1996. *Challenging the Growth Machine*. Lawrence: University Press of Kansas.

Firey, W. 1945. Sentiment and Symbolism as Ecological Variables. *American Sociological Review, 10*(2), 140–48.

Fischer, P. 1999. *Section 8 and the Public Housing Revolution: Where Will the Families Go?* Chicago: Woods Fund of Chicago.

———. 2003. *Where Are the Public Housing Families Going? An Update*. Chicago: Woods Fund of Chicago.

Fischer, W. 2006. *Public Housing Squeezing between Higher Utility Costs and Stagnant Funding: Low-Income Families Will Bear Brunt Shortfalls*. Washington, D.C.: Center on Budget and Policy Priorities.

Fratantoni, M., D. G. Duncan, J. Brinkmann and O. Velz. 2007. *The Residential Mortgage Market and Its Economic Context in 2007*. Washington, D.C.: Mortgage Bankers Association.

Frazier, E. F. 1957. *Black Bourgeoisie*. New York: Free Press.

Freeman, L. 2006. *There Goes the 'Hood*. Philadelphia, PA: Temple University Press.

Freeman, L. and F. Braconi. 2004. Gentrification and Displacement. *Journal of American Planning Association*, 70(1), 39–52.

Friedman, T. 2000. *The Lexus and the Olive Tree*. New York: Random House.

Fuchs, E. R. 1992. *Mayors and Money: Fiscal Policy in New York and Chicago*. Chicago: University of Chicago Press.

Fullilove, M. 2004. *Root Shock*. New York: Random House.

Gaines, K. K. 1996. *Uplifting the Race: Black Leadership, Politics and Culture in the Twentieth Century*. Chapel Hill: University of North Carolina Press.

Gans, H. J. [1962] 1982. *Urban Villagers*. New York: Free Press.

Gates, H. L. 2004. *America Behind the Color Line*. New York: Warner Books.

Gills, D. and W. White. 1998. Community Involvement in Chicago's Empowerment Zone. In C. Herring, M. Bennett, D. Gills, and H. T. Jenkins. (eds.), *Empowerment in Chicago: Grassroots Participation in Economic Development and Poverty Alleviation*, pp. 14–70. Chicago: University of Illinois Press.

Gittell, M., K. Newman and F. Pierre-Louis. 2001. *Empowerment Zones: An Opportunity Missed*. New York: Howard Samuels State Management and Policy Center.

Gittell, R. J. 1992. *Renewing Cities*. Princeton, NJ: Princeton University Press.

Gladstone, D. L. and S. S. Fainstein. 2003. The New York and Los Angeles Economics. In D. Halle. (ed.), *New York and Los Angeles*, pp. 79–98. Chicago: University of Chicago Press.

Goetz, E. G. 2003. *Clearing the Way*. Washington, D.C.: Urban Institute Press.

Gosnell, H. F. 1937. *Machine Politics: Chicago Model*. Chicago: University of Chicago Press.

Greenstone, J. D. and P. E. Peterson. [1973] 1976. *Race and Authority in Urban Politics*. Chicago: University of Chicago Press.

Gregory, S. 1998. *Black Corona*. Princeton, NJ: Princeton University Press.

Grimshaw, W. J. 1992. *Bitter Fruit*. Chicago: University of Chicago Press.

Grogan, P. S. and T. Proscio. 2000. *Comeback Cities*. Boulder, CO: Westview Press.

Grossman, J. R. 1989. *Land of Hope*. Chicago: University of Chicago Press.

Haddad, Y. Y. and M. J. Balz. 2006. The October Riots in France: A Failed Immigration Policy or the Empire Strikes Back? *Immigrational Migration*, 44(2), 23–34.

Halpern, R. 1995. *Rebuilding the Inner City*. New York: Columbia University Press.

Harris-Lacewell, M. 2004. *Barbershops, Bibles, and BET: Everyday Talk and Black Political Thought*. Princeton, NJ: Princeton University Press.

Hartung, J. M. and J. R. Henig. 1997. Housing Vouchers and Certificates as a Vehicle for Deconcentrating the Poor. *Urban Affairs Review*, 32(3), 403–19.

Hebert, S., A. Vidal, G. Mills, F. James, and D. Gruenstein. 2001. *Interim Assessment of the Empowerment Zones and Enterprise Communities (EZ/EC) Program: A Progress Report*. Washington, D.C.: U.S. Department of Housing and Urban Development.

Hirsch, A. R. [1983] 1998. *Making the Second Ghetto: Race and Housing in Chicago 1940–1960*. Chicago: University of Chicago Press.

Hoffman, L. M. 2000. Tourism and the Revitalization of Harlem. *Research in Urban Sociology*, 5, 207–23.

————. 2003. The Marketing of Diversity in the Inner City: Tourism and Regulation in Harlem. *International Journal of Urban and Regional Research, 27*(2), 286–99.

Hyra, D. 2006a. Racial Uplift? Intra-Racial Class Conflict and the Economic Revitalization of Harlem and Bronzeville. *City and Community, 5*(1), 71–92.

————. 2006b. City Politics and Black Protest: Economic Transformation of Harlem and Bronzeville. *Souls, 8*(3), 176–96.

Jackson, J. L. 2001. *Harlemworld*. Chicago: University of Chicago Press.

Jacoby, T. and F. Siegel. 1999. Growing the Inner City? *New Republic, 221*(8) 22–27.

Jargowsky, P. A. 2003. *Stunning Progress, Hidden Problems: The Dramatic Decline of Concentrated Poverty in the 1990s*. Washington, D.C.: Brookings Institution.

Jennings, J. 1992. *The Politics of Black Empowerment*. Detroit, MI: Wayne State University Press.

Johnson, J. W. [1930] 1991. *Black Manhattan*. New York: Da Capo Press.

Johnson, K. 2004. Community Development Corporations, Participation, and Accountability: The Harlem Urban Development Corporation and the Bedford-Stuyvesant Restoration Corporation, *ANNALS, AAPSS, 594*(1), 109–24.

Kantor, P. 2002. Terrorism and Governability in New York City: Old Problems, New Dilemma. *Urban Affairs Review, 38*(1), 120–27.

Katznelson, I. 1981. *City Trenches*. Chicago: University of Chicago Press.

Kelley, R. D. 1994. *Race Rebels*. New York: Free Press.

King, G., R. O. Keohane and S. Verba. 1994. *Designing Social Inquiry*. Princeton, NJ: Princeton University Press.

Landry, B. 1987. *The New Black Middle Class*. Berkeley: University of California Press.

Leland, S. 2001. The Political Climate of Devolution and the Implementation Game. *Journal of Regional Analysis and Policy, 31*(1), 39–47.

Lemann, N. 1991. *The Promised Land: The Great Black Migration and How It Changed America*. New York: Alfred A. Knopf.

Lenz, T. J. and J. Coles. 1999. *The Regional Rental Market Analysis*. Chicago: Metropolitan Planning Council.

Liebschutz, S. F. 1995. Empowerment Zones and Enterprise Communities: Reinvesting Federalism for Distressed Communities. *Publius, 25*(3), 117–32.

Logan, J. R. and H. L. Molotch. 1987. *Urban Fortunes: The Political Economy of Place*. Berkeley: University of California Press.

Manhattan Community Board 10. 1999. *The Village of Harlem: Manhattan Community Planning District 10 Central Harlem: 197-a Plan*. New York: Author.

Marable, M. 2002. *The Great Wells of Democracy*. New York: BasicCivitas Books.

Marcuse, P., D. Burney and E. Tsitiridis. 1994. New York City: Historical Perspectives, Current Policy, and Future Planning. In W. F. E. Preiser, D. P. Varady, and F. P. Russell. (eds.), *Future Visions of Urban Public Housing: An International Forum*. Cincinnati, OH: Conference Proceeding.

Marschall, M. L. 2001. Does the Shoe Fit? Testing Models of Participation for African-American and Latino Involvement in Local Politics. *Urban Affairs Review, 37*(2), 227–48.

Massey, D. S. and N. A. Denton. 1993. *American Apartheid*. Cambridge, MA: Harvard University Press.

Massey, D. S. and S. M. Kanaiaupuni. 1993. Public Housing and the Concentration of Poverty. *Social Science Quarterly*, 74(1), 109–22.

Maurrasse, D. 2001. *Beyond the Campus*. New York: Routledge.

McAdam, D. 1982. *Political Process and the Development of Black Insurgency, 1930–1970*. Chicago: University of Chicago Press.

McAdam, D., J. D. McCarthy and M. N. Zald. 1996. *Comparative Perspectives on Social Movements*. Cambridge, MA: Harvard University Press.

McMillen, D. P. 2003. The Return of Centralization to Chicago: Using Repeated Sales to Identify Changes in Housing Price Distance Gradients. *Regional Science and Urban Economics*, 33, 287–304.

McNickle, C. 1993. *To Be Mayor of New York: Ethnic Politics in the City*. New York: Columbia University Press.

McRoberts, O. M. 2003. *Streets of Glory*. Chicago: University of Chicago Press.

Medoff, P. and H. Sklar. 1994. *Streets of Hope: The Fall and Rise of an Urban Neighborhood*. Boston: South End Press.

Mele, C. 2000. *Selling the Lower East Side*. Minneapolis, MN: University of Minnesota Press.

Meyerson, M. and E. C. Banfield. 1955. *Politics, Planning and the Public Interest: The Case of Public Housing in Chicago*. New York: Free Press of Glencoe.

Mills, C.W. [1956] 2000. *The Power Elite*. New York: Oxford University Press.

Mollenkopf, J. H. 1991. Political Inequality. In J. H. Mollenkopf and M. Castells. (eds.), *Dual City*, pp. 333–58. New York: Russell Sage Foundation.

———. 1994. *A Phoenix in the Ashes: The Rise and Fall of Koch Coalition in New York City Politics*. Princeton, NJ: Princeton University Press.

Moore, K. S. 2005. What's Class Got to Do With It? *Journal of Urban Affairs*, 27(4), 437–51.

Moss, M. L. 1995. Where's the Power in the Empowerment Zone? *City Journal*, 5(2), 76–81.

Moynihan, D. P. 1973. *The Politics of a Guaranteed Income*. New York: Random House.

Nathan, R. 1983. State and Local Governments under Federal Grants: Toward a Predictive Theory. *Political Science Quarterly*, 98(1), 47–57.

Nathan, R. P. and D. J. Wright. 1996. *The Empowerment Zone Initiative: Building a Community Plan for Strategic Change*. Albany, NY: Nelson A. Rockefeller Institute of Government.

National Commission on Severely Distressed Public Housing. 1992. *The Final Report of the National Commission on Severely Distressed Public Housing: A Report to the Congress and the Secretary of Housing and Urban Development*. Washington, D.C.: Author.

National Council for Urban Economic Development. 1988. *Improvement Districts: A Tool for Business Self Help*. Information Service Report 51. Washington, D.C.: Author.

Newman, K. S. 1999. *No Shame in My Game: The Working Poor in the Inner City*. New York: Knopf / Russell Sage Foundation.

Newman, K. and E. K. Wyly. 2006. The Right to Stay Put, Revisited: Gentrification and Resistance to Displacement in New York City. *Urban Studies*, 43(1), 23–57.

New York City Department of Housing Preservation and Development. 2002. *Harlem Tour*. New York: Author.

New York City Economic Development Corporation. 2004. *Economic Snapshot: A Summary of New York City's Economy*. New York: Author.

New York City Housing Authority (NYCHA). 2001. *Special Tabulation of Tenant Characteristics*. New York: Author.

———. 2002a. *Capital Fund Program Presentation: Manhattan North Council of Presidents*. New York: Author.

———. 2002b. *Fact Sheet*. New York: Author.

———. 2006. *The Plan to Preserve Public Housing*. New York: Author.

New York State, Commission of Investigations. 1998. *An Investigation into the Creation of the Harlem Urban Development Corporation and Its Operations from 1981–1995*. New York: Author.

Oates, W. E. 1999. An Essay on Fiscal Federalism. *Journal of Economic Literature*, 37(3), 1120–49.

Oliver, M. L. and T. M. Shapiro. 1995. *Black Wealth/White Wealth*. New York: Routledge.

Orr, L., J. D. Feins, R. Jacob, E. Beecroft, L. Sanbonmatsu, L. F. Katz, J. B. Liebman, and J. Kling. 2003. *Moving to Opportunity for Fair Housing Demonstration Program: Interim Impacts Evaluation*. Washington, D.C.: U.S. Department of Housing and Urban Development.

Osofsky, G. [1963] 1996. *Harlem: The Making of a Ghetto*. Chicago: Elephant Paperbacks.

Ottley, R. 1943. *New World A-Coming*. New York: New World Publishing Company.

Paetsch, J. R. and R. K. Dahlstrom. 1990. Tax Increment Financing: What It Is and How It Works. In R. D. Bingham, E. W. Hill and S. B. White. (eds.), *Financing Economic Development: An Institutional Response*, pp. 82–98. Newbury Park, CA: Sage Publications.

Park, R. E. and E. W. Burgess [1925] 1967. *The City*. Chicago: University of Chicago Press.

Pattillo, M. 2003. Negotiating Blackness, For Richer or For Poorer. *Ethnography*, 4(1), 61–93.

———. 2007. *Black on the Block: The Politics of Race and Class in the City*. Chicago: University of Chicago Press.

Pattillo-McCoy, M. 1999. *Black Picket Fences*. Chicago: University of Chicago Press.

Peterson, P. E. 1981. *City Limits*. Chicago: University of Chicago Press.

Pinderhughes, D. 1997. Race and Ethnicity in the City. In R. K. Vogel. (ed.), *Handbook of Research on Urban Politics and Policy in the United States*, pp. 75–91. Westport, CT: Greenwood Press.

Plunz, R. 1990. *A History of Housing in New York City*. New York: Columbia University Press.

Popkin, S. J., L. F. Buron, D. K. Levy, and M. K. Cunningham. 2000. The Gautreaux Legacy: What Might Mixed-Income and Dispersal Strategies Mean for the Poorest Public Housing Tenants? *Housing Policy Debate*, 11(4), 911–42.

Popkin, S. J., V. E. Gwiasda, L. M. Olson, D. P. Rosenbaum, and L. Buron. 2000. *The Hidden War*. New Brunswick, NJ: Rutgers University Press.

Popkin, S. J., D. K. Levy, L. E. Harris, J. Comey, M. K. Cunningham, and L. Buron. 2002. *HOPE VI Panel Study: Baseline Report*. Washington, D.C.: Urban Institute.

Portes, A. and R. G. Rumbaut. 1996. *Immigrant America*. Berkeley: University of California Press.

Price, S. R. 2002. Changing Places: Race, Class, and Belonging in the "New" Harlem. *Urban Anthropology, 31*(1), 5–35.

Puentes, R. and D. Warren. 2006. *One-Fifth of America: A Comprehensive Guide to America's First Suburbs*. Washington, D.C.: Brookings Institution.

Putnam, R. D. 1993. *Making Democracy Work*. Princeton, NJ: Princeton University Press.

———. 2000. *Bowling Alone: The Collapse and Revival of American Community*. New York: Simon and Schuster.

Ranney, D. 2003. *Global Decisions, Local Collisions*. Philadelphia: Temple University Press.

Reed, A. J. 1999. *Stirrings in the Jug*. Minneapolis, MN: University of Minnesota Press.

Rich, M. J. 1989. Distributive Politics and the Allocation of Federal Grants. *The American Political Science Review, 83*(1), 193–213.

———. 1993. *Federal Policy Making and the Poor*. Princeton, NJ: Princeton University Press.

Riposa, G. 1996. From Enterprise Zones to Empowerment Zones: The Community Context for Urban Economic Development. *American Behavioral Scientist, 39*(5), 536–51.

Rubin, R. E. and J. Weisberg. 2003. *In an Uncertain World*. New York: Random House.

Rubinowitz, L. S. and J. E. Rosenbaum. 2000. *Crossing the Class and Color Lines: From Public Housing to White Suburbia*. Chicago: University of Chicago Press.

Sagalyn, L. B. 2001. *Times Square Roulette*. Cambridge, MA: MIT Press.

Sampson, R. J. 2001. Crime and Public Safety: Insights from Community-Level Perspectives on Social Capital. In S. Saegert, J. P. Thompson, and M. R. Warren. (eds.), *Social Capital and Poor Communities*, pp. 89–114. New York: Russell Sage Foundation.

Sampson, R. J., J. D. Morenoff, and F. Earls. 1999. Beyond Social Capital: Spatial Dynamics of Collective Efficacy for Children. *American Sociological Review, 64*, 633–60.

Sampson, R. J., S. W. Raudenbush, and F. Earls. 1997. Neighborhoods and Violent Crime: A Multilevel Study of Collective Efficacy. *Science, 277*, 918–24.

Sassen, S. 1998. *Globalization and Its Discontents*. New York: New Press.

———. 1999. *Cities: Between Global Actors and Local Conditions*. The 1997 Lefrak Monograph, Urban Studies and Planning Program School of Architecture: University of Maryland, College Park.

———. 2000. *Cities in a World Economy*. Thousand Oaks, CA: Pine Forge Press.

———. [1991] 2001. *The Global City*. Princeton, NJ: Princeton University Press.

Schatzman, L. and A. L. Strauss. 1973. *Field Research*. Upper Saddle River, NJ: Prentice-Hall.

Schill, M. H. 1997. Chicago's Mixed-Income New Communities Strategy: The Future Face of Public Housing? In W. V. Vliet. (ed.), *Affordable Housing and Urban Redevelopment in the United States*, vol. 46, pp. 135–57. Thousand Oaks, CA: Sage Publications.

Schill, M. H., I. G. Ellen, A. E. Schwartz and I. Voicu. 2002. Revitalizing Inner-City Neighborhoods: New York City's Ten-Year Plan. *Housing Policy Debate, 13*(3), 529–66.

Schill, M. H. and B. P. Scafidi. 1999. Housing Conditions and Problems in New York City. In M. H. Schill. (ed.), *Housing and Community Development in New York City*, pp. 11–52. Albany, NY: State University of New York Press.

Schwartz, J. 1986a. Tenant Power in the Liberal City, 1943–1971. In R. Lawson, R. and M. Naison. (eds.), *The Tenant Movement in New York City, 1904–1985*, pp. 134–208. New Brunswick, NJ: Rutgers University Press.

———. 1986b. Tenant Unions in New York City's Low-Rent Housing, 1933–1949. *Journal of Urban History*, 12(4), 414–43.

———. 1993. *The New York Approach: Robert Moses, Urban Liberals, and the Redevelopment of the Inner City*. Columbus: Ohio State University Press.

Schwartz, C., J. C. Leavy, P. A. Nolan., and J. P. Jones. 1999. *NCBG's Chicago TIF Encyclopedia: The First Comprehensive Report on the State of Tax Increment Financing in Chicago*. Chicago: Neighborhood Capital Budget Group.

Sellers, J. M. 2005. Re-placing the Nation: An Agenda for Comparative Urban Politics. *Urban Affairs Review*, 40(4), 419–45.

Sen, A. 1984. *Resources, Values, and Development*. Cambridge, MA: Harvard University Press.

Shashaty, A. 2007. Home Sales Fill Funding Gap for Mixed-Income Redevelopments. *Affordable Housing Finance*, 15(3), 47–48, 74.

Short, J. R. and Y. Kim. 1999. *Globalization and the City*. New York: Addison Wesley Longman.

Simpson, D. 2001. *Rogues, Rebels, and Rubber Stamps*. Boulder, CO: Westview Press.

Simpson, D., O. Adeoye, R. Feliciano and R. Howard. 2002. Chicago's Uncertain Future Since September 11, 2001. *Urban Affairs Review*, 38(1), 128–34.

Sites, W. 2003. *Remaking New York*. Minneapolis: University of Minnesota Press.

Small, S. 1999. The Contours of Racialization: Structures, Representations and Resistance in the United States. In R. D. Torres, L. F. Miron and J. M. Inda. (eds.), *Race, Identity, and Citizenship*, pp. 47–64. Malden, MA: Blackwell Publishers.

Smith, N. [1996] 2000. *The New Urban Frontier*. New York: Routledge.

Smith, L. V., F. Pafenberg, and L. Goren. 2006. *Mortgage Markets and the Enterprises in 2005*. Washington, D.C.: U.S. Department of Housing and Urban Development.

Snyderman, R. and S. D. Dailey. 2001. *Public Housing in the Public Interest: Examining the Chicago Housing Authority's Proposed Service Connector Model*. Chicago: Metropolitan Planning Council.

Spear, A. H. 1967. *Black Chicago: The Making of a Negro Ghetto 1890–1920*. Chicago: The University of Chicago Press.

Spence, L. H. 1993. Rethinking the Social Role of Public Housing. *Housing Policy Debate*, 4(3), 335–68.

Squires, G. D., L. Bennett, K. McCourt, and P. Nyden. 1987. *Chicago: Race, Class and the Response to Urban Decline*. Philadelphia: Temple University Press.

Stack, C. B. 1974. *All Our Kin*. New York: Harper and Row Publishers.

Stone, C. N. 1989. *Regime Politics*. Lawrence: University Press of Kansas.

Strauss, A. and J. Corbin. 1998. *Basics of Qualitative Research*. Thousand Oaks, CA: Sage Publications.

Sullivan, T. 2003. *Report 5 of the Independent Monitor*. Document provided by the View from the Ground, www.viewfromtheground.com.

Swyngedouw, E. 1997. Neither Global nor Local: "Globalization" and the Politics of Scale. In K. R. Cox. (ed.), *Spaces of Globalization: Reasserting the Power of the Local*, pp. 137–66. New York: Guilford Press.

Taub, R. P. 1988. *Community Capitalism*. Boston, MA: Harvard Business School Press.

Taub, R. P., D. G. Taylor, and J. D. Dunham. 1984. *Paths of Neighborhood Change*. Chicago: University of Chicago Press.

Taylor, M. M. 2002. *Harlem: Between Heaven and Hell*. Minneapolis: University of Minnesota Press.

Taylor, P. J. 2004. *World City Network*. New York: Routledge.

Thompson, J. P. 1999. Public Housing in New York City. In M. H. Schill. (ed.), *Housing and Community Development in New York City*, pp. 119–42. Albany: State University of New York Press.

———. 2006. *Double Trouble: Black Mayors, Black Communities and the Call for a Deep Democracy*. New York: Oxford University Press.

Turbov, M. and V. Piper. 2005. *HOPE VI and Mixed-Finance Redevelopments: A Catalyst for Neighborhood Renewal*. Washington, D.C.: Brookings Institution.

Turner, M. A. 1998. Moving Out of Poverty. *Housing Policy Debate*, 9(2), 373–94.

Turner, M. A., S. Popkin, and M. Cunningham. 1999. *Section 8 Mobility and Neighborhood Health*. Washington, D.C.: Urban Institute.

Tyre, P. 2004. Returning Seniors Revitalize Cities, and Themselves. *Newsweek*. October 11, pp. 44–45.

U.S. Department of Housing and Urban Development. 2000. *The State of the Cities 2000*. Washington, D.C.: Author.

U.S. Government Accountability Office. 1996. *Community Development: Status of Urban Empowerment Zones*. Washington, D.C.: Author.

———. 2004. Community Development: Federal Revitalization Programs Are Being Implemented, But Data on the Use of Tax Benefits Are Limited. Washington, D.C.: Author.

———. 2006. *Community Development Block Grants: Program Offers Recipients Flexibility but Oversight Can Be Improved*. Washington, D.C.: Author.

Venkatesh, S. A. 2000. *American Project*. Cambridge, MA: Harvard University Press.

———. 2002. *The Robert Taylor Homes Relocation Study*. Working paper, Center for Urban Research and Policy, Columbia University, New York.

Venkatesh, S. A., I. Celimli, D. Miller, A. Murphy, and B. Turner. 2004. Chicago Public Housing Transformation: A Research Report. Working paper, Center for Urban Research and Policy, Columbia University, New York.

Verba, S. and N. H. Nie. 1972. *Participation in America*. New York: Harper and Row Publishers.

von Hoffman, A. 2000. A Study in Contradictions: The Origins and Legacy of the Housing Act of 1949. *Housing Policy Debate*, 11(2), 299–326.

———. 2003. *House by House, Block by Block*. New York: Oxford University Press.

Walter, J. C. 1989. *The Harlem Fox: J. Raymond Jones and Tammany, 1920–1970*. New York: State University of New York Press, Albany.

Wallace v. Chicago Housing Authority. 2003. 321 F. Supp. 2d 968 (N.D. Ill. 2004). Filed, January 23, 2003.

Whyte, W. F. [1943] 1955. *Street Corner Society*. Chicago: University of Chicago Press.

Wille, L. 1997. *At Home in the Loop: How Clout and Community Built Chicago's Dearborn Park*. Carbondale: Southern Illinois University Press.

Williams, T. and W. Kornblum. 1994. *The Uptown Kids: Struggles and Hope in the Projects*. New York: G. P. Putnam's Sons.

Wilson, J. Q. 1960. *Negro Politics*. Glencoe, IL: Free Press.

Wilson, W. J. 1987. *The Truly Disadvantaged*. Chicago: University of Chicago Press.

———. 1996. *When Work Disappears: The World of the New Urban Poor*. New York: Sage Publication.

———. 1999. *The Bridge over the Racial Divide: Rising Inequality and Coalition Politics*. Berkeley: University of California Press.

Wong, K. K. 1990. City Choices: Education and Housing. Albany: State University of New York Press.

Wong, K. K. and P. E. Peterson. 1986. Urban Responses to Federal Program Flexibility: Politics of Community Development Block Grant. *Urban Affairs Quarterly*, 21(3), 293–309.

Wylde, K. 1999. The Contribution of Public-Private Partnerships to New York's Assisted Housing Industry. In M. H. Schill. (ed.), *Housing and Community Development in New York City*, pp. 73–91. Albany: State University of New York Press.

Wyly, E. K. and D. J. Hammel. 1999. Islands of Decay in Seas of Renewal: Housing Policy and the Resurgence of Gentrification. *Housing Policy Debate*, 10(4), 711–71.

Yin, R. K. 2003. *Case Study Research: Design and Methods*. Thousand Oaks, CA: Sage Publications.

Zielenbach, S. 2003. Assessing Economic Change in HOPE VI Neighborhoods. *Housing Policy Debate*, 14(4), 621–55.

Zukin, S. 1987. Gentrification: Culture and Capital in the Urban Core. *Annual Review of Sociology*, 13, 129–47.

———. 1995. *The Culture of Cities*. Malden, MA: Blackwell Publishers.

Index